- SELF -
A Study in a Circle

by
P. Krishan Kaul
BE MSc CEng FIStructE MICE MIE FGS

Aum Sai Publications

First edition published in 1995 by
Aum Sai Publications,
34 Perth Avenue
London NW9 7JT
United Kingdom
Tel: (0181) 205 0295

Copyright © P. Krishan Kaul, 1995

All rights reserved. No part of this book may be reproduced or utilized in any form or by any means, electronic or mechanical, including photocopying, recording or by any information storage and retrieval system without permission in writing from the publisher, except for brief passages quoted in a book review.

British Library Cataloguing-in-Publication Data

Kaul, Parduman Krishan
Self: A Study in a Circle
I. Title
126

ISBN 0-9524018-0-0

Printed in the United Kingdom

DEDICATION

Eternal Existence *(Sat)*, Total Awareness *(Chit)* and Absolute Bliss *(Aananda)* are the very nature of the Essential Man (the Self). In spite of the false identification of the Immortal Self with the evanescent body-mind complex which covers the Truth in a veil of ignorance, it is this ever pulsating essential nature that has, since the beginning of time, prompted man to seek knowledge, immortality and happiness. In this quest, experiences of others are the best guides and one's own, the best teachers, with each life but a step towards the eventual victory of the indomitable spirit of man.

This humble effort is dedicated at the **Lotus Feet** of **SAI**, the motivator, the inspiration and the very source of strength, with all my love, reverence and a heartfelt prayer that those whose curiosity takes them through the pages of this book may find within it something to reflect upon.

ACKNOWLEDGEMENTS

The knowledge about the Self is the common heritage of all mankind and to share that knowledge the duty of all spiritual aspirants. It is with this faith that I have, in writing this book, drawn freely from the various sources listed in the Bibliography. Equally gratefully do I record my heartfelt thanks to all those sources.

I offer my loving and respectful salutations to my late father, Shri Dina Nath Kaul, who has been an example to me and many others in self-discipline, self-sacrifice and self-less service, to my mother, Shrimati Padmavati Kaul, whose love, prayers and blessings have given me strength and much more besides, and to my late uncle, Shri Radha Krishan Kaul and my aunt, Shrimati Gunwati Kaul, to whom I owe a great deal, for their blessings, prayers and love.

The painstaking task of typing the manuscript was undertaken, always with a smile I hasten to add, by Miss Daxa Yadav to whom I owe a deep debt of gratitude. I can express nothing but admiration for the patience she has shown throughout.

My grateful thanks are due to Mr Manohar G. Bhojraj, Ms Nina O'Connell, Mrs Sara McNern and Mrs Sylvia Bishop for their efforts in adorning the chapters with beautiful theme sketches. I am also indebted to James A. Ratcliff for his invaluable assistance with the production of the camera-ready copy of the manuscript.

I am deeply indebted to Prof Vishwanath Pandit for going through the manuscript and making invaluable suggestions for its improvement, and to Dr H. V. Sathyanarayana Shastry and Dr P. G. Shukla for their help with and the editing of the Glossary of *Sanskrit* Words.

I would also like to record with love and affection the contributions of my wife, Shibni, who patiently sifted through the manuscript and helped with the proof reading, and our son, Prashant, who helped with the general presentation and whose dexterity with the word processor has shaped the manuscript into its present form.

Finally, my heartfelt thanks go to all friends and well-wishers whose good wishes have been a constant source of encouragement to me during the compilation of this manuscript.

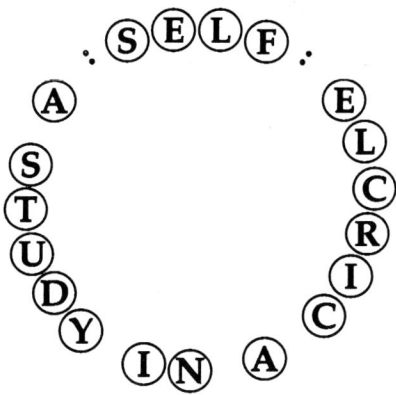

CONTENTS

i.	Foreword	*i*
ii.	Preface - A Glimpse of Sai	*iii*
1.	Study Circle	*1*
2.	Integration	*10*
3.	The G * A * M * E	*19*
4.	The Enemy Within ?	*29*
5.	Human Values	*40*
6.	Ceiling on Desires	*53*
7.	Aspects of Meditation - I	*61*
8.	Aspects of Meditation - II	*73*
9.	A Dream Within a Dream	*84*
10.	Sound of Silence - I	*90*
11.	Sound of Silence - II	*97*
12.	Sanathana Dharma	*104*
13.	Law of Karma	*114*
14.	Symbolism	*128*
15.	From 'i' to 'I'	*136*
16.	Knowledge of Self - I	*146*
17.	Knowledge of Self - II	*156*
18.	The Master Within	*168*
19.	Principle of Surrender	*178*
20.	Road to Destiny	*187*
21.	The Spirit of Numbers	*195*

Appendices

A.	A Suggested Format for a Typical Study Circle	217
B.	Yoga, Kundalini and the Chakras	219
C.	Nirvaana-Shatkam (An English Rendering)	223
D.	Key to Alphabetical Code	225
E.	Interesting Facts and Figures	226
F.	Bibliography	232
G.	Glossary of Sanskrit Words	234

Education is a wasteful process unless knowledge is transformed into Wisdom and Wisdom is expressed as character. Character is the most precious gift of education. Without character, wealth, education and social status are of no avail. Character makes life immortal ... Education is the awareness of the Immortal Spirit; education is not the acquisition of burdensome information regarding objects of men ... Education must endow man with humility. The wise are humble that they know no more; the fool is proud that he knows so much. Humility and reverence are the genuine fruits of education ...

I am not so concerned about the 'marks' a student gains at college as the 'remarks' made about his character ... Education should be about how to live, not how to make a living ...
          – Sri Sathya Sai Baba

FOREWORD

"The notable advances in science and technology we witness represent the essence of the Upanishads."

Bhagawan Sri Sathya Sai Baba

When asked "Does God exist?", a sage replied very promptly,"My saying 'Yes' would serve no purpose. You must seek for yourself and get the answer." Howsoever conceptualized, God is beyond sensory perception and hence beyond any description and definition. Books, discourses and even the holy scriptures are only dim indicators of that Reality which surpasses man's intellect. Yet, the enquiry must begin and go on. No wonder the *Brahma Sutra* begins with the aphorism, *"Athaato Brahma Jignyaasa"* - "Henceforth the enquiry into the *Brahman*."

Mahatma Gandhi once remarked that to understand the unknown we must begin with the known. Properly motivated and applied, the mind and the intellect must serve like the launching pad for a satellite - necessary but only up to a point. Their task is to pose the correct questions. Whether and to what extent a seeker in the domain of spirituality is on the right trail is very well indicated by the kind of questions he asks. It is in this context that study circle in general and the present work in particular, assumes significance by stimulating and motivating the mind and the intellect to pose appropriate questions to oneself and to others.

In this age of science, men are prone to demand rational arguments in support or in refutation of vital propositions. There is a widely held but mistaken view that faith and reason are mutually exclusive. *Sanathana Dharma* which has been the sheet anchor of Indian civilization has never given cause for conflict between science and spirituality, between state and religion or, between welfare and liberation. In all cases the two are the two sides of the same coin - complementary and strengthening each other, as it were, assuredly an aspect of *adwaita* (non-duality). Every principle of *Sanathana Dharma* is, as indeed emphasised in the text, logical and well reasoned. As far as so called rationality is concerned modern science recognises that rationality itself is subject not only to inherent severe limitations but also to multiple interpretations. Be that as it may, one must distinguish faith with lack of faith on the one hand and from blind faith on the other. One must also guard against self deluding as well as self denying influences of the intellect. That the Creator has blessed man with the power to discriminate is because faith is meant to be based on reason, contemplation and experience.

My modest experience with study circle activity has been that presentations often turn into intellectual gymnastics leaving the listeners untouched and cold, or into routine hyperboles and *clichés* avoiding meaningful questions. The distinguishing feature of the present monograph is that it neither shies away from reason nor understates faith. It covers concisely, clearly and systematically a large variety of topics which frequently come up for discussion in study circles. By offering it at the Lotus Feet of *Bhagawan Sri Sathya Sai Baba*, Krishan Kaul has put to the most befitting use his erudition, experience and above all devotion. I have no doubt that seekers of Truth in general and those engaged in study circle activity in particular will find it extremely useful.

Prof. Vishwanath Pandit
Prashanti Nilayam
Dec. 04, 1991

> *Wake up my children: wake up to the dawn of knowledge, wake up to your Divine Duties, wake up to your Divine Rights and wake up to your Divine Reality.*
> — *Sri Sathya Sai Baba*

PREFACE

A Glimpse of Sai

Man's preoccupation with acquiring and adding to his material comforts has assumed such proportions that his belief in God and his native divinity are dismissed as primitive, irrational and unscientific sentiments. In his mad and unbridled pursuit of power and pleasure, man has lost his sense of direction. However, the concept that Spirit is at the very core of even matter is gaining currency now. For example, in ice we find coldness, weight, form; it is visible. Melt the ice, it becomes water. Pass electricity through water, it becomes invisible H_2 & O which, when analysed further, are nothing more than forms of electronic vibrations. One may therefore proclaim, scientifically, that ice does not exist, even though it is perceptible to our senses of sight, touch and so on. In reality, its essence is invisible electrons or form of energy. In other words, that which can be dissolved into invisibility, Baba says, cannot be said to have valid existence. In this case, matter can be considered as not existing, but having relative existence.

So, matter exists but only in relation to our mind and as an expression of the invisible electronic forces that do exist being unchangeable and immortal. Mind and matter therefore have only formal existence; in reality, only Cosmic Mind exists. Remove the mind, matter will disappear too. Is there any wonder why Bertrand Russell, the famous philosopher remarked: "Materialism as a philosophy becomes hardly tenable in view of the evaporation of matter." Never before in the history of mankind has there been felt, on a global scale, such a need and urgency for a well-wisher and a friend, a guide and a master, to revitalise the spiritual values in the heart of man and reverse the trend of moral degeneration and blind pursuit of materialism, as it is today.

At this critical time in the history of mankind, when strife and discord have robbed man of peace and harmony and when the forces of evil are relentlessly pushing him close to the brink of disaster, we are uniquely fortunate to witness, walking on earth, the Embodiment of Divine Love and Light, *Bhagawan* Sri Sathya Sai Baba, who has come to raise the consciousness of man and guide him to his spiritual unfoldment.

Who is Sai Baba? If, in answer to this question, the mind were to proclaim that Sai is God, it would imply one of two things: either that the mind is God-realised or that it is a step above God to be able to claim to know all that there is to know about Him. Before letting it jump to any such conclusion, however, it would be appropriate to examine, first, the credentials of the mind.

The mind on its own is not Self-sufficient; it is corruptible. We also know that it suffers from, to name but a few, the diseases of lust, anger, greed, delusion, pride and jealousy. However, by far the most malignant of all its ailments is 'desire'. Desire is the root cause of all troubles. As one desire is fulfilled, instead of assuaging the hunger, ten more sprout in the wings. If desire is not controlled and curbed, it spreads like cancer destroying the native peace and equanimity. It is like the drug which only increases further the pain and suffering that the addict hopes it would remove.

Hunger, thirst, etc, likewise are the diseases that the mind suffers from and which also bring it pain. As Baba says, "The worldly pleasures are, at best, counter-actions against pain. You feel thirsty, you drink water; you are hungry, you eat food. It is not positive pleasure that water and food bring; they merely negate the pangs of thirst and hunger." If this was not so and they were truly the bringers of pleasure, then non-stop eating, drinking or sleeping would bring unending happiness. But such is not the case. "Raja Bhartrihari, while he was the king of a prosperous kingdom, wallowed in pleasure. However, he gave up all when he understood that the worldly pleasures were no more than a sort of counter-action ...". His experience is summed up in the following verse *(Shloka)* from his *'Vairagya Shatak'*:

> *"Trishaa shushyatyasye pibati salilam swadu surabhi;*
> *Kshudhaartah san shaaleen kawalayati shaakaadi walitaan;*
> *Pradeepte raagaagnau sudridhatarama shrilashyati wadhoon;*
> *Prateekaaro vyadhih sukhamiti viparyasyati janah."*

Translation: "When the mouth is parched, one drinks water, sweet and scented; tormented by hunger, one takes a morsel of food, that is rice with condiments; when the fire of passion catches the heart, one embraces one's wife fondly; thus counter-action of pain is really misunderstood by people as some positive happiness."

So, how can such a finite ailing mind, with its preferences and prejudices, which is apt to blowing hot and cold, prone to mistaking a rope for a snake and confusing counter-action of pain for positive pleasure, ever be expected to know or comprehend the infinitude of God? It is beyond the reach of the mind; Infinite alone can comprehend the Infinite; only the soul, which is immortal, can comprehend immortality. Just as a droplet, upon losing itself in the ocean, assumes the characteristics of the ocean, so also the mind, if made to dwell on and merge in the Infinite (God), can verily become that Infinite; thereafter all questions about the identity of God

O LORD!

*Make me an instrument
of your Peace;*

*Where there is hatred, let me sow Love;
Where there is injury, Pardon;
Where there is discord, Unity;
Where there is doubt, Faith;
Where there is error, Truth;
Where there is despair, Hope;
Where there is sadness, Joy;
Where there is darkness, Light;*

O Divine Master!

*Grant that I may not so much seek
to be consoled, as to console;
to be understood as to understand;
to be loved, as to love;*

*for it is in giving that we receive,
it is in pardoning that we are pardoned,
it is in dying that we are born to Eternal Life.*

Saint Francis

become redundant. This, however, implies and requires the annihilation of the mind. To confer God-hood on Sai solely on the speculation of the mind therefore, is as meaningful an exercise as expecting a monkey to testify to the secrets and subtleties of meditation!

With the inability of the mind to reliably explain away the Sai mystery thus laid bare, let us turn towards the intellect and its powers of reasoning and logic.

We read and hear about and witness numerous, inexplicable phenomena associated with Sai. For example, merely by blowing his breath, Sai transformed in a trice, a piece of stone into an entrancing figure of Lord Krishna with a flute, under the watchful eyes and to the utter amazement of a geologist. Not only had the shape of the stone completely changed, the atoms too had metamorphosed into sugar candy! "Professor! According to your science, you said that there were any number of constituents in this stone. Physicists would delve into the atoms and go down to the electron, proton and neutron. But within them all is the Primordial Power. The same Power appears as all different objects. God does not stop with being the physical power of the electron and proton. He inheres as the live power of Love too. It is to show this, that the Primordial Power is playing the flute here. To show the sweetness of His heart, He has turned it into candy"– explained the miracle-master, as if to underline the words of *Sri* Aurobindo that what is 'logic of the Infinite is magic for the finite.' As Baba says, "What you call miracles are in the very nature of the *Avataar*."

Would it ever be possible for anyone to so rearrange the constituents of the rock as to form an edible statue in candy if one did not possess the necessary control over the primordial elements? It stands to reason that none other than the Primordial Power Itself could conceivably rearrange the primordial elements merely by wishing so. So, whenever we see Sai perform miracles, what we really witness is a glimpse of the Primordial Power in action.

Likewise, multiplication of food manifold, resurrection of the dead, materialisation of, amongst other things, a live monkey, dispersing rain clouds by a mere wave of His hands, 'cancelling cancer', assuming different forms and appearing in different places simultaneously, and so on, are some of the other miracles performed by Sai. In fact, books written by people from all walks of life, eg, scientists, psychologists and scholars, doctors, lawyers and professors, pundits, politicians and preachers, from all parts of the world, are replete with documented accounts testifying to His extraordinary miraculous powers.

On one occasion in 1982, when my family and I were graciously called in for an interview just a few minutes before the *bhajans* (devotional singing) were due to start in the *Prashanti Mandir* (temple), I recall feeling my enthusiasm a trifle dampened to think that it would be no more than those very few minutes before we would be out again. In the event, however, Baba spoke to us for many times more than the few minutes I had dared hope for, and we came out brimming with joy and happiness and full of His Love. As we opened the door and stepped outside the interview room, expecting the half-hour *bhajan* session to have been over by then, the thought of making our way towards some quiet spot to take in and savour the love and joy we had the unique fortune of experiencing, crossed my mind. Imagine then my utter amazement to hear the three AUM's signalling, not the conclusion but, yes, ... the very start of the *bhajans*!

But how could this be? Had we stepped into a different dimension of time upon entering the interview room; or was it that within the confines of that room the time had somehow got stretched or slowed down, or simply stood still? Whether it was one thing or the other, it mattered not. What was singularly fortunate was to have been able to witness Time itself waiting upon the Lord and Master of Time.

I have often pondered over why it is that even a handful of us, however alike in our temperaments, when left on our own, invariably find enough excuses not to see eye to eye with one another and yet, in their relation with Sai, even a million people with wildly dissimilar temperaments and in spite of numerous misunderstandings arising amongst themselves, experience nothing but love towards Sai welling up within themselves. What else can it be attributed if not to the unconditional and unconditioned Divine Love flowing from Sai which dissolves all our negativity, cleanses and uplifts us and removes the obstacles against the free flow of our love.

Our powers of reasoning and logic, such as they are, when used to analyse the available documentary evidence thus, would overwhelmingly lead us to conclude, among other things, that Sai also has total control and absolute supremacy over elements, that He transcends time and space and is omnipresent, omnipotent and omniscient and that He is the embodiment of Love. All this leads us to infer that He must be God. But mere inference on its own, however well reasoned and well-founded cannot be equated with direct experience because rational Sai, after all, is not the Essential Sai. In our bid to understand the Sai phenomenon therefore, if we can neither rely exclusively on the testimony of the mind nor solely on the ratiocination of the intellect and, at the same time, find ourselves unable to ignore or dismiss the phenomenon either, how then are we to relate to Sai? Let us now turn to the testimony of the heart – not the biological organ which pumps blood, but the spiritual centre which is the seat of intuitive feeling and love.

It is a well known fact that no one loves anyone else more than one's own self. In our relationship with others, the feeling of attachment prompted by a sense of possessiveness is often mistaken for love. Such 'love' is conditional and is based on relationship. Take the relationship away and the so called 'love' would find no basis to exist. On the other hand, in our relationship with Sai, there can be no possessiveness and therefore there is no attachment. What then causes the uncontrollable stream of tears to well up in our eyes when we find ourselves in His immediate presence physically or mentally? It is difficult to explain or rationalise and assign reasons to it. This spontaneous outpouring from the heart which happens without any prompting from or calculation by the mind, or any act of deliberation or reasoning on the part of the intellect, is the miracle of love. Not a word may pass between the lips and yet the tears speak volumes. Summarised in those joyful tears of love is the sum total of all the aims and aspirations of man and reflected in them is the fruition of all the prayers, penances and pilgrimages. It is obvious then that Sai is closer to us than even our own mind or the intellect. Who is it that wipes our tears and drives away our fears? Who is it that shifts a mountain-load of sorrows from our hearts? His one glance brings sunshine into our lives; His one smile showers unparalleled blissful joy.

In Sai, we witness the confluence of the human and Divine. In His actions do we not only have the glimpse of the Divine at work, we also witness the fulfilment of the highest aspiration of man. In Him and through Him, we have a chance to see our own Real Self.

Sai is the food that we eat; He is the air that we breathe. He gives meaning to our lives; He is the sum and substance of our lives. I know not who or what God is but I know this that Sai is none other than my own Self.

Let us also remember that "To but One Goal are marching everywhere all human beings though they may seem to walk on paths divergent; and that goal is I, the Universal Self, Self-Consciousness."

In the eighteen topics that follow, an attempt has been made to turn the enquiry towards the Self in the hope of catching a glimpse of Sai.

PKK

O Divine Mother Sai! May everyday of our lives be a pilgrimage unto Thee.

NB:

In the course of studying Sai literature, one comes across a number of *Sanskrit* words which keep coming up repeatedly and which, for want of exact English equivalents, may require long explanations. The words themselves are short, sweet and easy to pronounce. To ensure that our non-familiarity with the *Sanskrit* language does not detract us from enjoying the full benefits of the Sai literature, it is in our best interests to build up a small vocabulary of at least the most commonly occurring words. An attempt has, therefore, been made not only to maintain the flow of the narrative by giving English equivalents or explanations alongside the *Sanskrit* words (italicized) wherever they first appear in the text, but also to compile a glossary of all such words at the very end, under Appendix G, for easy reference.

> *Man is mislead into believing that Nature is his rival which has to be defeated and conquered; he struggles and suffers loss and pain in the process. He considers it heroic to undergo travail in what he calls the 'conquest of Nature'! But, if only he feels kinship with Nature, as equally saturated with Divinity, and proclaiming with equal clarity the immanence of God, he can be happier and much more restful and content.*
>
> *When you see everywhere, on every inch of ground, in every being, small or big, the footprint of God, Nature is seen in a new Vesture of Glory, a manifestation that demands worship, rather than exploitation and enslavement ...*
>
> — *Sri Sathya Sai Baba*

"A little learning is a dangerous thing;
Drink deep or taste not the Pierian Spring;
There, shallow draughts intoxicate the brain,
And drinking largely sobers us again."

Alexander Pope

1. STUDY CIRCLE

The single most glorious achievement of human mind has, undoubtedly, been the recognition of the fact that latent within one's own Self, transcending the barriers of caste, creed and colour, is the divinity which is the repository of *Sat* (Eternal Existence), *Chit* (Total Awareness) and *Aananda* (Absolute Bliss). The lives of great sages and the masters of the spirit bear testimony to this achievement of man. However, with the supervention of mind casting a veil of ignorance, man has allowed himself to forget his lofty heritage and divine destiny. Nevertheless, the innate thirst to manifest his native divinity is ever pulsating in his subliminal Self and, in spite of all his passions and prejudices, it is this intuitive urge in man to achieve immortality, attain supreme knowledge and experience total happiness, that drives him on, inexorably, towards the discovery of his Higher Self.

Mind has no existence as such except as a collection of thoughts it entertains or dwells upon. Through its continual contact with the phenomenal world the mind, unfortunately, keeps our consciousness tethered to the physical plane, identifying the material world outside, instead of the Self within, as the main focus of attention. This, incidentally, is the reason why man masquerades as a beggar betraying poverty of spirit, displaying a lack of imagination and running after tinsel and trash. Stronger the influence of our mind and deeper the infatuation with the material world, the greater our ignorance and distortion of vision. In fact, the caprices of ignorance are too well known to need elucidation; it can delude any one into seeing a snake for a rope and strike terror in the looker-on. Removal of ignorance through education is, therefore, necessary to drive out the fear and correct the imbalance. This can be achieved through the study and discussion of appropriate topics in the company of like-minded seekers and aspirants in a study circle.

'Study within a circle' is the definition given by Baba for a study circle. "It is not just reading books. Study in a circle means taking up a point and each person discussing what the meaning of that point to them is ... Each offers a point of view and finally, values are derived from this". In this way will there be not only a sharing of experience but also an appreciation of one another's point of view.

It is important to recognise, at the very outset, the kind of knowledge worth pursuing in a study circle. With every advancement in the scientific research and addition to the pool of our temporal knowledge, it is only the extent of our ignorance that is sharply brought into focus; we realise how little we know and how much more there is to learn. With every single puzzle solved, ten new ones surface; instead of gaining ground and getting closer to the end (of knowledge), the destination becomes progressively remote. By extending the frontiers of our physical knowledge, it becomes increasingly clear that we do not necessarily progress towards the ultimate bounds but only succeed in enlarging the horizon of our ignorance like ever increasing circles. This state of affairs is eloquently summed up by T. S. Elliot:

>**"Endless invention, endless experiments,**
>**Bring us knowledge of motion, but not of stillness,**
>**Knowledge of words, and ignorance of the world,**
>**All our knowledge brings us nearer to ignorance;**
>**Where is the life we have lost in living?**
>**Where is the wisdom we have lost in knowledge?**
>**Where is the knowledge we have lost in information?**
>**The cycle of heaven in twenty centuries,**
>**Brings us further from God and nearer to dust."**

It was this kind of realisation that moved the lips of ancient sages to supplicate: "Oh God! What is that which once known, everything else becomes known." (*"Kasmin Tu Bhagavo Vijnaate Sarvam Idam Vijnaatam Bhavati?"*) That supreme spiritual knowledge is the knowledge about the underlying, unchanging Reality which is masked by the ever changing, manifold diversity. It is this knowledge that should be the aim of a study circle and all those topics which will help towards the realisation of our *atmic* (of Self) Reality should form the source material for the study. Of such knowledge it is said:

>*"Na chora–haaryam na cha raaja–haaryam,*
>*Na bhraatar–bhaajyam na cha bhaarakaari;*
>*Vyaye krite vardhata eva nityam,*
>*Vidyaa dhanam sarva–dhana pradhaanam."*

Translation: "Knowledge cannot be stolen by thieves nor appropriated by kings (as tax); it is not subject to division (as part of inheritance) amongst brothers, nor does it weigh heavily (on the mind of one who carries it). As it (knowledge) is spent (by sharing with others), (far from experiencing any diminution) it goes on ever increasing; (that is why) the wealth of knowledge is (considered as) the supreme wealth."

It is a well known scientific fact that electric current flows between two points in a circuit only as long as there is a potential difference between the two points. In a study circle group, likewise, spiritual current can be expected to flow in the circle of its membership only when there exists a potential difference in the knowledge of the various participants. Hence the need for evolving a proper composition of membership for a study circle cannot be overemphasised. Besides, for effective participation and communication, the circle should not be unduly large. A suggested format for study circle is given in Appendix A.

For the success of study circle in general, and entering the spiritual quest in a meaningful way in particular, it is essential to appreciate the essence of, and bear in mind, the following key principles.

(1) We must divest our minds of all preconceived notions keeping our minds ever open. Even in the scientific world, it is now an accepted principle that, a student in search of knowledge should free himself from all his predispositions, and keep an open, unbiased mind ready to receive whatever unfolds itself as being true. A good illustration of such a requirement is given in a Zen story. "There was a Zen monk in Japan who was an adept in meditation. Because of his reputation as a teacher, a well-known professor was drawn towards him. The professor went to see the monk, who offered him the customary tea. Placing a cup in front of the distinguished visitor, he poured tea into it until it became full. He continued pouring even as it overflowed. Seeing the tea spilling over, the startled professor asked for an explanation. The monk said: 'I can fill that which is empty, but not that which is already full. You have come to me with your mind already full of ideas of *'meum'* and *'tuum'*, ambitions and desires. If you seek my instruction, empty your mind, forget all that you have learnt and rid yourself of all harmful and useless matter; then return and I will teach you'. We often fill our minds with desires which are pernicious and which arouse passions that obscure the truth." This prevents us from assessing the values and exercising our powers of discrimination correctly. We need to empty our mind of body-consciousness so that it can be saturated with *atma*-consciousness.

(2) We must gratefully welcome the light of knowledge and wisdom from whichever direction it may be forthcoming. The quality of a teaching or a statement should be judged by the Truth it enshrines and not by the age, attributes and attainments of the 'teacher' or the author. To underline this,

the scriptures have categorically laid down the wholesome dictum:

*"Yukti–yuktam vacho graahyam baalaadapi shukaadapi,
Yukti–heenam vachas–tyaajyam vriddaadapi Shukaadapi."*

Translation: "Whatever is consistent with right reasoning should be accepted, even though it comes from a little boy or even a parrot; whatever is inconsistent therewith ought to be rejected even though emanating from an elderly person or even the great sage Shuka himself".

(3) Spiritual enquiry transcends the barriers of caste, creed and colour. Truth or knowledge related to God, Man and Universe is our common heritage and not an exclusive preserve of any one sect or community. It is revealed to man for the benefit of all mankind irrespective of the language or scripture it may, from time to time, be written in.

(4) We must approach the process of learning with prayerfulness and humility, as humility alone behoves and befits the real seeker after Truth. *"Vidyaa Dadaati Vinayam"*. "True knowledge confers humility", declare the scriptures; the more we learn, the more sharply into focus is brought our own ignorance. Higher secrets unfold themselves to us only in a spirit of prayerfulness and in the purity of our heart.

(5) We must ensure that the dialectic discussions and discursions do not degenerate into pedantic displays of pomposity. One must beware arid polemics parading as logic. "Erudition, well-articulated speech, a wealth of words and skill in expounding the scriptures", says Shankaracharya, "are the things which give pleasure to the learned, but they do not bring liberation". "A buried treasure is not uncovered by merely uttering the words 'come forth'. You must dig and work hard to remove the stone and earth covering it. Then only can you make it your own. In the same way, the pure truth of the *atman* (the soul), buried under *maya* (illusion) and the effects of *maya*, can be reached by contemplation, meditation and other spiritual disciplines such as the one who knows *Brahman* (God) may prescribe – but never by the subtlety of arguments".

(6) We must learn to suspend judgment and adopt an open-minded neutrality until the subject matter is objectively examined. Notwithstanding this, we must recognise that given the differences in our angles of perception, our respective experiences in relation to a particular subject matter may not be identical. This may, at times, prevent our reaching a common understanding. However, this difference must be respected.

(7) For benefit to accrue from participation in a study circle, regular attendance is essential. Irregularity of attendance can, inevitably, subscribe to repetitions and a slowing down of progress. By our attendance can be measured our commitment to this discipline and what priority we accord it. Our yearning has to have strength to inspire endeavour. When yearning is weak, endeavour also declines.

The study of philosophy in the absence of a longing for salvation, says *Tripura Rahasya*, is like dressing up a corpse. The desire must be strong and abiding in order that it may bear fruit. "Just as a man scalded by fire runs immediately in search of soothing unguents and does not waste his time in any other pursuit, so also must the aspirant run after emanicipation to the exclusion of all other pursuits. Such effort alone will be fruitful." The thirst for the knowledge of the Self and, in the furtherence of that aim, the desire to attend the study circle must therefore be heartfelt and spontaneous. If the reason for attendance happens to be no more than doing favour to or pleasing someone else, then the pretence cannot be sustained for long and soon the enthusiasm will fizzle out. It is therefore not proper to put pressure on anyone to attend the study circle. "Those who are hungry", Baba says, "will themselves come seeking places where food is available; those who have no hunger will not be impressed, even when a variety of tasty dishes is placed before them."

Study circle sessions should be conducted in an atmosphere of mutual love and understanding and bearing in mind the following objectives:

(a) **Removal of ignorance and controlling the waywardness of mind through disciplined study:** Ignorance (of our physical self), in this case, can be bliss but only if it is accompanied by the awareness of the spiritual Self. According to Drummond, "He who will not reason is a bigot; he who cannot is a fool; he who does not is a slave". Our efforts in the study circle must be aimed at driving out the bigot, the fool and the slave in us.

Through *maya* (Grand Illusion), Baba says, the pure consciousness which is our essential nature gets wrongly identified itself with the body. The two get mixed up as closely as the iron bar in the fire which becomes so red hot as to look like fire itself, and even partakes of some qualities of fire such as emitting heat, sparks and light. Even as the fire takes the shape of the object it catches, so too does the Divine consciousness assume, under the spell of *maya*, completely the same form as that of the body. The wrong identification creeps into the body gradually, step by step, as it were, like the layers of heat getting into the red hot bar. These layers are: (i) *Aavarna* or the layer of ignorance which makes it forget its inherent Divine Self-illumined state;

(ii) *Asmita* or turning the attention of the consciousness outside for experiencing its lost glory or bliss; (iii) *Raaga* or fondness for external sense objects (related to sight, sound, smell, touch and taste) for experiencing happiness; (iv) *Dwesha* or aversion to objects which deprive the body of sense pleasures or cause pain to the body, and (v) *Abhinivesha* or complete identification of one's consciousness with the body and the feeling "I am young/old, tall/short, dark/white, weak/healthy" and so on.

How then are we to cast off the spell of *maya* and realise our true Self? The answer lies in constantly reminding ourselves of the following truths regarding the Self :–

- "*Sa vetti sarvam, nacha tasya vettaha*". Self is the Knower of all; It cannot be known by any one.
- "*Adreshto dreshtaha*". Self is the Seer but not the object of It's own sight.
- "*Ashroto shrotaha*". Self is the Listener but not Itself the object of hearing.
- "*Maanaso antaram yam mano na veda*". Self illumines the mind but is not Itself cognisable by the mind.

Just as the hand that holds the pair of tongs cannot be caught by the tongs, so too the mind and the intellect which are the "instruments" of the Self cannot grasp the Self.

Realization of the Self is not attained by intellection but by cessation of thought. So, as long as one is caught in the mire of 'i' and 'mine', and is unable to shake off the notions of 'myness', viz, 'my body', 'my mind', 'my intellect', etc, the Self which transcends cognition, will not be found, for it cannot be realised as 'my Self'. "Retire into solitude", says *Tripura Rahasya*, "Analyse and see what those things are which are cognised as 'mine'; discard them all and transcending them, 'look' for the real Self."

(b) **Developing clarity of vision:** Consider the example of a number of people seated along the perimeter of a circle looking at an object placed at the centre. Depending upon the location of each individual in relation to the object, only a limited, particular aspect of the object can be seen from any given location, other aspects remaining hidden. So, the attributes or characteristics of the object as revealing themselves to and therefore defined by every individual will differ from that of every other individual along the perimeter. Whilst every single definition will be valid and correct, it must be recognised that no single definition will, on its own, represent the whole truth exclusively, nor even may all of them collectively, fully exhaust the totality. Given the relative differences in our temperaments, our likes and

As My devotee you have taken a step that is incomparable in magnificence and magnitude - even greater than the giant step forward which was acclaimed by man when he first walked on the moon.

I am here beside you. I am within you. I am in your Heart of Hearts. I am here to help you and guide you. Turn to God; I cannot do that for you; you must do that yourself.

I can draw the God in you towards Me, but you must come to Me. You must become one with Me and try to see God everywhere. See his Love in all people. Feel His Love in you, for it is above all other love.

When I go about My work, I impart the Love of God. My Love is God's Love. Am I not giving you a hint as to the real glory of God's Love that reposes within you? Let Me awaken you from your slumber. Let Me help you open your eyes for you to see the Love of God that awaits you. This is My work. This is My joy. I am tireless in my quest to let you be filled with the Love of God.

As I look on you, I see the Lord within you. His Divine sweetness bathes you. I want you to know that this Divine Heritage is yours. Know this and come to the Lord's Kingdom. You will live for evermore in a treasure house of blessed happiness.

A rare chance to find God is in your grasp. Do not sacrifice even one breath without coming closer to your own God-Self. Benefit from every means I give you to find God. Become ever aware of the Love of God. Impart God through your Love to all.

Your dawn of knowledge is approaching. Each day is your chance to achieve the greatest of all earthly accomplishments: to become Yourself - God.

Sri Sathya Sai Baba

dislikes, our strengths and weaknesses, etc, as we view truth, we can get only as much of it as the circumstances we find ourselves in will permit, understand only as much of it as our intellect will comprehend and know only as much of it as we are able to experience. This then makes the difference between man and man. Whilst we perceive the truth in different ways thus, we must never lose sight of the fact that we all belong to the same Universal Truth. It is important to bear this in mind all the time; only then will we develop catholicity and universality of vision.

(c) **Becoming steady in our spiritual discipline:** Discipline is the first rung on the spiritual ladder. Certain measure of discipline is needed even to cross and reach safely the other side of a road; how much more so will be required to wade through the gross, the subtle and the causal bodies in order to reach the Self? Steadiness of mind is the yardstick by which our progress can be measured.

(d) **Strengthening our faith:** It is often said that "For those who believe in God, no explanation is necessary; for those who do not, no explanation is possible". However, it must be recognised that, at the lower rungs of spiritual quest, reason is often seen accompanied by an in-built doubt. This is only to be expected. Voicing a genuine doubt must not be construed as lack of faith. As one poet-philosopher remarked:

> **"There lies more faith in honest doubt,**
> **Believe me, than in half the creeds".**

"Believing, where we cannot prove," will of course come through personal experience and such a belief will, in course of time, draw certainty to itself. However, when a doubt does arise, every attempt should be made to clarify it rather than to allow it to fester and add to the confusion. We must, of course, recognise that spiritual quest often takes an aspirant beyond intellectual reasoning. As Pascal has aptly remarked: "The heart has reasons of which reason has no knowledge". We must not expect everything to be possibly explained away by the head (ie through rationalisation); remember, the most brilliant logic can only approach the truth but never attain it; certain facts may therefore have to be accepted on trust on the testimony of the heart (ie intuition).

The *Bhagavad Geeta* (Song Celestial) has laid down that "the man of earnest faith acquires supreme wisdom" ("*shraddhaavaan labhate jnaanam*"), and "the one filled with doubts perishes" ("*samshayaatma vinashyati*"). When life flows between these two guiding principles, Baba says, then it will be blessed with peace and happiness. "It is only when man is guarded by earnest faith (*shraddha*) on one side, and freedom from doubt (*nissamshaya*) on the other, that he will be able to reach the goal of life."

Faith should not be underestimated. If it were not for faith, man would not dare even breathe for fear of catching some pathogenic infection and would perish in the process. Faith, claims *Tripura Rahasya*, is like a fond mother who can never fail to save her trusting child from dangerous situations.

(e) **Bringing about our transformation:** Study Circle sessions should not be turned into venues for collection of information. They must inspire us to bring about our transformation. Baba emphasises the fact that an ideal study should have the following three components:

- *Shravana* : Reading of books or listening to the reading of books or listening to discourses. Dispassion for the pleasures of life arises in an aspirant who gradually begins to long for knowledge of the Truth and becomes absorbed in its search.

- *Manana* : Ruminating over and contemplating what has been read, listened to, or discussed. One is impelled to turn over the whole matter in one's mind until one is able to ascertain the truth with clearness and certitude.

- *Nidhidhyaasana* : Absorbing fully the meaning of what has been read or listened to, and then putting the ascertained knowledge into practice until the experience of Truth is realised.

To make study sessions meaningful, it is essential that the knowledge acquired is put to the right use; only then will the knowledge acquired blossom into wisdom. Baba says that, in spite of great advances in science and technology, human character and morality have not made commensurate progress. "Knowledge without discrimination is dangerous. Atomic power is being harnessed for destructive purpose. How much could be done for improving production and raising the condition of the people if all this energy could be used for peaceful and productive purposes. Knowledge should promote people's well-being and not cause harm to them."

"Through knowledge, you acquire humility. Through humility, you become worthy of responsibility. Through responsible positions, you get wealth. Through wealth, you must practice righteousness. Righteousness ensures your well-being in this world and the one beyond it."

O Divine Mother Sai! Deliver me from the sleep of Ignorance into the dawn of Wisdom.

QUESTIONS :

(1) What is the destiny of man? What keeps him from achieving it?
(2) What is the need for study circle?
(3) Preconceived ideas are often a hindrance in the process of learning. Discuss.
(4) Discuss the main principles responsible for the success of study circle.
(5) In what ways can irregularity of attendance affect the quality of study circle?
(6) What causes our ignorance and how does it manifest itself?
(7) How can one attempt to remove ignorance?
(8) Discuss the main objectives of study circle.
(9) Why is it that different people have different perceptions of the one and only eternal Truth?
(10) Discuss the different aspects of the human personality.
(11) List the importance of discipline for spiritual progress.
(12) How does intuition operate?
(13) Transformation, not information, is the key to spiritual progress. Discuss.
(14) "Fools dwelling in darkness, wise in their own conceit and puffed up with vain knowledge, go round and round, staggering to and fro, like blind men led by the blind". Discuss.
(15) What is the supreme wealth and why?
(16) What is that which once known everything else becomes known?

Wisdom of the Wise

Faith	*is the*	*Threshold of the Wise*
Truth	*is the*	*Strength of the Wise*
Fearlessness	*is the*	*Nature of the Wise*
Steadfastness	*is the*	*Trait of the Wise*
Character	*is the*	*Hall Mark of the Wise*
Humility	*is the*	*Ornament of the Wise*
Silence	*is the*	*Language of the Wise*
Peace	*is the*	*Breath of the Wise*
Love	*is the*	*very Life of the Wise*

PKK

"Whither so ever ye turn, there is the Face of God."

Qur'an

2. INTEGRATION

What possible explanation can there be for two children begotten of the same parents to be temperamentally different from each other or indeed their parents? Why are all of us on this planet, begotten of the one and only Divine Father, of different colours, creeds, cultures and circumstances? Well, our infinite past is responsible for having shaped our present. This concept is based on the Principle of *Karma* (Law of Causation), which is explained in more detail in Chapter 13. This principle explains away, logically and comprehensively, the apparent injustices and differences in the world and enables us to reconcile the concept of an impartial and just God with these seeming inequalities. Burdened with our accumulated individual and collective *kaarmic* debt, one takes birth at a time and place which provide the necessary environment for working out the debt and lightening the burden. The character of an individual, or the 'human personality', is an expression of his or her deep-seated tendencies or latencies. Since these are developed and acquired over many life times, getting rid of the less desirable of these traits demands a great effort and commitment. Thought is a powerful creative force and actions are materialised thoughts. Through consciously directed thought-force, backed by appropriate action, it is possible to refine our character and generally bring about the unfoldment of our spiritual nature.

There is also a vague notion of idealism, of ridding the world of its ills and promoting the welfare of the humanity. However, being thrown together with our own innate tendencies and latencies, most of our solutions, however well intentioned, are conceived under the sway of our personal preferences and prejudices and are, therefore, not always universally accepted. Besides, our infatuation with the illusions of the material life is so strong that the very life-force which could be profitably directed towards establishing cohesion and harmony is, unfortunately, frittered away in the suicidal pursuit of unending dichotomy of desires. This preoccupation of the individuals towards their own exclusive needs, inevitably, breads clash and conflict. Yet it is this clash, this differentiation of thought that makes for light and love, strength and character, art and music, sacrifice and martyrdom. It is this flux, this movement, that is the essence, the very life and vitality of the manifested world. Variety is the very soul of life. Without flux, all life must cease. But, whilst it is impossible that all differences will cease, asks *Swami* Vivekananda, is there any reason why we should hate and fight each other? Whilst accepting contrariness or variety as an essential aspect, rather an inherent law of life, it should not degenerate into profanity and destruction but be seen as adding richness to life. If differentiation be the essence of life, what then do we mean by Integration?

Integration does not mean having the same colour of the skin or following the same religion or speaking the same language or donning the same dress; nor does it imply doing the same thing by all simultaneously. For all these things are not possible since the Creator, who knows better than you and I, did not Will it so. Commenting upon the religion of love, Gautam Sen remarks: "How often we slap a label on a person – 'Communist', 'Capitalist', 'Christian', 'Hindu', 'Negro' – and, by so doing refuse to acknowledge him as a separate human being. The fact, however, is that no two capitalists or Christians or Hindus or whatever – right down to two twins and two persons' fingerprints – were ever exactly alike or will ever be so. As long as we fail to realise this, how is it possible for us to love one another?" Thank God that we cannot make all conform to the same ideas. For, if we all thought alike, we would run out of thoughts to think and would look like the mummies in a museum staring blankly at one another's faces. Whilst differences must exist, there need be no discord.

Integration may be likened to threading together into a garland an assortment of flowers taken from different trees, with their own peculiar shapes and sizes, and colours and fragrances, worthy of offering at the Lotus Feet of the Lord. Differentiation is implied and inherent in integration. One cannot exist without the other. Without differentiation, human endeavour, indeed the very human life, would cease to exist; without differentiation, integration has no meaning.

Look at the breath-taking mozaic around us: a mountain here, an ocean there, a forest here, a desert there, flora and fauna, stars and planets in the firmament – some in perpetual motion while others apparently motionless, all performing their allotted, different functions like clockwork and without any conflict.

The society we live in is made up of individuals. What we think and how we behave as individuals and the way we interact with other members of the society, determine the state of health of the society. When there is harmony in thought, word and deed of the individuals, there is also peace and well being in the society. However, when we do not put into practice what we preach or stand by what we profess to be right, we lose credibility in the society. When our deeds are completely out of tune with our professed ideals, then it is not mutual trust and understanding but distrust and disbelief that grow resulting in friction and faction and an inevitable lack of integration. The stresses and strains resulting from the disharmony in our thought, word and deed also make it uncomfortable for us to live in peace with our conscience; an uneasy conscience is a nagging bedfellow. Furthermore, our innate tendencies and latencies, which are at work in a subtle way most of the time, find expression in our emotive linguistic, religious or cultural preferences and prejudices thus adding to the general confusion. When words like Europeans and Asians, Christians and Hindus, English and Sanskrit, etc, are branded about without due thought and consideration, purely to score points off each other and with a view to emphasising that "integration" is possible but only on the terms of one or the other, polarisation results and the professed aim of the "brotherhood of man" and integration itself become the casualty. Coming to terms with our conscience holds the key to our well being and has, therefore, been the prime urge of many a spiritual seeker.

The only way to improve the society we live in and change the world at large, is by bringing about the desired change within our own-selves and not by imposing our ideas of change or standards of improvement on others. Only by removing the conflict within our own-selves will we ever progress towards global peace and harmony. The necessary prerequisite, however, is to recognise that the need for improvement exists and to identify our own shortcomings through self analysis.

Most of the time we are not clear about our objectives. On rare occasions when we are, we do not seem to be able to muster the strength to see our convictions through. "The spirit may be willing but the flesh is weak". This is so because of our lack of faith in ourselves.

A saint poetess of Kashmir, Lalleshwari by name, once sang out (in *Kashmiri*):

> "*Ba kyah kara yiman panchan dahan ta kahan*
> *Yim yath lejje vokhun karith gayam*
> *Agar sari samahan ta akisai razi lamahan*
> *Ada kyaazi raavihay kahan gaav*".

Translation: "O, What am I to do with these five, ten and eleven that have run away and robbed this (earthen) pot? If only they were to tug at the same tether, why then would the eleven lose the cow?"

The five represent the five senses of perception, together with the five senses of action, they become the ten, and the mind makes up the eleven. The pot refers to the physical body. When the mind reaches out through the senses into, and pursues the diversity of, the objective world, its peace is gone. If only the mind and the senses integrated their efforts and turned their attention inwards, they would certainly find kinship with the *Atma*, the Real Self, the goal, and not stray away from it.

Bhagawan Sri Sathya Sai Baba has often reiterated that He has come to re-establish *Sanathana Dharma*, the universal highway to God. '*Sanathana*' means eternal and universal and '*dharma*' means code of conduct in thought, word, and deed based on Truth, and so, it is the heritage of all mankind and not just one religious group. Because it is a *Sanskrit* expression, does that alter its content, or, because of that, is its relevance and universality any the less? Would an apple rise heavenwards instead of falling down if the law of gravity were written in a language other than English? Can truth be selective in seeking out who should follow it? Of course not.

Truth is the basic tenet, indeed the very life breath of Sri Sathya Sai Organisation and its founder is Truth incarnate. It offers a unique opportunity to those who join it to demonstrate to the whole world how, in spite of their differences, people of different faiths, languages, ages and temperaments can come together in mutual understanding and love and march hand-in-hand towards the common spiritual goal. That indeed has to be one of its strengths also and that is why Sri Sathya Sai Organisation is not run by a 'show of hands'.

Seventy percent voting one way and thirty percent the other, does not necessarily make seventy percent right; nor does it imply that the minority are always right. These numbers merely indicate respective preferences at any given time. However, a show of hands is required but only to affirm that we are willing to join them together in pulling towards the common goal, complementing each other's efforts instead of putting up hurdles or giving substance to non-existent apprehensions.

If we want spiritualism but only at our own terms and to suit our own convenience, if we seek truth but only in so far as it accords with our preconceived notions based on our prejudices and preferences, it is not the spiritual path that we will be treading, it is not truth that we will get. These can be achieved only through disciplined enquiry and an open mind, and in a spirit of sacrifice and effacement of ego and false pride.

There is, very often, a tendency to adapt truth to suit one's own conception of it. All sorts of geographic, socio-cultural or even religious 'justifications' are advanced in support of our preferences. However, the fact remains that Truth does not change with time nor with the direction of the compass. We must also recognise that those of us who have joined the Sri Sathya Sai Organisation, have done so out of our own free will, not to change or modify the message and mission of Sai – which in any case we cannot even if we wanted to – but to bring about our own transformation. When the call came, we volunteered. When He takes us up on our word, we must not lay down the terms and conditions. Our commitment has to be total and unconditional. The object of our searches and researches, our prayers and penances and pilgrimages to *Prashanti Nilayam*, is to cast away our assumed limitations and false apprehensions in order to get closer and closer to the divinity. Why then pursue a course which might take us away from that goal?

We must stop talking in terms of Europeans and Asians, Hindus and Christians, etc, in a manner that might subscribe, perhaps not deliberately, but nevertheless damagingly, to division and confusion. It is not the real differences but the imagined ones that create problems. Sectarianism, bigotry and its horrible descendent, fanaticism, says *Swami* Vivekananda, have long possessed this beautiful earth. "They have filled the earth with violence, drenched it often with human blood, destroyed civilizations and sent whole nations to despair. Had it not been for these horrible demons, human society would be far more advanced than it is now". It is the ignorance in man that impels him to claim that his belief is the only belief and his path the only True path. Those who are the least faith-full are often the most vocal. It is the fanaticism and intolerance born out of such ignorance that have been responsible for many a shameful aberration of the human mind.

There is a saying (in *Kashmiri*):

> *"Yeli peeran hisaab mangan,*
> *Kata peeran natth atchi zangan."*

"When the preachers will be called by the Lord to account for the conduct of their own lives, false preachers", it is said, "will be seen shaking at the knees". Consider the example of Mr 'A' and Mr 'B'. Both run charity hospitals but with one difference; Mr 'A' does it out of compassion and a heart-felt concern for the plight of the poor, whereas Mr 'B' does so to build up for himself a good public image to catch votes for his election to the parliament. Externally, both their actions are similar and in the eyes of the people, both appear virtuous. In reality, however, one is a humanitarian, a humble God-seeker, and the other an inveterate self seeker! We must ever remember that man will not be judged by the faith he professes but by his actions and the motives behind them. Of what use then is it to be most religious in pretence if irreligious and uncharitable in action? We cannot become religious merely by professing a faith, however noble its tenets, but only by living that faith in our daily life.

In the rare moments of deep and silent reflection, when the realisation dawns that the apparent diversity of faiths has unity and harmony as its base, all doubts and apprehensions disappear rendering man speechless. From that moment onwards, he looses all interest in proselytising and preaching, his head bows down in humility and his silent actions become the most eloquent expressions of his true faith. According to Lao Tzu:

**"He who knows, does not speak;
He who speaks, does not know."**

"Why was man created one?" the Rabbis ask. They themselves reply: "In order that no man should say to another, 'My father was greater than thine'", thus stressing the fundamental equality of all men. However, without understanding fully our own human nature, how can we expect to fathom the inherent oneness or the nature of the divine or indeed recognise the divinity present equally in all beings? For instance, if we assert that God is omnipresent, and that He is therefore present as much in a donkey and a pig as in a man, why then feel slighted if someone hails us as "an ass" or "a swine"? Baba says that it is only when we have realised our oneness with God that we are entitled to speak about the equality and oneness of all beings. "Till then, a dog is a dog, a donkey a donkey, and a man a man. As long as you regard yourself as a human being, respect other fellow-humans, show love towards other creatures...."

Remember, the planets may be many and different, but the universe is One; the countries and continents may be different, but the world is One; people may be of different colours and temperaments but all mankind is One; modes of worship may be different but the essence of all prayers is One. In the words of *Swami* Vivekananda: "Every worship offered is received by Him whatever be the name or the form worshipped; every hand lifted heavenwards, every lip that moves in supplication, a prayer unto Him; all knees bending towards Qa'ba, or kneeling in a Hindu temple or a Christian church, are kneeling unto Him and, whether we are conscious of it or not, singing the glory of the same God, for He is the One Lord of all!"

Integration means a certain meeting of the minds. It implies understanding and, in spite of the apparent differences, knowing how to live together in harmony, helping each other's efforts on this pilgrimage of life. Integration is something that has to come from the heart. True integration can only come about from a spiritual understanding of the essential oneness of all life; to achieve this, feeling of separateness must go.

Swami Vivekananda says: "When man has seen himself as One with the Infinite Being of the universe, when all separateness has ceased, when all men, all women, all angels, all gods, all animals, all plants, the whole universe has been melted into that Oneness, then all fear disappears. Who to fear then? Do you fear yourself? Can I hurt or kill myself? Then will all sorrow disappear. What can cause me sorrow? I am the One Existence of the universe. Then all jealousies will disappear; of whom to be jealous? Of myself? Then all bad feelings will disappear. There is none in the universe but I... kill out this differentiation, kill out this superstition that there are many. He who, in this world of many, sees the One; he who, in this mass of insentiency, sees the One Sentient Being; he who in this world of shadow, catches that Reality, unto him belongs eternal peace, unto none else, unto none else."

Consider the example of concrete. The various constituents that make up concrete, eg, aggregates, sand, cement and water, come in different shapes and sizes, from different sources and have different individual properties. However, when they are mixed, they blend together complementing each other, assuming the properties of the homogeneous mass known as concrete. During this process of mixing, and as a result of the chemical reaction between the constituents, heat of hydration is given out. To ensure that this heat does not cause cracks in the concrete, the concrete has to be 'cured' with water and only then will we get concrete of the strength and durability that will stand up to the various stresses and strains. Likewise, in the Organisation, we have to integrate together into a homogeneous conglomerate. Inevitably, during this process of mixing, there is bound to be friction with the various components trying to segregate, but as long as the heat so generated is cooled and cured by the divine water, ie, Love of Sai, we can be assured of strength which will withstand all the vicissitudes of life.

In the words of *Swami* Vivekananda, "Just as individuals come into being to play out their own *karmas*, so also with nations. Each nation has a destiny to fulfil, a message to deliver – a message not of oppression and exploitation, difference and despair, but of hope, harmony and integration – each representing, as it were, a note, however peculiar, in the harmony of nations!"

Remember a body cannot enjoy sound health if any part of it is ailing; a family cannot enjoy happiness if one of its less fortunate members is

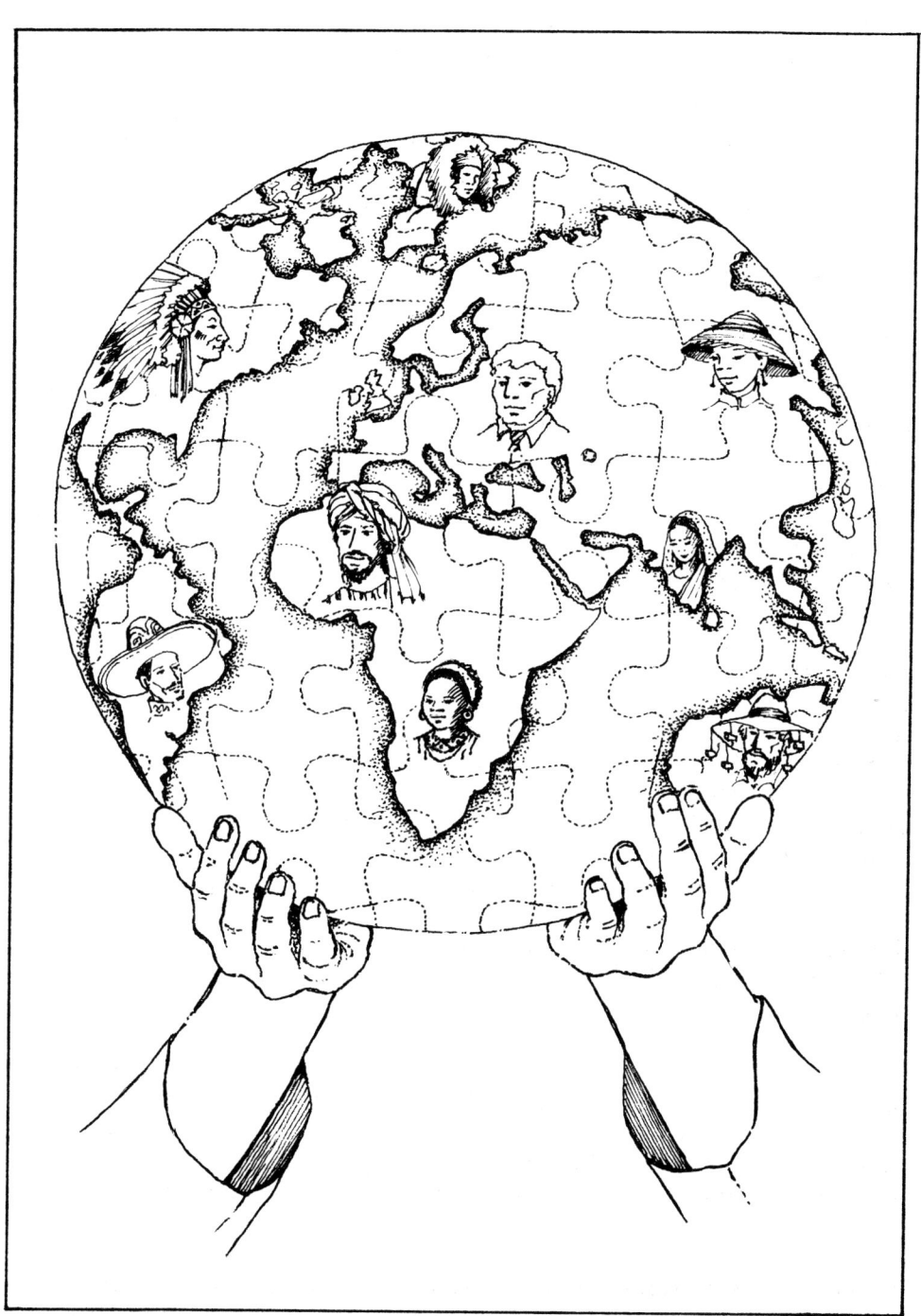

ignored; the world cannot experience peace and harmony, if even the tiniest part of it lives in abject poverty, be that of the body or the spirit.

In the Divine Plan unfolding itself before our very eyes, there are great works to be accomplished and great heights to be scaled. To become the instruments in the Divine Plan, we must make a conscious effort to bypass all the extraneous matter, the theology, the dogma, the ritual, that clutters up religion, and achieve clarity of vision. The tasks that lie ahead are beckoning us to throw away the blinkers, cast away the glasses of petty jealousies, unfounded apprehensions and veiled prejudices and to show to the whole world that the apparent differentiation has harmony as its base and in that firm belief march forward, hand-in-hand towards the goal of Integration. At the individual level, Integration has also to be consciously worked at in thought, word and deed. By each night-fall, our conscience must call us to account for our lapses during the day to ensure that with each dawn our resolve to spread light and love around and to recognise the brotherhood of man and the fatherhood of one omnipresent God, grows stronger and stronger. Only through the integration of the human personality can true integration in the society be achieved. In the words of Baba:

> " **There is only one caste, the caste of humanity.**
> **There is only one religion, the religion of love.**
> **There is only one language, the language of the heart.**
> **There is only one God and He is omnipresent.**"

"Mankind can be happy, peaceful and prosperous only through the knowledge and practice of unity; if man's thoughts, feelings and attitudes run along the bylanes of distinction and difference, his happiness is destroyed by fear, pride, suspicion, hatred and greed and then *Shanti* (Peace) is beyond reach. Consider the One Indivisible Ocean as your goal and gain; then what does it matter which current flows where - the Gulf Stream, the Arctic Stream - all merge in the self-same expanse. People may be adopting the *Bhakhti* (Devotion) path or the *Jnaana* (Wisdom) path or the Islamic or the Christian paths; they all reach the self-same Ocean of Divine Grace. There, all distinctions disappear and are known as invalid. All labels and identifications slip off by themselves. Names and forms to which each tiny little river was attached fade away when the waters merge in the Ocean. Keep the call of the Ocean ever echoing in the ear. That is The Inner *Sadhana* (spiritual practice) for every one, until he reaches the ONE."

O Divine Mother Sai ! May all my thoughts be centred upon Thee and may all my words and deeds be in accord with my thoughts ! May I see all in Sai and Sai in all !

QUESTIONS:

(1) "Root cause of unrest in the world is the differences in thought!" Do you agree? Give reasons.
(2) Understanding, not uniformity, is the essence of Integration. Discuss.
(3) Without differentiation there can be no integration. Discuss.
(4) Can Truth be established by a show of hands? Give reasons.
(5) Truth can be established by the one who is able to win an argument! Do you agree with this statement? Give reasons.
(6) How many races inhabit the earth and how many Gods are there?! What conclusions can you draw from your answer?
(7) List the fundamental differences between people of different races and religions!
Are these differences acquired or inherent, real or imaginary?
(8) How can mankind be happy and peaceful ?

The age span 16 - 30 is crucial, for that is the period when life adds sweetness to itself, when talents, skills and attitudes are accumulated, sublimated and sanctified. If the tonic of unselfish service is administered to the mind during this period, life's mission is fulfilled - for the process of sublimation and sanctification will be hastened by this tonic. Do not serve for the sake of reward, attracting attention, or earning gratitude, or from a sense of pride at your own superiority in skill, wealth, status or authority. Serve because you are urged by Love. When you succeed, ascribe the success to the Grace of God who urged you on, as Love within you. When you fail, ascribe the failure to your own inadequacy, insincerity or ignorance.
– Sri Sathya Sai Baba

*"There is one secret which, if known, lays bare all secrets.
There is one problem which, if solved, no problems remain unsolved.
There is one knot which, if untied, all knots are loosened.
There is one science which, when mastered, all is mastered ..."*

Sri Sathya Sai Baba

3. THE G * A * M * E

Seeds sown in a patch of land, nurtured with the same water and compost, tended by the same hands of the same gardener, blossom into flowers of different shapes, sizes, hues and fragrances. We know this to be so, but do we know why? Why are water-laden clouds wafted away from one spot only to pour down as rain somewhere else? What is the subtle secret of sound? When the grossest element is refined more and more, it becomes lighter and lighter and achieves, progressively, greater freedom of movement; if a human being is, likewise, purified of his ego which weighs him down, can he levitate or walk on water? By what means are the stars, the moon and the galaxies, strewn like shining pearls in the night sky, so precisely balanced?

The list of questions that have fascinated and engaged the human mind over the ages, is simply endless. However, the secret of solving these and myriad other mysteries surrounding man, lies hidden in the answers to the four fundamental questions. These are:

- What is the greatest **Gift** to man?
- What is the greatest **Achievement** of man?
- What is the greatest **Mystery** surrounding man?
- What is the greatest **Enquiry** facing man?

If these questions are correctly understood and satisfactorily answered, the 'mystery' of the universe can be seen in its correct perspective.

Baba says, "Life is a Game; play it". In order to play the game of life with confidence and well, we must not only know what the game is about and what the ground rules are, but we must also be aware of our own capabilities; only then can we play to our full potential.

Wealth, strength, beauty, scholarship, etc, although undeniably, enviable and welcome divine gifts in their own right are surely not the greatest gifts to man; the one gift that stands out above all other gifts is the one that separates man from the beast and characterises the humanness in him, ie, the power of discrimination between good and evil, right and wrong, etc. Even more than this, it is the power of discrimination between the changing and the changeless, time-bound and timeless and the evanescent and the eternal; that is undoubtedly the greatest gift to man.

Man, as we know, has been granted the freedom of thought; it is in exercise of, and in accordance with, this freedom that he is able to perform acts which may be construed as good, bad or indifferent. However, without the power of discrimination, the freedom of thought on its own, would be like an open licence without any guarantee against its wanton misuse. Furthermore, for this power of discrimination to be meaningful, it is axiomatic that, in the first instance, man also has the knowledge of what is native to his Self and, by extension and implication, the means to know what is alien.

The world of matter, time and space around us, indeed the whole universe, is subject to change. It is in perpetual motion, and motion implies change. Consider the body-mind complex; the body at birth does not, even remotely, resemble the state it is in when approaching death. It undergoes a continuous change through the various stages from birth till death, ie, childhood, youth, middle age, old age, etc. Mind, likewise, is ever changing. Mind is a collection of thoughts and desires; as the thoughts and desires change, so also does the mind. Even time is for ever changing; what will be 'tomorrow' is potentially 'today' in the making and what is 'today' will become 'yesterday' in a day's time.

The birth of the human body is intrinsically governed by the principle of cause and effect. The root cause of our present birth is the lingering, deeply cherished but unfulfilled desires accumulated through our previous lives. Our temperament, personality and general make-up are a direct consequence of our deep-seated latencies and tendencies nurtured in our past life. That, incidentally, explains why two children begotten of the same parents could have totally dissimilar temperaments and attitudes to life; they carry with them, and are the results of, two distinct causal bodies.

The aspect of human personality which is beyond any change, however, is the *atma*, the real Self. So, the changing body contains within it, for a while, the changeless, eternal spirit or the Self. The mistake lies in confusing the lifeless dwelling, the body (*deha*), for the immortal dweller, the Self (*dehi*), the very life itself. Baba says "The body gains its lustre from its indweller who is God. As long as the indweller resides in the body, it is full of fragrance and life. The moment this indweller leaves the body, the body becomes foul and obnoxious. Without its indweller, the body is a reprehensible thing; far from being fragrant, it just emits a bad smell from moment to moment. The body is given in order to understand the indweller. This power of discrimination is unique to mankind".

The precious gift of discrimination has been, mercifully, bestowed upon man so that he may use this in separating the body-mind complex which is impermanent, from the *atma* which is eternal, and then striving to realise the *atma*, the Self. It is indeed this gift that has moved the human lips to supplicate:

> *"Asato maa sat gamaya,*
> *Tamaso maa jyotir gamaya,*
> *Mrityor maa amritam gamaya,*
> *Aum shanti shanti shantihi."*

Translation: "O Lord! Lead me from untruth, (evanescence of the body and the manifested universe) to truth, (existence of the *atma*), from darkness (of ignorance covering the *atma*) to light (of effulgence of the *atma*), from death, (of the body-mind complex) to immortality (of the *atma*). Let there be Peace, Peace and Peace!

The greatest achievement of man is not the inroads he has made in the fields of science and technology however fantastic and breathtaking they may undoubtedly be by any stretch of imagination, such as, the discovery of the microchip, man's landing on the moon, etc, nor even the concept of zero without which our science and technology would not be where these are today. Man's researches into the fields of science and technology have, however, been orientated towards increasing the life span of the body at all costs, irrespective of its usefulness or otherwise, increasing the material comforts of the body, and in the production of the arsenals of mass destruction. With the alarming growth of the consumer culture, the spirit of selfless service, love and sacrifice, have become meaningless and wasteful concepts of ridicule. The selfishness and exploitation of others, at times cleverly disguised as charity, are stifling the very existence of human life on this planet.

The grandest, single most glorious achievement in the history of mankind has, undeniably, been the recognition and the conscious realisation of the fact that man does not have to look heavenwards to find God but that the germ of divinity, the seed of God-hood, verily lies latent within him as his own true Self. It is the presence of this true Self alone that is responsible for activating the body and its functioning. According to the *Vedic* wisdom, the Self, the Life-Principle in the body, is a concretised reflection of the Cosmic

Consciousness which has been designing and guiding the course of evolution from the very beginning. Even the scientists and psychologists are increasingly coming round to this way of thinking.

Microbiology traces the origin of life to what are called the DNA (Deoxyribonucleic acid) molecules in the cell which are supposed to control and regulate the development and growth of the body. The scientists tell us that there are about 10^{10} cells and therefore about 10^{20} macromolecules in the human brain. The biologists would have us believe that, with the appearance of the DNA molecule, the non-living started evolving into a living organism. With the further discovery of the 'genes', it is believed that there is a subtle 'gene' which is the 'carrier' of 'encoded messages' related to the way each molecule is supposed to behave and function. It is thus assumed that the genetic code is a special device which tells each cell how to carry out the process of life, step by step.

To the biologist, Ludwig Von Bertalanffy, however, "The ultimate reduction of the phenomenon of life to the molecular properties of DNA and related substances ...," appears "less convincing..." His view is shared by many other scientists as well, one of whom, the eminent biologist Paul Weiss, asks, "Could you actually believe that such an astronomic number of elements, shifted around as we have demonstrated in our cell studies, could ever guarantee your sense of identity and constancy in life without this constancy being insured by a super-ordinated principle of integration?" Modern psychologists too, are subscribing to the view that an extremely coordinated and ordered functioning of each of the 100 billion cells in the human body could not be possible without the presence of a non-physical, non-chemical, 'super-intelligence' which inspires each cell with the knowledge of design. This 'super-intelligence' is also referred to by many scientists and psychologists as the 'underlying reality', 'ground-stuff' or even 'cosmic consciousness'.

Man, verily, is the repository of the truth, the reality. Through his obsessive attachment to the comforts of the body and total disregard for the need of the spirit, however, man has lost the way. The overwhelming attachment with the body can destroy all powers of discrimination. Baba illustrates this point with the following story.

Once upon a time Indra, the lord of the celestials, was cursed to be born as a pig on earth. Being born thus, it was spending all its time living a family life in dirty, muddy water. The sage Naarada, while passing by and seeing this pig and its family, recognized Indra reduced to that form. Taking great pity on it, Naarada spoke to the pig, "Indra, look at the state you have

I never would have come, had I been asked!
When would I choose to go, if I were asked?
I would forswear this world, and would dispense
With coming, being, going, were I asked!

He brought me hither, to my great surprise;
From life I gather but a dark surmise;
I go perforce. Why come? Why live? Why go?
I ask these questions but find no replies.

Who was it that did knead my clay? Not I.
Who spun my web of silk and wool? Not I.
Who wrote upon my forehead all my good
And all my evil deeds? In truth, Not I.

'Twas writ at first, whatever was to be,
By pen unheeding bliss or misery,
Yea, writ upon the tablet once for all,
To murmur or resist is vanity.

With outward seeming we can cheat mankind,
But to God's Will we can but be resigned;
The deepest wiles my cunning e'er devised,
To shirk divine decrees no way could find.

When Allah mixed my clay, He knew full well
My future acts, and could each one foretell;
Without His fiat nothing can I do;
Is it then just to punish me in hell?

What eye can pierce the veil of God's decrees,
Or read the riddle of earth's destinies?
Pondered have I for years threescore and twelve,
And can but say these things are mysteries.

The Quatrains of Omar Khayyam
(Translation: E. H. Whinfield)

degenerated into. How did this happen? But never mind, I will get you out of this. I can use all my accumulated powers of penance to help you". He spoke to it very sympathetically, saying that one who should be enjoying all the luxuries of heaven has been put into such a miserable state. How very unfortunate its life had become. Indra, in the form of pig, replied, "Why are you coming in the way of my happiness? The joy that I am getting in this dirty water, I will not be able to get anywhere else. The wonderful life that I am enjoying with my family in this muddy water I cannot even get in heaven. Please do not meddle with my life and come in the way of the joy that I am experiencing most fully here. Go on your way, please". Indra, who was under the spell of the illusion of attachment, did not realise his pitiable condition. When one is under the spell of *moha* (attachment), one will be completely deluded. This delusion is due to the irresistible power of *maya* (Illusion).

In spite of all his lapses and disappointments caused by the supervention of the veil of ignorance weaved by *maya*, it is the intuitive urge, born out of an insatiable thirst to recover the 'lost' Self, ever flickering in man, that spurs him on, inexorably, towards the discovery of the Self attaining, in the process, the pinnacles of love, beauty, character, scholarship and sainthood, and sacrifice and martyrdom. The lives of great sages and masters bear testimony to this achievement of man. This is the Truth, Purity and Beauty (*Satyam, Shivam, Sundaram*) of the saints who take birth as mere mortals with their usual frailties and failings but who bravely fight their way to realise their innate divinity, leaving behind their indelible footprints on the sands of time for the benefit of all mankind. They demonstrate vividly that our life is a painful yet enjoyable game of hide and seek with God, culminating in the joy and ecstasy of one-ness with Him. How infinitesimal is the size of man and yet how infinite his potential! Could such a thing ever be possible if man were not divine?

The *Sanskrit* word *sharira* means that which wastes away; it refers to the body. Baba says that God has been called *shariri*, the one who lives in the perishable body. To penetrate through the veil of ignorance that hides this truth, one must make an effort to discover the immortal Lord, the Self, residing resplendently in the mortal body. It is only when that divine goal is realised that all agitation and activity for the body will cease.

Brahma, the Creator, it is said, once asked the sage Naarada what it was that he found most puzzling during his travels on earth. Naarada listed three things: Firstly, the dying are weeping over the dead. Those who are themselves approaching death every moment are weeping over those who have died, as if their weeping has any effect either to revive the dead or to prevent or postpone their own death! Secondly, everyone fears the consequences of sin but goes on sinning nevertheless! Thirdly, everyone craves for the fruits of *punya* (meritorious acts) but is reluctant to perform any meritorious acts! These are the three great paradoxes; what then is the greatest mystery surrounding man?

The mystery of the universe and its Creator, however awe inspiring it might be, is not the greatest mystery, but that, in spite of bearing the greatest gift, ie, the power of discrimination, and having made the greatest discovery that we are the immortal *atma*, we parade ourselves as the mortal bodies; in spite of being the repositories of the priceless gem, we masquerade as beggars, unable to keep pace with our desires, associating ourselves with death rather than life, and seeking tinsel and trash in the ever-changing material world which is never likely to offer us anything better than decay and death.

Baba says, "Wherever you look, whether it be here on earth, or in heaven, or even in the nether world, everything that you can find anywhere, is made up of some combination of the five primordial elements. Nothing else exists. Whatever you have ever desired, whatever you have ever used, whatever you have ever lost, all these myriads of things are nothing but changes in the manifestations of the five elements. All these countless variations of the five elements have been, and are, forever changing with the time; they are all temporary, endlessly cycling from one name and form to another". Remember, that which is subject to change, carries with it the seeds of disappointment.

"The flower which has blossomed today will be dried up tomorrow and decomposed a few days later. The beautiful form of today will become ugly tomorrow. Once every seven years all the atoms which constitute the human body undergo a total change. It would be foolish, indeed, for you to think that the body and the sense organs which are made up of the five elements, are permanent, or that any object made up of these elements has any lasting value".

"Whenever you make a search through the far corners of this world you will discover that you are really just seeking these five elements; they are all you will find in any of the things of the world.... There is only one entity which transcends the five elements, and that is what you should aspire for".

Instead of this, unfortunately, in our passion to add to our material prosperity, we allow our desires to run amok with unbridled impunity. There is an inverse relationship between our desires and prosperity.

Greater our wants and desires, the poorer we are; the lesser our wants and desires, the richer we are. The mistake, however, lies in equating our poverty or prosperity with a lack or an abundance of the material wealth or acquisitions.

The social norms that we lay down and the pulls that the society of our creation exerts upon us in return are responsible for our plight today. Inordinate emphasis is placed on our material prosperity and the needs of the spirit are given no consideration at all. There is a misguided notion that money holds the key to our well being and to the solution of all our problems. One of the arguments often advanced in support of this view, for example, is that money alone can buy the best medical care in the world and make all the difference between life and death. It is almost tantamount to saying that disease, and even death, can be kept at bay simply by the jingle of coins in our pocket! If that were indeed so, the richest men around would also be the healthiest and the longest lived in the world. But we know that not to be the case.

Money may buy us the best medicine, can it shower on us health? It may buy us fleeting pleasures, can it earn us lasting peace of mind? It may buy us the best education, can it bestow upon us wisdom and character? Money may buy us information, can it cause our transformation? It may buy us the worldly gifts, can it secure for us the grace of the Lord?

It is not suggested that we should ignore our material needs and comforts but merely that a sensible balance between the material and the spiritual needs should be struck. Furthermore, it is not wealth by itself that is to blame for our problems; it is how we earn it and with what motives, whether we use it or abuse it, and whether we control it or allow it to run and ruin our lives. Nevertheless, it is as well to bear in mind that "Money comes and goes; morality comes and grows."

Why is it that in spite of the tremendous advances in science and technology and material prosperity, man has still not assumed his rightful role in his own destiny? In spite of having added to his material comforts, why is man no nearer to a state of peace within or without? The answer that is fast gaining currency in the various parts of the world now is that our educational institutions are not geared up to meeting the challenge because of the conspicuous absence of a value-based education and training from their curricula.

Of what use is it to teach a child that a horse has four legs and a tail when it can find this out for itself as a matter of course as it grows up? Instead of persuading the children to cram meaningless nursery rhymes, such as, "Bah Bah Black Sheep...", would it not be far more profitable to inculcate in them the habit of prayers, respect for the elders and teachers, sense of responsibility and discipline, so that as they grow up they spread joy around instead of leaving a trail of disasters? In our hands, and in the way we educate and bring up our children, lies not only the future happiness of our homes and the general well being of our society and the world at large, but also the destiny of human race.

We have, however, allowed ourselves far too long to be duped into believing and brain-washed and hypnotised into identifying the perishable body, rather than the imperishable *atma*, as the reality. It is as if we are under the spell of somnambulistic amnesia, not knowing who we really are. What we do not realise is that the body on its own is never alive whereas the life-force, the *atma*, never dies. So, how can a piece of paper even in the shape of a bank note, or a coin, itself lifeless, infuse life into another equally lifeless object, ie, a body? What gives meaning and purpose to this otherwise a corpse of a body is the *atma* within it. Without it, it does not even have a scrap value. Without this life-force, no amount of wealth can even prevent the decay and decomposition of the body let alone breathe life into it.

Incidentally, regarding the locus of life (*praana*) in man, the *Vedas* declare : "He shines like a lightning in the heart of a dark blue cloud." Baba says, "Behind the back of a person, there is the spinal column with 33 vertebrae. Between the 9th and the 12th vertebrae, there is the *sushumna naadi;* which shines like a lightning. People imagine that life resides in the heart. The heart is like the main switch. But life does not reside there. What happens to life when heart surgery is performed? When the heart is transplanted, it is like changing the main switch. But it is because of the vital force in the middle of the spinal column that life exists."

What then is the greatest, most urgent enquiry facing man today? Surely not whether there is life on other planets, or how to land man on these planets, nor indeed what lies beyond the farthest planet. It is not to know who God might be or how He set about His creation. In attempting to address this enquiry, if we turn our attention outwards, the questions multiply, whereas if we direct it inwards, the whole enquiry condenses into one simple question: *Koham* (Who am I)? In the answer to this simple question, it is said, lies hidden the key to the mystery of the whole universe!

In order that 'I' may reveal itself, the spiritual aspirant has to develop three qualities:

- A deep yearning to find the Truth;
- An unshakable faith in the fact that he, verily, is the repository of the Truth;
- An application of disciplined effort towards recognising the Truth.

Furthermore, as behoves a spiritual seeker, the enquiry into the Self must be taken on only with humility and in an attitude of prayerfulness. Prayers, however, must not be allowed, on account of our impatience, to degenerate into a trade or pact with God. To have the right perspective of God and the right spirit of prayer are important. Periaval sums it up beautifully as follows:

> "The purpose of prayer is not to petition for benefit. Such petitioning implies either that God does not know what we want, which will militate against His Omniscience, or that He waits to be asked and delights in praise, which will degrade Him to the level of ordinary man. Why then do we pray? Though Omniscient, God is immanent in every creature and knows what is in the heart of every person. Yet, if what we wish to say in prayer remains unsaid, it afflicts our heart and so prayer heals that affliction. By prayer, we do not seek to change what God ordains; in fact, we cannot do so. We go to Him to remove our impurities. We attach ourselves to Him who has no attachments, to rid ourselves of our attachments. A devout consciousness that God exists will itself do the miracle of alchemising us into purity of nature. We obtain spiritual charge into our frame by being in His presence."

Patience is all the strength that one needs. And, of course, when one is good and ready, through His Grace, the Truth will dawn.

O Divine Mother Sai ! Illumine my heart and guide my steps towards Thee.

QUESTIONS:

(1) In what way is man different from an animal?
(2) How can you prove that the knowledge of the Self is native to man?
(3) Why are children begotten of the same parents seldom alike in their temperaments?
(4) What are the changing and the unchanging aspects of the human personality?

(5) Of what value is the power of discrimination to man?
(6) What price has mankind paid and is paying for the increase in its material comforts?
(7) What is the difference between the *deha* and the *dehi* or the *sharira* and the *shariri*? Why does our power of discrimination fail us in recognising this difference?
(8) What do you consider is the greatest achievement of man?
(9) What is the greatest mystery surrounding man and how does it compare with the greatest paradoxes?
(10) "Money holds the key to the solution of all our problems!" Examine the statement critically.
(11) What is the root cause of all the problems facing man today?
(12) "The more we reach out into the objective world, the less near will we get to the truth." Discuss.
(13) Whereabouts is the locus of life in man?

Realise the Heaven within you and all at once all desires are fulfilled, all misery and suffering is put an end to. Feel yourselves above the body and its environments, above the mind and its motives, above the thoughts of success or fear. The great cause of suffering in the world is that people do not look within, they rely on outside forces.
— Sri Sathya Sai Baba

"We are what we think,
Having become what we thought.
Like the wheel that follows the cart-pulling ox,
Sorrow follows an evil thought."

A Buddhist Verse

4. THE ENEMY WITHIN ?

It is not in the nature of man to seek ignorance, to crave unhappiness or to court death; all these are alien to man. Man, as we know, has a yearning for a life without death, an insatiable thirst for knowledge and he is ever engaged in an unending pursuit of happiness. Such preferences ever pulsating in man, however, could only be prompted by the inherent attributes of Eternal Existence (*Sat*), Total Awareness (*Chit*) and Absolute Bliss (*Aananda*) which are native to his real Self – the Essential Man. This then also is the reason why man so dislikes all that is likely to threaten his well being or bring him anything other than happiness and bliss.

An enemy, on the other hand, may be defined as someone whose interests are quite contrary to one's own and who is out to bring harm and cause pain and suffering. If such an enemy be truly 'within' us, how then could we reconcile its presence alongside the *Sat-Chit-Aananda* Self? For, it is not possible for the darkness of ignorance to co-exist with the effulgence of the Self. It stands to reason, therefore, that the 'enemy' cannot be an integral part of the Self but must be an alien, an intruder, which somehow gains entry 'within'. In order to get the measure of such an enemy, it is essential to recognise its identity, understand when and how it gains entry and establish its location habitation and modus operandi; only thereafter can a meaningful attempt be made to deal with it.

However, for our efforts to bear fruit, Grace of the Lord is essential. What better way to earn it and to feel His constant presence within than by treating Him as our partner for life. This is why *Aadi* Shankaraacharya used to pray to Lord Shiva, who is considered as the Master Hunter and who, it is said, enjoys that role, thus:

"O Lord! Thou art the Master Hunter and the forest of my heart abounds in wild beasts of all sorts. So, please come and hunt these beasts which roam about therein with unbridled impunity. That would offer both of us the greatest joy - to You the greatest sport and to me the salvation from my nightmare."

The six mental aberrations (the wild beasts) that cause us considerable harm and pain and are collectively referred to as the 'Enemy Within' have been described by *Bhagawan* Baba as follows.

(1) **Kaama**: *Kaama* is desire and attachment; desire for riches, property, honour, status, fame, children, etc; attachment for all things of this sensory world, this false, temporary, impure world. *Kaama* signifies transient pleasure based on worldly desires.

Desires are never fully satisfied. They multiply and always keep us in want and poverty and therefore in perpetual misery. In the ultimate analysis, even the yearning for liberation is a desire, but with one important difference; with the fulfilment of this one desire, no further desires remain.

Attachment or non-attachment does not mean anything in relation to our external body; it is all in the mind. A man may be on a throne and perfectly non-attached (like king Janaka); another may be in rags and yet very much attached. Attachment for the sensory world keeps the soul in the thraldom of matter.

(2) **Krodha**: *Krodha* means anger which manifests itself in one's yearning to harm others in thought, word or deed thereby causing ruin to them. When one is invaded by anger, one experiences a loss of reason; one forgets that by harming others who are, essentially, extensions of one's own Self, one will only be bringing harm to one's own self. Anger shortens a man's life. When a man gets angry, his temperature rises; the blood gets heated up; in the process the nerves get weaker and as a consequence all organs in the body also get weaker. This weakness may last for six months. One moment of anger will deprive a man of the energy got from six months of food. Every fit of anger shortens a man's life-span. Anger is prompted by fear and fear is born out of ignorance. But if all are One, what then is there to fear?

(3) **Lobha**: *Lobha* is greed that manifests itself as the determination that no one else should partake of even a small fraction of what one has earned or what one has; also, that even in times of distress and need, one's possessions should not be diminished by use. Just as desires multiply, greed also grows. When we save our first thousand pounds for times of need, it is the greed that prompts us to save another for a rainy day. But having succeeded in doing so, it is the growing greed, yet again, which then impels us to leave the two thousand pounds, thus saved, untouched, and to save, instead, a further thousand pounds, for the rainy day of course! And so, on and on, it grows, keeping one restless and discontented all the time.

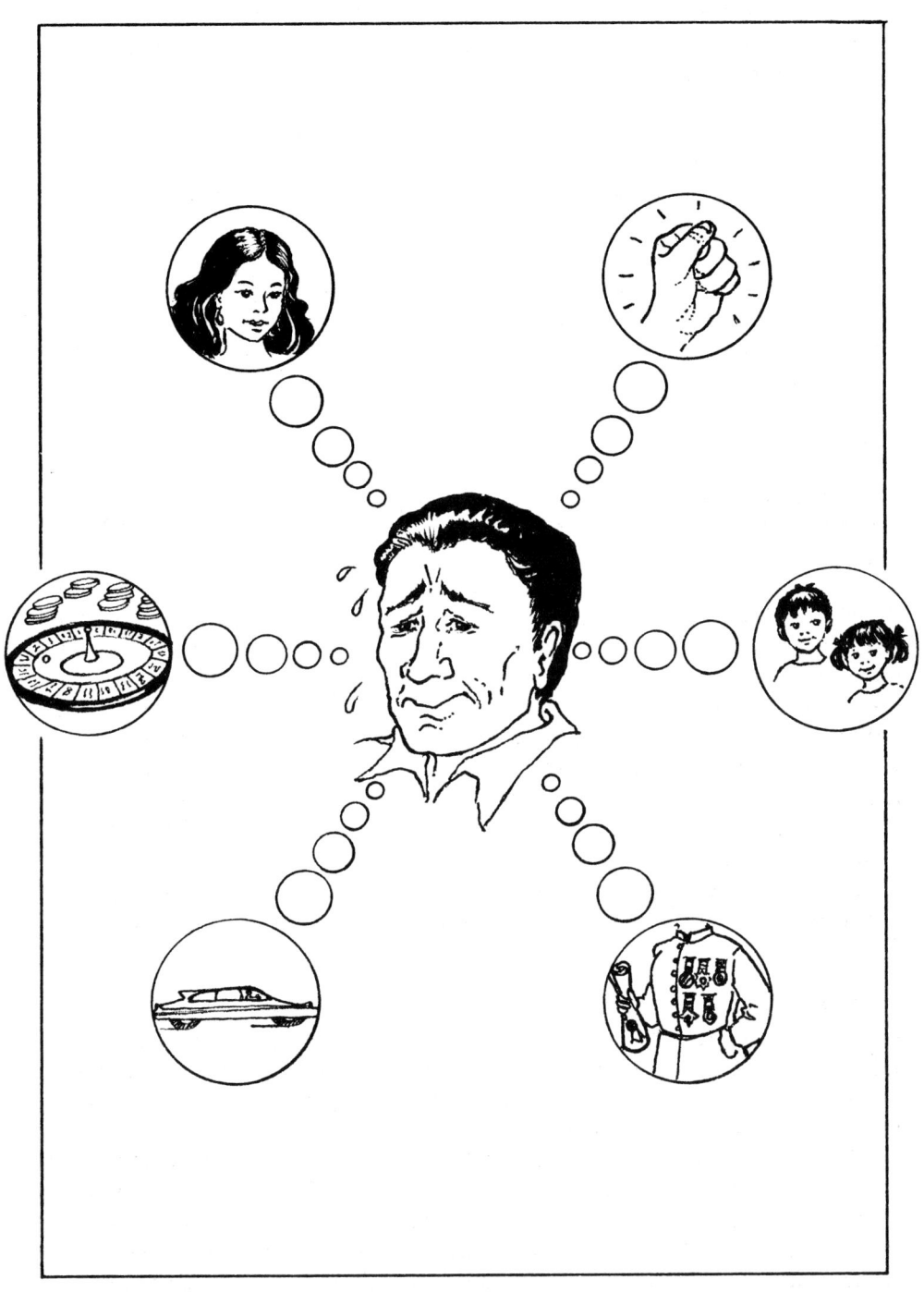

JOY AND SORROW

Your joy is your sorrow unmasked.
And the selfsame well from which your laughter rises was oftentimes filled with your tears.
And how else can it be?
The deeper that sorrow carves into your being, the more joy you can contain.
Is not the cup that holds your wine the very cup that was burned in the potter's oven?
And is not the lute that soothes your spirit the very wood that was hollowed with knives?
When you are joyous, look deep into your heart and you shall find it is only that which has given you sorrow that is giving you joy.
When you are sorrowful, look again in your heart, and you shall see that in truth you are weeping for that which has been your delight.
Some of you say, "Joy is greater than sorrow," and others say, "Nay, sorrow is the greater."
But I say unto you, they are inseparable.
Together they come, and when one sits alone with you at your board, remember that the other is asleep upon your bed.
Verily you are suspended like scales between your sorrow and your joy.
Only when you are empty are you standstill and balanced.
When the treasure-keeper lifts you to weigh his gold and silver, needs must your joy or your sorrow rise or fall.

"The Prophet" by Kahlil Gibran

(4) **Moha**: *Moha* is the infatuation which gives rise to the delusion that some people are nearer to one than others and the desire to please them more than others, leading to exertions for earning and accumulating for their sake. As long as we suffer from *moha*, we are in bondage and as long as we are in bondage, we can never be happy.

Baba has also explained *moha* in a different way. He says that *moha* does not refer to attachment to wealth, property or children. "*Moha* is derived from the words 'Maa', meaning 'finite', and 'Ooha' meaning, imagining that which does not exist. '*Moha*' means 'finite conception of the unreal as real'. It is divorced from any concept of divinity and is totally related to the phenomenal world.

(5) **Mada**: *Mada* means extreme arrogance and pride. *Sanskrit* word for sense-control is *dama* which is made up of two letters 'da' and 'ma'. *Dama* when turned around becomes *mada*. *Mada*, therefore, is indicative of lack of sense control. *Mada* means the swagger that develops when one feels that one has scholarship or strength, riches or fame, more than others.

Pride, it is said, is a subtle cancer of the soul; one knows not when it creeps in nor how it grows. Little achievements make us grow heady and giddy and we think no end of ourselves, strutting on the bubble of pride – a mere pin-prick away from bursting – as Shakespeare lamented:

> "But man, proud man! Drest in a little, brief authority!
> Most ignorant of what he is most assured!
> His glassy essence, like an angry ape! Plays such fantastic
> tricks before High Heaven, as make the Angels weep!"

Inevitably, when worldly attainments part company with one, as they must do one day or the other, the mansion built on the inflated ego comes tumbling down causing extreme pain. But even when one does not have these attainments in the first place, *mada* makes one move about without reverence for elders and consideration for others' feelings and craving only for one's own comfort and security. Man in his pride struts about blindly and the egoism or vanity that prods him on are of four main types: vanity of clan, vanity of wealth, vanity of youth and vanity of scholarship.

(6) **Maatsarya**: *Maatsarya* is extreme jealousy which makes one miserable when others are as happy as oneself; in fact one cannot tolerate it. Jealousy makes its appearance when one comes in contact with a person who excels one in terms of wealth, position, beauty, intelligence, and such other qualities. The moment jealousy enters a person, all the virtues which that

person might have cultivated over a long time, will be destroyed. Jealousy does not live harmlessly inside a person. It destroys all the great qualities and virtues in man. It develops a demonic nature; it destroys the human nature and strengthens the animal nature. It has no scruples. It is only a mean type of satisfaction to think that through one's jealousy and hatred one can impart trouble to others. In reality, one is torturing oneself only. Jealousy will, in a number of ways, create difficulties for the person who is infected with it.

Baba lists four other traits of mind which also rob us of our native peace and tranquillity and can, therefore, be readily added to the above six. These are:

(7) **Dambha**: This trait of hypocrisy prompts people to do, seemingly, holy and commendable works, ie giving away vast sums of money in charity, etc, but with the sole purpose of winning the applause of the world and gaining recognition. It takes away the sanctity of the act and degenerates it into trade.

(8) **Darpa**: *Darpa* is the pride that haunts man when he is rich and 'happy'. This mistaken happiness in fact prevents man from experiencing the true happiness.

(9) **Eershya**: *Eershya* is the desire that others should get the grief, the misery and the worry, which one is suffering from. Clearly, this indicates a lack of wisdom and distorted thinking. We must recognise that we cannot escape from, or pass on to someone else, the pain and pleasure which come our way in strict accordance with the divine dispensation and as a direct consequence of our past actions. For, as the holy Qoran says, "No soul bears the burden of another". To think otherwise is sheer hypocrisy and lunacy.

(10) **Asuya**: *Asuya* means thinking always of doing evil to others; the preparedness to put up with any trouble to satisfy this desire to harm others. When one harbours such demeaning thoughts, how can the agitation of the mind be stilled and peace of mind experienced?

All the above traits are also referred to as the Inner Foes. They reveal the beast in man utterly devoid of : *viveka* (discrimination), *vichakshana* (use of intelligence), *vairagya* (detachment), *dayaa* (kindness, compassion), *sathya* (truth), *dharma* (right conduct), *shanti* (peace), *prema* (love) and *ahimsa* (non-violence). In the sixteenth canto, verses 1 to 4 of the *Bhagavad Geeta* (The Song Celestial), *Sri* Krishna (The Lord) enumerates for the benefit of Arjuna (the representative man) the characteristics of the virtuous and the wicked. Fearlessness, truth, absence of anger, renunciation, uncovetousness, forgiveness, fortitude, purity, absence of hatred, absence of pride, etc, are listed as the hallmarks of the virtuous; hypocrisy, arrogance, self-conceit, anger, ignorance, etc, are the traits by which the wicked can be identified.

Man has been given life so that he may realise the divinity that is inherent in him. The main obstacle that stands in the way of that realisation is the body consciousness and the attachment to the body – the binding link of 'I and mine'.

Furthermore, man does not seem to have a steady mind at all; without the necessary firmness and steadiness of mind, he is unable to control its vagaries. A businessman who knows that he should not deceive, makes a resolution that he will limit himself to earning, honestly, only a fair and a modest profit; yet, the very next opportunity to test his resolution that comes his way, he seems to suffer from a strange lapse of memory. A man, knowing that it is wrong to lie may, at some time, resolve not to do so again that moment onwards; yet, what is it that impels him to reel off lies felicitously the very next conversation he gets into? It has to be some very powerful entity working inside man that constantly defeats his efforts forcing him to depart, repeatedly, from his own firm resolutions. For, had it not been for such a powerful instinct or urge at work within him, he would surely not have changed his resolve but would have been able to exercise his will to hold to his pledged discipline. This then points to the presence of some force hidden within man which he is not able to comprehend or control. However, "If he contemplates deeply and tries to discover just what exactly this power is," Baba says, "He will find that .... the first powerful urge which makes man give up all his resolutions is desire". "Desire acts as the leader or the captain of all the other evil traits or enemies which gain entry....."

One might plan stratagems to defeat one's external enemies, but this will be of little use until one has overcome one's inner foes. "Once you have yielded to the enemy within", Baba says, "How can you ever hope to conquer your external enemies?" "This captain of the evil traits, desire, has made a hole and entered the house; the others like hatred, anger, greed, etc, then follow it in. The moment these enemies have entered into you, you lose all your wisdom, you also give up your resolution. Therefore, the most important reason for not fulfilling your own firm resolution, is the welling up of desire."

Baba refers to jealousy and hatred as the twin thieves, adding that the one cannot live without the company of the other. "There is an inextricable relationship between them; they will always take shelter within each other..... Where there is no jealousy there will be no hatred. When hatred is visible, then you will also find jealousy lurking invisibly below the surface".

The road to man's liberation, Baba says, is barred by three gates: *kaama* (lust), *krodha* (anger, hatred), and *lobha* (greed).... "When man is subject to *kaama* (lustful desire), he loses all sense of right and wrong. Greed destroys man's devotion. *Krodha* undermines *jnaana* (wisdom). The man filled with anger and hatred becomes utterly thoughtless. He loses his sense of discrimination. These three destroy a man's spiritual practices – *karma* (action), *upaasana* (worship) and *dhyaana* (meditation). When there are no spiritual practices, man becomes a creature of whims.

Spiritual heart of man is referred to as the temple wherein resides God, as the *atma* (soul). The human body composed of bones, flesh and blood can be looked upon as the compound wall surrounding the temple. Just as with any other compound wall made out of bricks and mortar, there are likely to be a number of gates, so with this wall of bones and flesh also, there are a number of gates or doors in the form of the sense organs. It is through these doors of the senses that desire and other brood of enemies break in and invade the inner sanctuary.

We thus know the route the enemy takes to gain entry; as to the time when it chooses to do so, a moment's reflection will reveal the fact that the presence of the enemy can be experienced during the 'wakeful' state but never during the 'deep-sleep' state. The single, most important difference setting the two states of awareness apart is the mind, ie, the presence of mind in the former state and its absence in the latter. Presence of mind in the 'wakeful' state and its absence in the 'deep-sleep' state can, thus, be directly linked with the presence or the absence of the enemy in the two respective states. It follows therefore that the entry must be gained by the enemy only through the active connivance of or the welcome accorded by, the mind. But what is mind?

Unfortunately, this may not be as easy to answer as it might sound because, most of the time, we identify our mind with the Self or Reality and we find it difficult to tell the two apart. That is the tragedy. We have, however, to realise that mind as such has no existence except as a concept which is often used to explain away the incoherence, the irrationality and the general malaise of human behaviour. Mind is nothing but a collection of thoughts and desires. Its form at any given time, therefore, is the same as that of the thought it entertains at that time. A thousand stray thoughts in the mind, both maleficent as well as beneficent, are constantly battling for supremacy – sometimes this one gains ascendency and sometimes that, sometimes bad, degrading thoughts and sometimes good, uplifting ones.

If we examine the list of the inner foes closely, one thing becomes unmistakably clear – the presence of the enemy is felt only after the contact with the outside objective world is established. For example, jealousy (of someone), desire (of something), etc, could not exist on their own but are likely to follow only after the contact with that 'someone' or 'something', ie, the sensory object, is first made; sever the link with the sensory objects, the enemies like jealousy, desire, greed, etc, will have no basis to exist. Whatever thought the mind dwells upon, that thought the mind becomes ("*yadbhaavam tad-bhavati*"). Allow the mind to dwell upon the objects of the sensory world, it loses itself in the sensory world, becoming a slave to the senses and giving free rein to the alien thoughts causing considerable pain and harm; allow it to dwell on the Self, it must, *ipso facto*, lose itself in and become the Self. In the former case, it is referred to as the lower or impure mind (*manas*) and in the latter, as the higher or pure mind (*chitta*). It would therefore appear that the mind is capable of serving two masters – the Self within as well as the sensory world without; it is in this context that the mind can also be referred to as the Double Agent.

A doubt that often arises is that thoughts have no awareness of their own, why then should they bring any consequence at all? Baba confirms that thoughts are insentient; they are like passing clouds overhead and, however demeaning they may be, they are, by themselves, unable to threaten any harm whatsoever. However, He warns us, that damage can be wrought but only when we allow our mind to **dwell** on the thoughts. To illustrate this point, consider the example of a news flash informing us that our next door neighbour has landed a pools win of a million pounds. The news by itself is harmless enough; it does not concern us in any way and should therefore cause us no pain. Nevertheless, if we allow our mind to dwell on it and allow ourselves to ponder over thoughts like: our neighbour will be able to buy things that we could only dream about, he will live in the lap of luxury whereas we will merely scrape through, why did we not win that money instead of our neighbour, we wish he loses the whole lot, etc, the jealousy will soon rob us of our peace of mind and become the cause of sleepless nights for us. The envy will simply consume us away by allowing ourselves to dwell negatively on someone else's good fortune! If only we are able to shift our thought process on to something worthwhile and uplifting, we would escape all damage. What we allow our mind to dwell upon, therefore, will become the cause of our happiness or unhappiness. This is why, in the "*Amrit Bindu Upanishad*", it is said: "*Mana eva manushyaanaam kaaranam* *bandha mokhshayoh*", "Mind itself is the cause of bondage as well as of liberation for man".

It is also interesting to note that, at any given time, demeaning and uplifting thoughts do not coexist; when one is present, the other appears to be conspicuously absent. This, therefore, implies that by constantly dwelling on the uplifting thoughts, it is possible to keep the demeaning thoughts at bay; by keeping the mind constantly engaged on the Self, senses will no longer hold the sway and will, in fact, die of inanition.

"No one ever found the walking fern", it is said, "Who did not have the walking fern in his mind." If we have love in our mind, we will find love in our heart. If we entertain hate, hate is what we shall meet. If we expect selfishness and deceit, we shall not be disappointed; from all sides will selfishness and deceit confront us. "Fear not, then;" says *Swami* Ram Tirth, "have holiness and purity in you; you will never come across anything unclean ...". There is a popular belief that when a wasp brings into its hole a particular kind of insect, the latter, out of fear, constantly thinks of its assailant till it is transformed into a wasp itself. So also if a person meditates upon *Brahman* (God) with all his mind, in course of time, it is said, he will become aware of his own God-hood.

Clearly, to achieve victory over the 'Enemy Within', mastery of the mind is held essential. This requires purging the mind of all evil, says Baba, by cultivating the following four chief virtues:

(1) *Maitri* (**Friendliness**): Comradeship and the company of the humble and good; love for the name and form of the Lord. One should not cultivate friendship with all and sundry. Friendship should be cultivated only towards those who are one's equal in age, status, culture, etc. Baba says, "Friendship with those above or below should be avoided. When you try to befriend those above you in status, they may try to patronise you. When you do not like to be lorded over, the friendship will break. When you develop friendship with those below you, you may attempt to boss over them. When they do not acquiesce in this, again the friendship will break up. Therefore, friendship will be enduring only when it is between equals in age, wealth, status, etc."

(2) *Karuna* (**Compassion**): Feeling of kindness towards afflicted. Kindness or compassion should be shown towards those who are in a lower position than ourselves in respect of age, wealth, health, status, education and the like. Only then does compassion become meaningful and valuable. Kindness justifies itself in such cases.

(3) **Mudita** (**Appreciation**): Joy one feels when meeting people who are charitable, who serve others, who help those in distress, etc. This quality relates to the attitude to be shown towards those who are better off than you..... *Mudita* means freedom from envy and feeling happy over better fortunes of others.

(4) **Upeksha** (**Disinterestedness**): Non-involvement; the feeling of unconcern at the wicked; neither loving them nor hating them. Distinction should be made between *apeksha* (liking) and *upeksha* (disinterestedness). We should keep at arms length all those who indulge in bad deeds and entertain bad thoughts.

Friendship with equals, compassion towards the lowly, rejoicing in the good fortune of those who are better off and keeping away from the wicked – these are the objectives worth pursuing in life. It is because of the failure to observe these directives that the quality of life, these days, has deteriorated.

Furthermore, to ensure steady progress towards the victory, one must also recognise, and steer clear of, the obstacles one is likely to face. The obstacles can be of the past, of the present and of the future. Recollecting and remembering the past and getting affected by it represents the obstacle of the past. We cannot recreate, relive or in any way alter our past; any time spent on dwelling on the past, therefore, will be wasteful and a hindrance to the future progress.

The obstacles of the present are of four types: attachment to sense-objects, cynical criticism and crookedness, dullness of understanding and exaggerated conceit. The first is the cause of our attachment to objects that attract the senses. The second makes one attend more to the peculiarities of textual criticism than to the sense of the teaching and makes one discover wrong meanings in the teaching of the *guru*. The third causes confusion which prevents one from grasping the words of the elders, the wise and the *guru*. The last obstruction makes one feel that one is a great scholar, pundit, or ascetic, mistaking the body and the senses for the *atma* (soul) and justifying one's own statement as correct through an exaggerated conceit. Baba says that attachment to sense-objects can be removed by developing purity, self-control, withdrawal of desires and the ability to suffer. "Dullness of understanding can be removed by listening again and again. Constant meditation on the things heard will abolish the habit of cynical criticism. All absurd conceit will vanish through the teachings one gets."

Obstructions of the future always come through sinful deeds. They may come and obstruct unawares or the obstacles may be created by anticipating troubles and worrying about them even before they come. Baba says that the spiritual aspirants can, to some extent, be cognizant of the approaching wrong and its origin. "It creates a desire which puts on the cloak of mercy. Then you must recognise it as an 'obstruction of the future'."

To conclude then, the 'Enemy Within' is, in reality, an alien intruder which works its way into our subtle body and, if not arrested and driven out, can establish itself in the shape of deep seated latencies and tendencies as part of our causal body also. However, it is not, and can never be, a part of the Self, the Essential Man. The enemy is able to sneak inside us only under the cover of darkness of *ajnaana* (ignorance). Thieves break into a house only when it is dark and unguarded. If the house is kept lighted all the time, they dare not steal into it. If we keep in our mind the light of Truth ever ablaze, no devil of fear or temptation will approach us. Baba says, "Ajnaana is the mental attitude that has reference to the external object. Under the glaring light of *vijnaana* (knowledge, wisdom), such clandestine entry can be prevented. *Vij*naana is the mental attitude that has reference to the internal subject". When the mental activity and attitude turn inwards and are constantly focused on the Self, the effulgence of the Self will permit no dark spots for the enemy to lurk in. "Turn your thoughts outwards and you gain the flux known as the world with all its agitations; turn it inwards and you realise the calmness, the serenity, the Bliss of the Self."

O Divine Mother Sai ! Let not other people's sorrows make my joys, nor their joys my sorrows; let their joys and sorrows be my joys and sorrows !

QUESTIONS:

(1) Why does man hate unhappiness and dread death?
(2) What are the Inner Foes? Discuss their nature?
(3) Is the 'Enemy Within' part of the Self? Give reasons.
(4) What is the purpose of life and what stands in the way of its realisation?
(5) How and when does the Enemy gain entry?
(6) Where exactly within the human personality does the enemy find a location habitation?
(7) How does the 'Enemy' operate?
(8) What is the connection between the mind, states of awareness and the enemy? Discuss.
(9) Why is mind referred to as the Double Agent?
(10) What are the twin thieves and why are they so named?
(11) What is mind? Explain.
(12) 'We become what we think'. Discuss.

(13) How can mind be purged of evil?
(14) What are the obstacles experienced in trying to master the mind? How can these be overcome?
(15) List how many of the enemies you can recognise within yourself and explain how, in your opinion, they were able to gain entry. How can they be uprooted and thrown out?
(16) "No one ever found the walking fern, who did not have the walking fern in his mind." Discuss .

Have no thorn of hate in your mind, develop love towards all. Desire is a storm, greed is a whirlpool, pride is a precipice, attachment is an avalanche, egoism is a volcano. Keep these things away so that when you recite the name of God or do Meditation, they do not disturb the equanimity. Let love be enthroned in your heart. Then, there will be sunshine and cool breezes and gurgling waters of contentment feeding the roots of faith.

– Sri Sathya Sai Baba

> *"Much is our preaching but not the word of Truth,*
> *Much is our building but not the man of Character,*
> *So why build cities glorious if man unbuilt goes?"*

.... *Anon*

5. HUMAN VALUES

Man is capable of functioning on three planes: the instinctive, the intellectual and the intuitive planes. When man is guided by instinct, ie when we talk and act in terms of the 'survival of the fittest', when we believe in 'going for the grabs', we function on the 'plane of the beasts'. When man uses his intellect to discriminate between good and bad, right and wrong, and uses this discriminatory power to pursue the good and shun the evil, when he lives in peace and harmony with his environment in a caring and sharing way, we then see man operate on a human plane. However, when man recognises and allows himself to be guided by the promptings of his conscience, the 'inner voice' arising from the very core of his being, ie, when he is guided by intuition, he is then on the 'plane of angels'.

In other words, we can say that man has three faces: that of a beast, that of a human being and that of an angel. As Baba says: the one that others think we are, the one that we think we are and the one we really are. The one others see is, generally, the beast in us; the one we see is the human face, and the one we really represent is the Divine Self.

When we have sublimated the beast in us, we shall see the emergence of the human face and when we have allowed the human values to blossom and flower fully in us, we shall begin to realise the Self, our innate divinity. That is the goal – indeed the sole purpose of life.

We have, however, wallowed long and deep in our baser instincts and, inevitably, find ourselves in a mess. Whichever way we turn, the ghost of war and the scourge of hatred, hunger and disharmony seem to haunt every part of the globe. In fact the whole environment seems to reek with war hysteria. In this troubled and torn world of today, where clash and conflict are the order of the day, a concerted drive for the fostering of human values on a global scale, the remaking of man, holds out the only ray of hope for our very survival.

We know more about the physical world today than we did in the past. In

What we must strive for today is not a new religion or a new society or a new code of morality; they are there already, in each race and country. We also have the basic plans for spiritual training already laid down in most religions. But we need persons who have attained purity in all levels of consciousness. Man can reach perfect bliss only when his heart becomes free from envy, egoism, greed and other evil traits. We need persons who can recognise and relish the recognition of the kinship and the identity between man and man, as well as between one society and another. They have to move beyond the limited 'i', to break loose from the entanglements of the senses. they have to jump over the battlements of the fort called 'body', and enter enthusiastically the wide world beyond. From the narrow vision of the 'individual need' man must voyage out into the broad vision of the 'universal'. When a drop of water falls into the ocean, it loses its narrow individuality, its name and form, and assume the form, name and taste of the ocean itself. If it seeks to live separately as a 'drop', it will soon evaporate and be soon reduced to non-existence. Each one must become aware that he is part of the one Truth that encompasses everything in the Universe. It is reprehensible to stick for one's whole lifetime to the low narrow paths of selfishness, envy and greed. Make the heart big and the mind pure. Then only can peace and prosperity be established on the earth.

Sri Sathya Sai Baba

spite of the tremendous strides in science, we are no closer to world peace, nor indeed a state of peace within our own selves. We may have penetrated the outer space, millions of miles away, we may have reached the stars and the moon, but we have not bothered to penetrate a mere 2 inches within to explore our inner space. The result is that we are ignorant even of our own identity.

There is a story of the three lazy men who were paragons of sloth and inaction. Even if they had a push-button keyboard in front of them to get anything they wished for, pushing the button itself would have been an effort. The house they lived in once caught fire. Thereupon, their conversation (in *Kashmiri*) went on as follows:

> "*Aalatchyo tember kaas.*"
> "*Yeth gari sukhi aas.*"
> "*Oho, baqawaas.*"

One lazy person said to the other: "I smell fire; put it out you lazy so-&-so." "Well, it hasn't reached me yet", replied the other, "Why spring into action while I can continue to enjoy few more moments of blissful inaction?" To the third person however, even this talk between the other two was an unwelcome intrusion because, for him, even moving the lips was an unnecessary effort. In anger he yelled: "Oh! The pointless prattle (just shut up the two of you)".

Unfortunately, the story has ceased to be a joke; it has a parallel in real life today. Our planet is afire with anger and hatred and yet we refuse to be stirred out of our cosiness because we mistakenly believe that the flames are miles away from our doors. This sense of indifference and smugness is dangerous; it is taking us closer and closer to the precipice. We have to change our outlook and thinking before it is too late; we must spring into action before we are consumed by the flames.

Look at the human body: feet which do the walking on dust and dirt are not, because of that, any the less important. If they sustain an injury, the hands massage them with loving care, the eyes shed tears of pain and the mind concentrates on finding the means to alleviate the pain. All this is spontaneous – there is no calculation, no trade. See the incredible coordination, caring and sharing. Our society, the human family, is likewise a body, with all of us as its cells, its component parts, but how unfortunately disorientated.

The monkey mind ever full of itself, sets out to refashion the world after its own heart's desire; sometimes the intentions are good, sometimes consciously bad. "But whatever the intentions may be, " says Aldous Huxley, "the results of action undertaken by even the most brilliant cleverness, when it is unenlightened by the divine nature of things, unsubordinated to the spirit, are generally evil."

Selfishness, greed, jealousy, vanity and many other degrading tendencies in man are the obstacles which prevent his innate goodness to surface and his love to flow freely. Root cause of all these tendencies is the ego born out of ignorance (of his true reality). It befogs the intelligence of man, blurs his vision and keeps him spinning in the mire of 'I' and 'mine'.

To eliminate this ego, Baba says, the belief that all objects belong to God, and that we are only holding them on trust, has to be strengthened. "This would prevent pride; it is also the truth. Then, when you lose a thing, you would not grieve. God gave; God took away. Of course you hear almost all talking in this strain and advising this reaction. But few follow that advice themselves. This is the sin of all sins; saying one thing and acting quite the opposite, denying in practice what you assert as precept." Regeneration of man can come about only through the denial of his assumed (false) identity; only through the sublimation of ego will come the blossoming of those values which truly characterise us as human beings.

A 'value' may be defined as a characteristic, an attribute, cultivation of which gives worthiness to life, enhances its sweetness and beauty and makes it fragrant. The five basic human values, under which all other values can be grouped, are: *sathya* (truth), *dharma* (right conduct), *shanti* (peace), *prema* (love) and *ahimsa* (non-violence).

Sathya (Truth)

Truth does not mean just testifying to facts as perceived by the senses. By Truth is not meant walking up to a man who has lost his sight and telling him that he is blind. If it is distasteful and offensive, it cannot be the Truth. Truth is the unchanging, unmanifested essence of the changing, manifested universe.

"Man looks outwards, inwards or heavenwards in search of the knowledge leading to his own reality or to the clues unravelling the mystery of God and Creation. These have been the rationalistic, the idealistic or the theistic ways of exploring the Truth. The Truth, however, has managed to remain transcendent to all these approaches for, it is neither outside, above nor exclusively inside. It is everywhere, at all times, and it subsists in everything. Truth cannot be the object of an individual's exclusive enterprise which attempts to treat it as an object of its own exclusive understanding or perception."

Consider the example of the 'dream' and the 'wakeful' worlds. Both are dreams; dreams of different dimensions may be, but dreams nevertheless. One is a dream of the individual conscience and the other that of the Cosmic Conscience; one appears when we close our eyes and the other appears when we open our eyes. Put another way, the manifested world does not exist when we close our eyes and the dream world does not exist when we open our eyes. The key seems to be the opening and closing of our eyes. That which exists only part of the time and which vanishes or appears with the blinking of an eye, how can such an arbitrary thing be the Truth? That alone is Truth which is valid for all time – past, present and future – which is unchanging, eternal and unaffected by variations in time or place (ie *sanathana*). It remains the Truth for all places and for all beings irrespective of their caste, creed or colour. That is the Truth which sustains the universe.

The world we are born into is in a state of continuous flux. It is ever changing; nothing in it is stationary. We were children yesterday, we are young today and we shall be old tomorrow. What was referred to as future yesterday, is present today and will be the past by tomorrow. In fact, all that is 'born' in the dimension of time and space, is bound by the laws of time and space and is subject to change, decay and 'death'. The change that we observe in an object is nothing but a different definition assumed at a different point in time. Baba says that the change from one specific point in time to the next is a projection of the passage of time. The delicious food welcomed and eaten with relish the night before becomes abhorrent the morning after. If we were able to remove the influence of time or somehow step outside the dimension of time and space, there would be no change and we would perceive timelessness or eternity. But comprehension of such a concept poses problems as long as we attempt to perceive timelessness through ill-equipped instruments, ie, our senses and the mind, which are time-bound and not of the same mould as timelessness or eternity.

There is often a vague notion that our mind and the senses represent our true identity. However, a moment's reflection could easily disprove this. In the 'deep-sleep' state, the mind and the senses are defunctionalised and yet 'I' continues to live. So, it is clear that the reality 'I' is not dependent upon the existence of the mind and the senses. Baba says, "A person whose eyes are closed declares that he cannot see anything; it is all dark. So, he sees darkness! Something in him sees both darkness as well as light – darkness when the eyes are shut, and light when they are open. If the eyes, in reality, do not themselves do the seeing, who is it that sees the light as well as darkness? It is that witness, that life force, which sees even when the eyes are closed, which continues to live even when the senses and the mind are defunct, which lives for ever even though in a body which is subject to death, it is that 'I' which persists alone in the deep-sleep state, that is the Real I – the Truth".

"In reality", Baba says, "light contains darkness and darkness has light in it; when one is present, the other is not evident, that is all". "The sun illumines the world but hides the stars. The child contains the old man, the old man has childhood persisting in him. Grief has joy latent in it; joy has the potency to lead the person to grief. When one is evident, the other is hidden, that is all".

"God is minuter than the minutest. When we are unable to see the air which we know is all round us, how can we see God who is even minuter? God is vaster than the vastest. When we are unable to picturise the cosmos which astronomy has not succeeded in unravelling, how can we see or imagine that which is vaster than the vastest. Yet the reality that sustains the cosmos as well as the cell is only One, the all pervasive *Brahman* (God). When the infinite vastness is spoken of in relation to cosmos, it is called as Overself, Supersoul or *Paramaatma*; when it is conceived as the core of all beings, it is the Self, the soul, *atma* or real I. All three are essentially One entity; delusion is seeing the One as many".

Evanescence, or impermanence of the body and the manifested world, and the immanence, transcendence and permanence of *atma*, the real I – that is the first and foremost human value of Truth.

Baba says: "Root cause of birth is *karma* (action); root cause of action is sorrow; root cause of sorrow is ignorance; root cause of ignorance is *bhrama* (delusion). As long as delusion persists, Truth cannot be recognised. Rid delusion, sorrow will cease and ignorance will disappear and then Truth will prevail".

Dharma (Right Conduct)

Dharma is derived from the *Sanskrit* verb-root *dhr* – which means "to hold". Having identified the Truth as the purpose of life, realisation of that goal, through the harmony of thought, word and deed becomes our ordained duty or *dharma*. Having established that the Truth is eternal, *sanathana*, it stands to reason that the conduct, *dharma*, that will enable us to realise it must also be eternal or *sanathana*. *Dharma* cannot be described as duty which changes with time.

The code of conduct that we live by in the society is the code related to the body and the manifested world. It not only varies from person to person and place to place, but even for the same person and place, it also changes from time to time. The ground rules and the norms change. This code is based on personal preferences. For example, getting up at 7 in the morning in the western world is commonly referred to as the "civilised" hour and, by implication, getting up at 4am would be decidedly uncivilized. In a country like India, the opposite might be the case. Similarly, our conduct towards other members of our society is based on our relationships with them and since our physical relationships are not permanent, our conduct likewise, keeps changing. Such a conduct is related to body-consciousness. Since, like the body, it is time and place bound, it is not *sanathana* or eternal.

The code of conduct or *dharma* that we refer to is unaffected by the vagaries of the weather, nor is it subjected to the direction of the compass. It is not time-bound; it must have currency at all times. Such *dharma*, Baba says, is *dharma* related to the soul, *dharma* for the realisation of the Self or Truth. This path, this code of conduct, this duty, is the path of disciplined Self-enquiry, and that duty is the same for all peoples in all places and at all times; that duty is *Sanathana Dharma*. This self-enquiry is the enquiry of the Self, the real I, which we know to be distinct from the body-mind complex.

In following the right path on the pilgrimage of life, Baba says, "Whoever subdues his egoism, conquers his selfish desires, destroys his bestial feelings and impulses, and gives up the natural tendency to regard the body as the Self, is surely on the path of *dharma*". "In all your worldly activities, you should be careful not to wound propriety or the canons of good nature. You should not play false to the promptings of inner voice, that is, you should at all times be prepared to respect the dictates of your conscience. You should watch your steps to see whether you are in someone's way. You should be ever vigilant to discover the truth behind the scintillating variety of this world". "When *dharma* is not used to transmute human life, the world is afflicted by agony and fear; it becomes tormented by stormy revolutions". In 'The Second Coming', W. B. Yeates remarks:

> **" Things fall apart; the centre cannot hold;**
> **Mere anarchy is loosed upon the world,**
> **The blood-dimmed tide is loosed, and everywhere**
> **The ceremony of innocence is drowned;**
> **The best lack all conviction, while the worst**
> **Are full of passionate intensity."**

Absence of *dharma* (right conduct) at the very core of human affairs has led to the disintegration of the society; the values have been thrown overboard. The good lack faith in themselves and the fanaticism of the wicked appears to be gaining ascendency. Observance of *dharma* keeps the society on an even keel.

He who upholds *dharma*, it is said, will in turn be guided and guarded by *dharma* itself. "The field of *dharma* is heart and what emanates from a pure heart as a pure idea when translated into action is *dharma*. If there is righteousness in the heart, there is beauty in the character; if there is beauty in character, there will be harmony in the home; if there is harmony in the home, there will be order in the nation and when there is order in the nation, there will be peace in the world".

Shanti (Peace)

Mind is the seat where desires take shape. It is important to control the forays of mind into the outer objective world and to prevent it from running amok. Mind has to be trained to be the servant and not the master of man. Without this, peace cannot be realised. Excesses and unbridled pursuit of passions and pleasures disturb the equipoise, the natural balance of man, resulting, inevitably, in fatigue, exhaustion, anxiety and diseases of all kinds. If we fritter away our energies in pursuit other than the one of truth, we will have no peace.

Man is beset with various problems which give rise to frustrations, dejections, disappointments, fear, and anxiety, and rob him of his peace of mind. What we perceive is simply the projection of our mind, and the way we react is a reflection of our own heart. With the thoughts of anger, falsehood and greed, we pollute the atmosphere much more than any other pollutants are ever likely to. We soil the firmament of our own (spiritual) heart, the very seat of love. We find ourselves bereft of love and so we reflect unhappiness. If the boss in an office happens to be in a good mood, even major lapses by a staff member are forgiven. However, if he is in a bad mood, even a minor omission is severely dealt with. This is but a small example of how we project our state of mind and reflect the state of our heart.

We often confuse peace with sense gratification. For some, having a hearty meal in a nice restaurant is a gratifying experience; for someone else, owning a Rolls Royce, and for yet another, living in a mansion. But does 'happiness' derived from such experiences endure for any length of time? Such forms of happiness are ephemeral. All matter is time-bound and so how can the happiness associated with the materialistic objects be anything other than fleeting, like daffodils – here today and gone by the morrow? How can pleasure, supposedly offered by the object and enjoyed by the subject be a permanent experience when they themselves have no permanent base?

Peace comes from within and not without; peace is what we exude and not what we abstract. Peace is a state of no agitation, the absence of conflict; it is an emotional equipoise. Peace is a continuous stream of unbroken calm that is the innate nature of man, the unperturbed state of the inner Self. There is no way to peace; peace itself is the way!

How can we realise this commodity called peace? Everyone of us clamours: I want peace ! Baba says: "Cross out the 'I', give up the 'want' and you will be left with peace!" We have to become zeros in the material sense in order to emerge as heroes in the spiritual sense. The ego has to be negated, the little self has to be effaced and the temporal desires eliminated, only then can we rediscover peace; otherwise, it will continue to elude us. Peace cannot be bought with riches or threats. It lies, and has to be found, within our own self!

Purity of motive and righteous action based on love and sacrifice can keep us at ease with our conscience. It is therefore the best guarantee for our peace of mind, for, an uneasy conscience is a tormenting companion.

"We have to welcome with equal mindedness, fame and blame, respect and ridicule, profit and loss, and such other responses and reactions from the society", says Baba. "Fortune is as much a challenge to our equanimity as misfortune ...." "once you have acquired the attitude of unaffectedness and non-attachment, you will have unshakable *shanti* (peace), self-control and purity of mind". Furthermore, "the most precious possession is mental equanimity, and it is one thing you cannot give, even if you have it. Each has to acquire it the hard way. But you can enlighten people on the discipline through which mental equanimity can be gained, and peace can be won. It cannot be earned through a higher standard of life; it cannot be got through riches, through the acquisition of power and authority, through developing physical strength and endurance. When you plan for service, remember this estimate of comparative values. The rich, the healthy, the strong, the powerful, the influential – all are afflicted with discontent, worry, fear and anxiety. They have no peace of mind. Peace comes from within; contentment is a mental condition. Do not feed the roots of attachment to worldly comforts, more than is absolutely necessary. They lead only to anxiety and fear; they can never satisfy the innermost craving of man.

them into the path of devotion and dedication; that will be for them the path of content and joy. Emphasise the universal *atmatattwam* (*atmic* principle); encourage prayer, meditation, quiet contemplation of the grandeur and glory of God, reflected in nature; repetition of the name of the Lord; encourage silence and solitude for the sake of introspection and contact with the springs of joy inherent in man".

Prema (Love)

Love may be seen in different forms: love between a mother and a child, a husband and a wife, a brother and a sister, teacher and a disciple, a friend and a friend. But all these forms of 'love' are conditioned and conditional. They are based on relationships; remove the relationships and the 'love' will have no basis to exist.

We are generally brought up on a diet of double standards. We expect our children to behave in a certain way with the rest of the family and within the confines of the home; but their behaviour outside – well that is a different story! Whereas we are expected to be helpful and disciplined within the house, there is no discouragement to grabbing whatever we can from the society and the environment. Our success in life may, in fact, be measured by how good we are at it. Is it any wonder then that some of the humankind whilst being helpful within the home can turn out to be monsters when let loose in the society. Clearly the love we bear towards the various members of the society is conditioned by our upbringing. It is also conditional because its very existence is based upon our relationships and our likes and dislikes. Such love is motivated by selfish considerations and is liable to change with the changes in time and circumstance. When our child commits a crime in the society, we try to shield him from facing the consequences because that is the reflection of the conditioned, rather ill-conditioned love that we bear towards him. By love is not meant blind attachment, affection or lust. It is not getting and forgetting. Love is giving and forgiving; it is spontaneous, selfless, unwavering, ever pure and unsullied.

Love is not merely a word; it is not just an experience. Love is more than living; love is life itself. One must not mistake love for an emotion. It is an energy that comes from the psychic centre in a human being. It is unconditional and unconditioned. As Baba says, "No reason for love, no season for love ; love for its own sake !" In the words of Elizabeth B. Browning : "Love me for love's sake that we may love on through love's eternity."

Just as cool, refreshing waters from the mountain tops flow without recognising the terrain, the land over which they flow, but nurture life and give sustenance; just as the cool breezes recognise no direction of the compass but merely bring coolth to all parts of the globe; just as the fragrance of a flower has no colour but is fragrance pure and simple; just as the smile of an innocent child knows no barriers of caste, creed or colour but is a spontaneous reflection of its inner joy and bliss, so also, *prema* (love), has to flow with freedom and without restriction; it must transcend all the man-made barriers of preferences and prejudices. Such love, Baba says, can emerge from the heart only after anger, pride and ego-sense are put out of action and removed. Cow is bereft of all these traits and that is why it is full of the milk of love and life. Is there any wonder that it is revered as the mother by the Hindus.

Captain Freddie Guest, an officer of the cavalry, describes in his auto-biography an incident that he witnessed in 1944 near Bangalore in India. He saw the bewildering sight of a fat cobra that had entwined itself around the hind legs of a cow, sucking milk direct from its udder. The cow too suckled the snake as if it were her own calf. At the sight of the well nourished snake, Guest was convinced that the drinking session must have been a daily occurrence. This exemplifies self-less love – love for its own sake. If animals are capable of such selfless love, how much more so should the humans be?

"Those saturated with Love are incapable of spite, selfishness, injustice, wrongdoing or misconduct; but, in those who have no love, above qualities are always above everything else".

"Passion, agitation, anxiety", Baba says, "degrade human nature". "They are born out of hatred, greed, malice of envy which love alone can counteract. When you have here the very embodiment of love, as your dearest treasure, why welcome into your hearts the waves of hatred, faction, fear and doubt? Why turn them into volcanoes of cruelty and wickedness, when they can smile as green valleys of fragrant flowers".

Ahimsa (Non-violence)

When we say that there is violence rampant in the world today, we commonly refer to its manifestation in a physical form. But violence can find expression in three ways: in thought, word or deed. Violence not only results from a physical assault or verbal abuse but injury can also be caused through the thought process of wishing ill or harm. Indeed, this can be the worst form of violence. It is easy to escape or stay away from a person given to physical or verbal violence, but how can one run away from the thoughts of violence directed against one? Just as prayers generate vibrations and have potency, so also do evil thoughts.

Non-violence is not running away from a tyrant or turning the other cheek out of fear; it is not passive inaction; it is not a negative attitude. It is a divine quality. Non-violence is a positive state of mind which impels one to desist from all forms of violence – not out of fear – but because of the conscious realisation that by causing injury or violence to others, one would only be causing pain and harm to one's own self. If there is kinship, how can we bring ourselves round to inflicting injury on others?

Cause of violence is fear and fear stems from ignorance. Beast in us resorts to violence when our physical or mental well being feels threatened. But if we dispel the ignorance which causes fear, then there shall be no need for violence. This can be achieved, by strengthening our powers of discrimination between the real and the unreal, between that related to the body and that related to the *atma*.

Peace and non-violence go hand-in-hand. If there is a state of peace within ourselves, it will manifest in a state of non-violence in our society. One cannot exist without the other.

Conclusion:

Baba says that the enumeration of *Sathya, Dharma, Shanti, Prema* and *Ahimsa* as five distinct human values is not correct. They are all facets of real humanness. They grow together; they are interdependent and inseparable. He says: "Love as Thought is *Sathya*; Love as Action is *Dharma*; Love as Feeling is *Shanti*; Love as Understanding is *Ahimsa*. So, Love must suffuse our very existence.

The value of Truth in us must reflect fearlessness, courage, detachment and humility; the value of Right Conduct must reflect duty, discipline, self-control, patience and perseverance; the value of Peace must reflect contentment, equanimity and cheerfulness; the value of Love must reflect kindness, forgiveness and spirit of sacrifice and service, and a person who professes to be non-violent must exude compassion and fellow-feeling.

Baba says, "The only way of hope in the enveloping gloom of fear, violence, and cruelty of enforced conformity, of hatred and persecution, is the peace that one can win, through self-control and *sadhana* (spiritual exercise). That peace will pervade and purify the inner consciousness as well as the outer atmosphere. *Sadhana* is the life-breath of man; struggling for power, pelf and pomp is but the breath of poison. Poor silly man craves for the air that will destroy him, the food that will torment him and the drink that will defile him! He revels in ruining his nature and denying his excellence! That is the tragedy of civilisation".

"See God in every one you meet; see God in everything you handle. His Mystery is immanent in all that is material and non-material; as a matter of fact, it has been discovered that there is no matter or material. It is all God, an expression of His Mystery! Derive joy from the springs of joy within you and without you; advance, do not stand still or recede. Every minute must make a forward step. Rejoice that it is given to you to recognise God in all and welcome all chances to sing His Glory, to hear His chronicle, to share His presence with others. God has His Hands in all handiworks, His Feet on all altitudes, His Eyes beyond all horizons, His Face before every face".

On the horizon, right now, is shining in all its splendour and glory the Light of Love. We must make contact so that we may infuse new life into our flickering candles and then the whole world will become one great ocean of Light and Love and the Sun, the Moon and the stars in the firmament will envy our planet and in that destiny alone lies the salvation of mankind

O Divine Mother Sai ! Let Prema be my feeling, Ahimsa my thought, Sathya my word, Dharma my conduct and Shanti my strength.

QUESTIONS:

(1) Discuss the three 'faces' of man.
(2) What reasons can you think of that have brought man so close to brink of disaster?
(3) What is the root cause of the unhappiness and inequality in the world today? What lessons can the human body teach us?
(4) Explain, through examples, your concept of *Sathya*. To which aspect of the human personality can this concept be applied and why?
(5) What is the difference between the eyes, the sight and the seer?
(6) What is it that hides the Truth from us?
(7) Explain, through examples, your concept of *Dharma*.
(8) Everyone hankers after *Shanti* (peace) but why do we find it difficult to attain?
(9) What is counteraction of pain? Give examples.
(10) How can world peace be attained?
(11) Explain through examples what is meant by conditioned and conditional love.

(12) Why is there so much hatred in the world? How can it be overcome?
(13) "A non-violent person negotiates from a position of weakness whereas a powerful person from position of strength." Examine critically.
(14) Describe the various forms of violence. What is the root cause of violence and how can it be overcome?
(15) How can the five basic human values be applied in the day-to-day life?
(16) To achieve global peace, one needs to discover peace within one's Self; to understand the mystery of God, Creation and man, one must first discover the Truth of one's own Self. Discuss.
(17) "The louder we laugh, the harder we may have to cry". Discuss.

> *Motherhood is the most precious gift of God. Mothers are the makers of a nation's fortune or misfortune, for they shape the sinews of its soul. Those sinews are toughened by two lessons they should teach: fear of sin, and fondness for virtue. Both these are based on faith in God being the inner motivator of all. If you want to know how advanced a nation is, study the mothers: are they free from fear and anxiety, are they full of Love towards all, are they trained in fortitude and virtue? If you like to imbibe the glory of a culture, watch the mothers, rocking the cradles, feeding, fostering, teaching and fondling the babies. As the mother, so the progress of the nation; as the mother, so the sweetness of the culture.*
>
> *— Sri Sathya Sai Baba*

"Life with desire is Man;
Life without desire is God"

Sri Sathya Sai Baba

6. CEILING ON DESIRES

Implied in the theme of the topic is a certain limitlessness of desires and a potential lack of control over them.

Desires are like pebbles thrown in the calm, pellucid waters; they create waves of agitation and rob us of peace. To underline the grief that following a trail of desires can bring, Baba relates the story of a pilgrim who accidentally sat under a wish-fulfilling tree. The pilgrim was thirsty and he longed for a glass of water. Lo and behold, a glass of water to quench his thirst appeared instantly. He then wished for a meal and his hunger too was satiated. After a fiesta – a siesta! A cot materialised in a trice and as he reclined on it, his thoughts turned to his wife to massage his tired legs. But as his wife appeared, thinking her to be an apparition, he exclaimed that she was an ogress and that she would gobble him up. Sure enough, she duly obliged! Such then is the nature and the ultimate result of desires.

Baba says that this world is itself a wish fulfilling tree; whatever we may desire will most assuredly be granted and so we have to be extremely careful about what we desire.

Under a cloak of mercy our desires persuade us to manufacture excuses to justify all sorts of endeavours. When we perform something that is worthwhile, we waste no time in declaring our ownership to the act and staking our claim on the expected reward thereof. However, when we indulge in something which is less than desirable we, unashamedly, transfer the responsibility and ownership to the devil. If we honestly believe that the almighty Lord is One without the second and that He and He alone permeates the entire cosmos, where then is the room for the devil or satan. It is only our imagination that gives shape, substance and existence to such names in order to serve as a convenient pretext to unload our own guilt on to or as a scapegoat for carrying the can for our own aberrations. We enjoy the freedom of thought and action. We must stop passing the buck and learn to own up to our actions prompted by our desires, and their consequences. Only then will we develop and sharpen our powers of analysis and discrimination which will hold us back from taking a blind leap into the bottomless pit of desires.

Desires come alive during the wakeful state. In the deep-sleep state, we are in a state of desirelessness. It follows therefore, that the desires have body-mind complex as the base; or, put another way, it could be said that desire is the basis of and the cause for the body-mind complex. If we did not have a desire, we would not need a body. Desires have no relationship with the *atma*. But desires can be realised only through the medium of the body. Body is not only the vehicle for the fulfilment of desires, it is also necessary for attaining salvation. It is like a launching pad, necessary for the take off but useless thereafter.

Mind, on the other hand, is not a physical or a biological organ like heart, lungs, etc. In fact, it has no existence except as a collection of thoughts – thoughts which derive their sustenance from the objective world. When thoughts turn into craving, they become desires.

He who has desires and feels wanting is ever poor, however rich he may be materially, whereas he who is contented is ever rich even when adorning the garb of material poverty. Contentment is generally mistaken for being satisfied with having very little or nothing at all, and is therefore seen as an easy substitute for lack of drive and motivation. However, once we taste the nectar (*sat, chit, aananda*) that is native to us, and touch the richness that we are the repositories of, the mind will lose its fascination and craving for the baubles of this material world. Contentment, therefore, is a reflection of our native fullness (*purnattvam*) and not of our material poverty.

What is the origin of desires? In a sense, it is the happiness or bliss which we have experienced in the past but have somehow lost, and our search for that lost bliss. We grope in the dark (in the material world through ignorance) and in the mistaken belief that the lost bliss can be recovered through the acquisition of wealth, riches, power, etc. And so, we set in motion and blaze a trail of desires.

Mind is veritably the breeding ground for thoughts and desires and, of necessity, the battle for controlling the desires has, therefore, to be fought and won in the mind itself.

In the normal course of "living", we have desires. We attempt to fulfil one desire after another. Some of these get fulfilled, others do not. Why not leave matters at that? Why bother to put a ceiling on desires? Well, the question itself and the fact that we should even contemplate such an option, implies and underlines a measure of our disillusionment and experience of futility in attempting to satisfy an endless stream of desires. When we see the fruit laden trees of the sensory world, we are lured by them and we run towards them. But howsoever close we might appear to get to this 'Garden of Eden' and however tantalisingly close the fruits might appear to be, the farther these fruit laden trees appear to recede! In other words, in spite of tasting one fruit after another, insatiable craving for more grows. And, because of the desires, further and farther the mind strays into the objective world, the more difficult and daunting the trek back into the *atmic* reality becomes. The ultimate aim of putting a ceiling on desires is to help towards the rediscovery of the *atmic* reality – to make contact with our Divine Self.

Our thoughts shape into desires; desires give rise to craving and when craving is strong, action follows. However, our endeavours do not always bear fruit. This is because we do not have the exclusive rights to this planet. We have to share it, and live in harmony, with other people and life forms. There is an interdependence and interaction. Just as what we think, utter or do might effect others, so also are their thought, word and deed likely to influence us. Furthermore, because different people have different individual perceptions of life, their thoughts and desires are bound to be different and, at times, at variance with one another. If we pursue our desires disregarding the problems of interaction or the sensitivities of others, what results then is conflict and confusion.

If our endeavours are thwarted and our desires remain unfulfilled, we experience frustration and anger which results in the loss of our peace of mind. If our desires do get fulfilled, however, for every single desire fulfilled there will be ten new ones sprouting in the wings. In the mad pursuit of this unending dichotomy of desires, we once again part company with our peace of mind. So, whether our desires find fruition or remain unfulfilled, either way, the end product is the same – we end up disturbing our native equipoise and losing our peace of mind.

Driven by desire, the mind flogs the body until it is no longer able to sustain the burden and drops dead. When we receive the marching orders, our unrealised but deeply cherished desires appear in the form of deep rooted tendencies and latencies in our next life.

Unless and until we put a stop to the forays of the mind into the objective world and apply some restraint on its vagaries and a ceiling on our desires, we will never achieve liberation and escape from the cycle of birth and death. When we cultivate proximity with the *atma*, the desires of the body-mind complex drop off. When complete identity with the *atma* is realised, the encumbrance or the encasement of the body-mind complex, which is the carrier for our ego and the means for fulfilling desires, is no longer needed and we achieve freedom, liberation from bondage, *mokhsha* – annihilation or death of delusion.

Is man enslaved by external objects and the attractions they exercise over him? Or, is it some inner impulse that urges him forward to shackle himself to sorrow? Baba explains this with an example thus: "There are professional monkey catchers in the village who employ a crude device for their purpose. In the places infested by the marauders, they place a number of narrow necked earthen pots, with a handful of peanuts inside each. The monkey approaches the pot, knows that it has the delicious nuts inside, puts its long hand in and grabs a fistful of nuts. It then finds that it cannot retrieve its arm; the neck is too narrow for the nut-full fist! So, it sits helpless and forlorn and is easily caught and transported! It thinks that there is someone inside who is holding back its arm, when it tries to pull it out! If only it had loosened the grip and got rid of the attachment to the nuts, it could have escaped! So, too, you are the victims of desire and the shackles you have yourselves fastened around you! Liberation, too, is in your hands. Contemplate the unchanging glory of God; then desire for the transient baubles of the earth will fade and you can be free".

When the body dies, it is said, that the whole panorama of all the events of its entire life, flash back in front of it like a movie on the screen. Providence thereby, mercifully gives us yet another chance to learn the lessons from our past so as to modify and improve our tendencies for the future.

Ceiling on desires is often confused with ceiling on waste. Of what use is it to force ourselves to trim down spending if our inner desires continue to multiply unabated and the craving continues to consume us away? Of what use is it to withhold action if we allow the desires prompting such action to run amok with impunity and unbridled freedom? Mere withdrawal or withholding of action cannot necessarily be an indicator of a ceiling or control on desires. By putting aside some money by not spending on this, that or the other, we must not delude ourselves into thinking that we are observing a ceiling on desires. Whilst frugality and the habit of saving are commendable and useful, ceiling on desires has to be applied where desires take shape, ie, in the mind itself.

Let us consider the example of a tricycle – a contraption with three wheels; the front wheel is the leading and the guiding wheel and the two rear wheels are the free wheels. The driving force is directly transmitted to the leading or the guiding wheel and if the free wheels are properly aligned, movement and progress is assured. However, if they are misaligned, the power will be wasted in the wear and tear of the various parts and no worthwhile progress is possible.

There are those who give little of the much which they have - and they give it for recognition and their hidden desire makes their gifts unwholesome.
And there are those who have little and give it all.
These are the believers in life and the bounty of life, and their coffer is never empty.

There are those who give with joy, and that joy is their reward.
And there are those who give with pain, and that pain is their baptism.
And there are those who give and know not pain in giving, nor do they seek joy, nor give with mindfulness of virtue;
They give as in yonder valley the myrtle breathes its fragrance into space.
Through the hands of such as these God speaks, and from behind their eyes He smiles upon the earth.

It is well to give when asked, but it is better to give unasked, through understanding;
And to the open-handed the search for one who shall receive is joy greater than giving.
And is there aught that you would withold?
All you have will some day be given;
Therefore give now, that the season of giving may be yours and not your inheritors.

"The Prophet" by Kahlil Gibran

Again, if we wish to prevent movement in a particular direction there are, seemingly, three ways of achieving this:

- by artificially preventing the movement of the free wheels by placing obstructions in their path;
- by applying brakes on the leading wheel; or
- by utilising or directing the leading wheel to guide the tricycle in a different direction altogether.

The first method will fail in its objective as soon as the resistance to the movement of free wheels is overcome. The second method will be successful only as long as the brakes are on; but we must remember that at some stage the brakes have to be released. The third method avoids the pitfalls of the first two and is assured of full success.

The three wheels are analogous to thought, word and deed. The motive force is the desire. If the word and deed are out of tune with the thought, energy is wasted and there is no progress. If we apply constraints to our words and deeds but allow our mind to work overtime and gain in momentum, the grip of the restraints will progressively loosen and our desires will hold sway once again. If we suppress thoughts, it will not be long before the desires spring up again. Suppression, therefore, is not a permanent solution and is doomed to fail. However, if we guide our thoughts constructively and direct the resulting desires towards one goal, progress can be achieved.

For achieving a ceiling on desires, consider therefore the three possibilities:

(1) Suppression of desires
(2) Sublimation of desires
(3) Spiritualisation of desires

(1) Suppression of desires:

Consider an obstruction, such as a dam or a retaining wall put in the path of flood waters. As the flood waters well up, the build-up of the 'pressure-head' can reach such proportions as to breach the dam unleashing, in the process, forces of such magnitude as will cause havoc and devastation. Similarly, desires, if allowed to multiply indiscriminately or gain in intensity but kept suppressed from being realised will, sooner or later, erupt like a volcano bringing in their wake trouble and turmoil. Suppression , therefore, can be counter-productive; it will add to, rather than help in achieving a ceiling on, desires.

(2) Sublimation of desires:

If in the retaining wall, we were to introduce weep holes to enable controlled release of water through them, excessive pressures would be prevented from building up. The release of the hydrostatic pressures through the weep holes is akin to the process of reasoning the desires out of the system before they inflict any damage. But for it to be successful, it has to be analysed and reasoned out of the system. It is conceivable that with this approach and persistence, desires will get lesser and lesser and eventually sublimated.

(3) Spiritualisation of desires:

If, in addition to the idea of the weep holes, a drain were also to be introduced to collect the water behind the wall and channel it away to serve a useful purpose, then all the problems and dangers could be avoided altogether. The concept is to spiritualise all our thoughts and desires into the single supreme desire of unfolding our own innate divinity.

Frugal habits, ceiling on waste and saving can also have a far reaching influence on the whole course of our life. Directly or indirectly, it can have a sobering influence on our desires. Saving has to be exercised at three levels:
- the physical or the material
- the mental or emotional
- the spiritual

At the physical level, there are two aspects to be considered; firstly, saving of the material resources of our planet, and secondly, saving of the resources at the personal level. With regard to the former, there is the need to save food, materials, clothing, natural resources, etc, in order to achieve a more equitable distribution throughout the world, to eradicate starvation and poverty and to ameliorate the standard of life on our planet. At the personal level, our own physical energy has to be conserved without being abused and wasted away, so that it can be utilised for the welfare of mankind. Lack of proper exercise, wrong eating habits and unrestrained living sap our physical vitality which leave us unable to cope with our own day-to-day problems let alone be of any help to others.

Money, for all practical purposes, is one of the important things in the world. Among the four principal aims of the human endeavour, ie, *dharma*, *artha*, *kaama* and *mokhsha*, (right conduct, material well-being, desire and liberation), it can be seen that *artha* or the material well being, the economic soundness of man, is also given a prime place. The injunction, however, adds that the acquisition of wealth and fulfilment of one's desires are to be based on, and are to be orientated always towards, the attainment of *mokhsha* or liberation, which is the ultimate goal, and not bondage.

Man should save up physically and materially in order to face up to not only the vagaries of the weather but also the vicissitudes of destiny in the form of misfortunes, ill health, loss of job, accidents, etc. By such prudence and forethought, one can avoid being a burden on others.

At the mental level, there is the need to conserve our mental energy and to strengthen and enrich our intellectual faculties, such as, sense of discrimination, will-power, power of concentration, etc. In the *Bhagavad Geeta*, the Song Celestial, it is said that the mind itself can be one's powerful ally or the worst enemy. It can degrade a person down and ruin him, or uplift him to divine heights. Humility, forbearance, friendliness, compassion and love are aids to conserving our mental energy and poise. Feeding ourselves vulgarity and obscenity through touch, taste, sight, smell and sound can, on the other hand, dissipate our mental energy.

On the spiritual level, there is, in all of us, the deep-rooted longing to contact the very core of our being. This thirst must not be stifled or smothered. It has to be fostered and nurtured through discipline and devotion to attain enlightenment. Observing silence and doing meditation can help in this direction.

To conclude, there is no profit in starving the mind of desire; indeed, we cannot exist as a body without one. So, let us give it a desire to feed on. But let that desire be to make our latent divinity manifest in all our thoughts, words and deeds. Only then will the Divine Principle be the controlling and guiding light of our life and only then will we have truly achieved a "ceiling on our desires".

O Divine Mother Sai ! Grant me but one desire that I may serve Thee in thought, word and deed .

QUESTIONS:

(1) What is the nature of the desires?
(2) "Man does not enjoy desires, desires enjoy man". Comment.
(3) How do desire operate?
(4) Where do the desires flee in the deep sleep state?
(5) "Show me a person without desires and I will refuse to see the body".

Discuss this statement.
(6) What is the origin of desires?
(7) Is it ever possible to fulfil all our desires? Give reasons.
(8) "We could add to our happiness if only we could fulfil greater number of desires!" Do you agree with this statement? Give reasons for your answer.
(9) It is said that when a person is about to die, the friends and relatives gathering around should not cry. Why?
(10) Can a ceiling on desires be achieved through their suppression?
(11) In what way can frugality of habits and a ceiling on waste help us towards a ceiling on desires?
(12) What is the result of our indiscriminate desires with regard to the world resources? Of what significance can the concept of ceiling on desires be in world today?

The morning shadow moves in front of you. However fast you run, you cannot catch it, on plain or mountain. Or, the shadow may pursue you and you cannot escape from it. This is the nature of desire. You may pursue it or it may pursue you - but you cannot overcome it or catch it. Desire is an insubstantial shadow. But turn desire inward, towards spiritual treasure, then it yields substantial results.

— Sri Sathya Sai Baba

*"When the veil of mind dissolves,
the Self has the vision of the Self"*

Sri Sathya Sai Baba

7. ASPECTS OF MEDITATION – 1

Man stumbles along in life caught up between two worlds – the finite world of limitation on the one side and the world of infinity and eternity on the other. The outside objective world, in spite of all its diversity and multiplicity, is the finite limited world which is subject to the laws of time and space. The world within us, on the other hand, is infinite and beyond the laws of time and space. Further discussion on this can be found in chapter 15.

The outer world is the world of senses, the world of touch, taste, sight, sound and smell. It can be observed and it comes alive only through the activity of mind and senses. Render the mind defunct and shut the senses off, the world outside will cease to exist. The inner world, on the other hand, is beyond the senses. It cannot be comprehended or experienced through the senses. In order to reach this inner world – the very core of our being, we must therefore transcend the mind and the senses.

Physics teaches us that potential and kinetic energies can coexist in different proportions. However, the sum total of all the energy remains constant, so that if hundred percent of the total energy is potential then the kinetic energy must be zero and vice versa. In much the same way, when we experience the world of spirit, the finite world of matter ceases to exist and when we are hundred percent engrossed in the material world, we find it difficult to comprehend the eternity of the spirit.

Liberation (*mokhsha*) is the release from the shackles of the finite into the freedom of the infinite; the process culminating into this release may be called meditation. Meditation is a retreat into our real Self away from the hassles of the body, mind and the senses.

We have only to look around dispassionately to realise how badly we need a rational approach to life. The mad and unbridled pursuit of power, the inordinate emphasis on the fleeting pleasures of life, the ready compromises with evils of all kinds, are sapping the very sinews of our spiritual life resulting more and more in the general malaise and discontent. The inner conflicts, tensions and the lack of equipoise, says Taimni, which are the inevitable results of this inner poverty of spirit are sought, in many cases, to be drowned in the mental numbness produced by drink or drugs or to be forgotten in the artificially created excitements of all kinds, thus increasing further the unhappiness they are meant to remove. The only way of breaking this stranglehold and living full and integrated lives at peace with ourselves and in harmony with our surroundings lies in making contact with our innate divinity, the Real I.

Who or what is this Real I? Let us consider an example:
"Knock, knock".
"Who is there?"
"It is I, Tom", or "It is I, Dick", or "It is I, Harry".
In each of these answers, there are two components – the invariable component: "It is I", and the variable component: "Tom", "Dick" or "Harry". The statement: "It is I" should have been enough but, on its own, it would not have enabled us to recognise the person. That is to say, it would not have enabled us to recall to mind the shape and form of the body known as Tom, Dick or Harry. So Tom, Dick and Harry merely identify the shapes and forms which are subject to change from person to person. It stands to reason , therefore, that what changes from person to person must bear different names but that which does not change cannot be so differentiated. So, we must conclude that there are two aspects to the human personality: the body-mind complex which changes from person to person and the I-principle which is the same in all. Identity with the changing aspect subscribes to differentiation, whereas the 'I'-principle emphasises the underlying Oneness and integration . So, Tom, Dick, or Harry may be my names yet, in reality, 'I' am neither Tom, nor Dick, nor Harry. If we lived in the awareness of this real 'I', would we also not be able to proclaim, as Baba does: "All names and forms are Mine"?

Note that although the spirit is encased in the body-mind complex, yet the two things are distinct. Aim of meditation is to make contact with the core – the reality. This is possible only after the shell of the body-mind complex is duly penetrated. This involves transcending the gross, the subtle as well as the causal bodies. The gross body is the physical body which is the result of the food we eat. Our vital airs, mental and the intellectual make up constitute the subtle body, and the embedded inclinations and latencies which are the cause of the human birth represent the causal body.

These three bodies are associated with the three states of awareness. In the wakeful state, which is associated with the gross body, one is conscious of functioning through the sense organs. Dream state is associated with the subtle body. In this state, consciousness from the body and sense organs is withdrawn, but the mind projects its own world of suppressed desires and wallows in its own creation. This is associated with the subtle body. In the deep-sleep state, which is associated with the causal body, all objective awareness is lost. Even the mind subsides and the intellect perceives nothing. In this state, although there are no thought agitations, yet we do not have pure awareness since all the proclivities of the mind are still there latent ready to manifest the instant right stimulus is encountered. It is a state of ignorance and therefore of pseudo-bliss.

Beyond these three states, however, lies the *atmic* state or "*turiya* state". It is also known as the "fourth state". It is beyond mental consciousness and so no thought agitations subsist. It is a state of objectless awareness. It is said to be a superconscious "state" wherein one is blissfully aware of the spirit and totally unaware of the objective world and the encumbrances of the body-mind complex or one's egotistic personality. It is not actually a state, it is total awareness. That is why it is also referred to as the "beyond state". It represents the common totality of all the states. To attain that experience, that awareness, meditation is the means. Baba says: "The very purpose of meditation is the purification of the mind and intellect and withdrawal of sense perceptions from contact with the objective experiences".

Losing or forgetting the body-consciousness and reaching a state of trance cannot, by itself, be described as meditation. If this were not so, all the drunks around, oblivious of their physical presence (through helplessness rather than by design!) after drinking two bottles of hooch, could claim to be *yogis* (realised souls) in meditation! However, a drunk who falls out of a carriage may neither be conscious of riding in the carriage, nor of falling out of it. Ideas of life, death, fear and the like do not appear to penetrate him and so, he does not suffer from contact with the objective existence. If such apparent security is to be got from wine, says Chuang Tzu, how much more is to be got from God? However, loss of body consciousness has to yield place to the experience of the *atma* or super-consciousness, then alone can it be a state of meditation.

The main pastime of mind is thinking. In fact mind has no existence except as a bundle of thoughts. Thoughts, in turn, influence our feelings and emotions. The quality of our life at any given time will, to a large extent, depend upon the quality of thoughts ruling our mind at that time. Good thoughts cannot evoke bad feelings, nor can bad thoughts good feelings. Therefore, if we are able to control our thoughts, we will be able to exercise control on our feelings and so also on the quality of our life.

Thoughts keep us tethered to the objective world thereby preventing us from experiencing the Self. Thus, the primary aim of meditation is the controlling of thoughts and the ultimate aim, their total elimination. When the thoughts are completely extinct and the mind is laid to rest, what one experiences then is the Self in its *Sat, Chit* and *Aananda* state. The four-fold aim of meditation could therefore be summarised as follows:

(i) To observe, study and understand the mind and the thought process.

(ii) To gain control over the mind by making it discard the degrading thoughts and dwell on the uplifting thoughts.

(iii) To gradually lessen the thoughts and focus on just one thought to the exclusion of all other thoughts.

(iv) To eliminate all thoughts and abide in the Absolute Knowledge, Total Awareness and Eternal Bliss of the Self

So, the mind has to be weaned away from its forays into the objective world and turned inwards in the firm belief that by turning towards the very source of light within us, it will get illumined. The first step, therefore, in the process of weaning away of mind is: emptying the mind. The ground must be prepared for the purification of mind by the expulsion from the mind of all that is mean and degrading, all desires which impede spiritual progress.

During the early stages, an aspirant is likely to face two obstacles. These are : *vikshepa* (unwanted thoughts) and *laya* (a state akin to sleep). *Laya* has to be avoided like plague as it robs us of all our efforts. Controlling the mind, however, which has had its own way for a long time is not going to be an easy task, more so as one has to reckon with one's latent tendencies. Mind has to be purified by replacing the thoughts which produce harmful agitation by introducing thoughts which are noble and uplifting. Putting a ceiling on one's desires will go a long way in achieving this. Getting rid of unwanted thoughts thus demands determination, discipline and continuous effort. Force should never be used with mind; use of force can be counterproductive and harmful; it will further strengthen the resolve of the mind to go its own way. Remember that it is the very nature of mind to produce thoughts and we are gradually training it to operate the way we wish it to. This will require great deal of patience. Use of discrimination and reasoning will help sublimate the waywardness of mind and see the unwanted thoughts through to their extinction but only if accompanied by heartfelt yearning and an attitude of prayerfulness and humility. Always remember that no effort can ever attain fruition without the grace of the

Lord.

Let us now consider the three components of meditation:

- The Meditator – Subject (***Dhyaata***).
- The Object of Meditation – Object, the Self (***Dhyeya***).
- The Process of Meditation – Relationship, Rapport (***Dhyaana***).

When we mention subject and object, we inevitably refer to two things separated by a space, either known or imaginary, ie, the seer and the seen. As an example, we posit the Creator as being distinct from His creation. If the subject approaches and merges with the object, then there is no distance or difference between the two; then there is no seer and no seen. So the process culminates into meditation only when the three factors, ie, the subject, the object and the process coalesce and merge into one unified experience without the experiencer being conscious of himself.

Let us look at the object of meditation, the real I, further. Consider the example of a building site. On the site, there is a team of part-time and full-time workers. The brick-layers, carpenters, steel fixers, etc, are the part time workers whereas the Engineer, the Architect and the Quantity Surveyor are full time workers. Yet none of these can call himself the boss. It is the Developer, who assembles the team of workers and activates the project and who disbands the team when the job is done, who is the real boss. He does not himself lay a single brick nor move a single stone; whether he is on site or off it, whether he is seen by the workers or not, yet he is acknowledged as the undisputed lord and master of the development. The developer was there before he assembled his team and gave it a corporate identity and he continues to be after disbanding the team.

Human personality bears an analogy to the construction site in as much as, it also has part-time and full-time workers and the real boss. Mind, for instance, is a part-time worker with the various senses as the labourers under it. Can it lay claim to being the reality, the boss? Well, the mind does not exist in the deep sleep state. Besides, it does not take a great deal of effort to realise that it is possible to kill our mind without, in any way, endangering our fundamental well being. Clearly then, mind cannot be the real I since it can be made redundant.

Our heart, on the other hand, could proclaim: "I am the Reality since I am part of the human personality from birth till death; if I cease to be so will the human being". But then similar claims could be made by the lungs, the respiratory system, the digestive system, the nervous system and so on. So, can all of these be the bosses? Intuitively, we know it not to be so because if you have more than one person in charge of the same job, it is a sure recipe for disaster. And we know that the destiny of the human life is certainly not disaster.

The real I has to be the One who:

- was present before the assembly of the team, ie, before the birth of the 'corporate body';
- will continue to be present after the disbanding of the team, ie, after the death of the 'corporate' body ;
- activates the 'corporate' body as a team;
- does not work on the site himself, yet witnesses everything that goes on.

This leads us to three important principles:

- "I" activate the body but "I" am not the body;
- "I" do not act, "I" am the witness;
- "I" am beyond birth and death, "I" am eternal.

Let us now consider the three stages of meditation: Before we enter the portals of **Meditation**, we must pass through the stages of **Concentration** and **Contemplation**. When the mind reaches out into the objective world through the senses, its attachments and activities multiply because of the multiplicity of the attractions. However, when the senses and the wayward mind instead of taking off in all directions, are directed inwards towards one point, one goal, the effect will be like the concentration of the rays of sun through a magnifying glass. This one-pointedness of mind is concentration. It is a function or activity which is subservient to and dependent upon the functioning of the senses, and the senses, in turn, are the contact points with the outer world.

Meditation, on the other hand, has to do with the inner firmament and demands transcending senses. So, whilst concentration must not be mistaken for meditation, it is an important first step. For one to be able to take in what is printed on a piece of paper, four things are necessary: (1) hands must hold the paper, (2) eyes must be focused on the text, the letters, (3) mind must think, and (4) the intellect (*buddhi*) must enquire; the intellect, the mind, the eyes and the hands must all work in unison, only then is it possible to concentrate. Only with such coordination of senses (ie, concentration), Baba says, is it possible for one to read and so, concentration is necessary for reading; so also for writing, walking, eating, etc. Similarly,

The mind is like a clean mirror. It has no intrinsic power of its own to directly experience the sense objects except through the concerned sense organs. For instance, it can see only through the eyes and hear through the ears but can neither see nor hear by itself independently. Consequently, the offences commited by the senses are reflected in the mirror of mind. No blame attaches to the mind per se. It is the association with the wayward senses that pollutes the mind. According to the Scriptures, the mind is subject to three kinds of pollution: Mala, Vikshepa and Avarana.

What is Mala? Man commits many offences, knowingly or unknowingly, not only in this life but also in previous lives. The imprint of these actions is carried by the memory (Chitta) life after life, like the dust accumulating on the surface of a mirror day after day. Thus the mirror of man's mind gets covered up by such dirt, which is technically named as "Mala". On account of this Mala, man is unable to see clearly the reflection of his real identity in the mirror of his mind ...

The second distortion of the mind called Vikshepa is due to the constant wavering of the mind, like the movements of the reflective image in a mirror that is kept moving or shaking frequently. To control this waywardness of the mind, one should undertake various spiritual practices like meditation, prayer and the nine modes of devotion mentioned in the Scriptures ...

The third distortion of the mind is called Avarana. This may be likened to a thick cloth covering the mirror of man's mind, which does not at all permit of any reflection whatsoever of the image of the Self. Thus, while Mala does not enable us to have a clear and correct image of the Self, and while Vikshepa results in seeing the Self as wavering, Avarana altogether hides the Reality - Self, and makes one identify oneself wrongly with one's body.

Sri Sathya Sai Baba

to drive a motor car, concentration is essential. Over a period of time, however, it turns into a routine and becomes a daily habit needing no special effort. It is obvious then that, to achieve this concentration, it is not necessary to go into meditation; concentration cannot therefore be equated to meditation. However, for concentration to develop and stabilise itself, three things are important: purity of consciousness, moral awareness and spiritual discrimination. Concentration is below senses and meditation is beyond senses. If we are to reach the portals of meditation, we must undertake the journey from below the senses to beyond the senses. From concentration, one must progress towards contemplation.

When our divine Self is identified as the goal and when the one-pointed thought force is directed towards that goal and that goal alone, to the exclusion of every other thought, that stage is contemplation. It is an intermediate step between concentration and meditation.

During the stages of concentration and contemplation, the awareness of the "meditator" persists. It is only through persistent efforts and His Grace, when the awareness of being the "meditator" drops off and when what remains is nothing other than what, in reality, was there all the time, ie, blissful consciousness, that experience is meditation.

Let us consider the example of a person on a carousel. As it goes round and round, the speed of the various objects flashing in front of his vision makes him giddy. If he lets go of the hold, his only contact with the centre of the contraption, he would shoot off at a tangent and come to grief. The way to counteract this nausea is to turn our gaze away from the diversity of objects, towards the centre of the carousel about which it rotates. But that is not the end of the problem. The minute we let go of our hold, we will again crash down. To overcome this problem we need to move away from the outer periphery of the carousel where the speed, and hence the centrifugal force, is the greatest, and inch towards the axis or the centre where the speed of rotation is the least, with our gaze constantly fixed on it. Once we reach that centre, there is then no danger of headaches nor of falling off.

Similarly, the entire universe is like a stupendous carousel with all the planets, etc, going round and round and prevented from crashing down because of the "force of attraction" from the universal axis. This force of attraction is Divine Love.

In much the same way, an individual life is like a carousel, with the gross body as the outer periphery. If we look outwards through the senses, the attractions of the objective world flashing in front of us give us all sorts of headaches. However, if we turn our gaze inward, towards our very core, the spiritual axis, the real I, then there is no agitation, no multiplicity and no headaches. Turning the gaze towards the centre, the axis, is concentration; inching towards the centre is contemplation, and reaching the very core is meditation. Just as *atma* (the individualised soul) forms our individual axis or centre, *Param-Atma* (the Universal or Super Soul) is the universal axis. When the individualised soul is released from the encumbrance of the body (the gross, the subtle and the causal), there is the mergence of the "individual" with the "universal". That is known as *mokhsha* or liberation. When the individual awareness is released from the clutches of the 'body-mind' consciousness and loses its identity in and merges with the universal or divine consciousness, that is meditation. Meditation is the means, liberation (*mokhsha*) is the goal.

Let us now briefly consider the principles of the three types of meditation:

(a) JAPA SAHIT DHYAANA (Name and Form Type)

Japa means a repeated and continuous (mental) chanting of a chosen Name of the Lord or a *mantra* (mystical formula) representing an aspect of divinity, with intense devotion and concentration.

Waywardness of mind often becomes the impediment to meditation. By its very nature, the mind has the tendency to flit, to move from one object to another. To tame it and gradually bring it under control, as a first step, we give it certain amount of freedom to wander. "When the mind wanders away from the recital of the Name, take it on to the Form and vice versa. Let it dwell either on that sweetness or this." Baba says, "Treated thus, it can be easily tamed. The imaginary picture thus drawn will, with practice, get transmuted into the emotional picture dear to heart and fixed in the memory". This is the principle of Name and Form type of meditation.

(b) JYOTI MEDITATION (Meditation on Flame)

The principle of this type of meditation uses the means of symbolic light. We perceive light permeating our entire being, driving away all the negative tendencies, then extending this light of Love to our kith and kin, friends and even foe and finally bathing the entire universe in this light. Baba says that, to see and think of the form most dear to one's heart in the flame, and see that flame in all, is the best form of meditation.

Baba emphasises *Jyoti* (Light) to be the best medium for meditation. The main reasons for this choice are as follows:

- It burns dross
- It dispels darkness of ignorance
- It energises
- It suffers no diminution or dilution
- It symbolises progress, evolution, auspiciousness

Out of the One Eternal Flame (*Parabrahma Jyoti*), a million life sparks (*jeevan jyotis*) may be kindled and yet the original primordial flame suffers no dilution or diminution. *Parabrahma Jyoti* is the one that kindles and the *jeevan jyoti* is the one that is kindled. When *jeevan jyoti* (life spark) makes contact with the *Parabrahma Jyoti* (Eternal Flame), it not only acquires the glow of, but also becomes identified with, the Flame itself, just as a lump of coal upon its contact with a live ember also becomes a live ember. It is this truth that is conveyed by the *Vedic* statement: "*Brahmavid brahmaiva bhavati*", "One who knows *Brahman* becomes *Brahman* Himself ultimately."

(c) SOHAM MEDITATION *(Ajapa or Hamsa Gayatri)*

Meditation should not be a ten minute, once a day affair. It should be an on-going continuous effort. We often complain that it is not possible to meditate if we are otherwise engaged in performing our worldly duties. Well, when we are engaged in the act of talking, eating, drinking, working, why even sleeping and dreaming, does our breathing stop? No! Does it in any way interfere or, is it in any way interfered with? No! Well then, if we could use our breathing as the medium of *japa* (continuous mental chanting), then we would achieve non-stop meditation in a manner which would neither interfere with nor be interfered by any action whatsoever. When *japa* thus merges with the breath, it is called *ajapa - jap*.

The compound phrase *So-ham Ham-sah* underlines the unification and oneness of the individual consciousness with the Universal Consciousness. Each phrase comprises the same two words *Sah* and *Aham* but with different emphasis. *So-ham* stands for '**That** am i' whereas *Ham-sah* proclaims '**I** am that'. These two phrases refer to the alternate but complementary assertions: one by the individual consciousness (i) of its identity with the Universal Consciousness (**That**), and the other by the Universal Consciousness (**I**) with the individual consciousness (that). In the words of Taimni, "... it is these assertions which produce and are at the basis of the two centripetal and centrifugal currents which are flowing in opposite directions and which in the physical body are routed along (two separate, subtle channels) the *idaa* and the *pingala*." This is analogous to the Father and the Son, as it were, calling each other across the barrier until they are united.

"When the *sushumna naadi* (the fine, invisible, ethereal chord in the spinal canal) is opened by the practice of *Yoga*, conditions are produced for the partial merging of the two opposite kinds of currents and their flowing in a single channel. The two alternate assertions implied in the *So-ham* and the *Ham-sah* along independent lines now take place in one joint assertion of oneness and thus is accomplished the union of 'I' and 'That' in Self-realization." (For a diagrammatic representation of *idaa, pingala* and *sushumna*, see Appendix B).

With each breath, Baba says, we are averring '*Soham*', I am He; *So* (He) as we inhale and *Ham* (I) as we exhale; He is I my Self. "If we harmonize the breath and thought thus, slowly, the 'I' and 'He' will merge, there will be no two, and *soham* will become transformed into **OM** which is the symbol of the attributeless Supreme." The continuous recitation of *So-Ham* with every breath is referred to as *Ajapa or Hamsa Gayatri*. The ever vibrant *anaahata* (ever new, never old, constant) sound in the *sushumna naadi* which our gross hearing faculty cannot hear is said to be 'OM'.

We must realise that the success of our meditation cannot be measured by the number of minutes we decide to meditate for because, in meditation, we are supposed to be beyond the sway of time. So long as one is aware physically, ie, when one is conscious that one is meditating, and keeping a track of time, it is no meditation at all. Because, in reality, there is no seeker and no sought. It is the mischief of the mind that projects this duality and which becomes apparent in the dimension of time. It is only when the consciousness of the body, mind, thought, ie, the senses, becomes totally extinct and only when we step into timelessness where the experience of the blissful Self alone subsists, that we can claim to be in meditation.

Understanding the mechanism of meditation is only the beginning. The real test comes in its application. We have to ask ourselves whether we are really serious about the business of unveiling the great mystery or whether our aspiration is merely an escape from the temporary disappointments, disillusionments and frustrations of life. Many seemingly enthusiastic aspirants find their enthusiasm fizzling out under the impact of the outer and inner difficulties and find it difficult to keep up the determination. Progress can be made only when we develop an indomitable will to learn to grapple with and overcome all kinds of difficulties. Remember, by the very nature of things, realisation of the Self cannot be attained by relying on help from outside agencies; we have to place that crown on our head ourselves.

Notwithstanding the above, it is abundantly clear that, with the advent of the *Avataar* of the age, Sai has become the focal point, the *sine qua non*, for millions around the globe today. Irrespective of their ages and allegiances, tastes and temperaments, cultures and creeds, faiths and fancies, He is commanding their unconditional attention. They are gathering their wayward thoughts which have hitherto strayed in all directions and are turning them towards Sai. This, clearly, is an exercise in concentration on a global scale. Having thus turned their gaze towards the form of Sai, and having pitched their ears towards the word of Sai, they find themselves singing the glory of Sai in a variety of tunes and languages. With this spontaneous, inexplicable upsurge of love for Him welling up in their hearts, they are beginning to see in Sai the reflection of their true Self. Recognising that Sai is none other than our own Self and affirmation of that essential One-ness is the state of contemplation. Experiencing that One-ness with Sai is the true meditation. The Lord Himself, in His infinite compassion, is teaching us, and taking us step-by-step towards, meditation. How uniquely fortunate and blessed we are !

O Divine Mother Sai ! Show me the way to the stillness of mind that I may feel Thy presence within and without .

QUESTIONS:

(1) What are the inner and outer worlds? What are their characteristics?
(2) Why do we find it difficult to "see" the inner world?
(3) What is meditation? What is the need for it?
(4) What is the connection between the name and the form?
(5) To whom can the statement "All names and forms are mine" be attributed and why?
(6) Why are the gross, the subtle and the causal bodies so called? What is their relationship with the three states of awareness ?
(7) What is the "Beyond State"?
(8) What are the three components of meditation?
(9) What is the object of meditation and what are its characteristics?
(10) How far can the mind take us along the path of meditation?
(11) In meditation, what thoughts should be uppermost in your mind?!
(12) Does deep-sleep state or loss of body consciousness represent a state of meditation?
(13) In meditation, what do you see, hear, smell, feel or taste?! Give reasons.
(14) Can you describe your state of meditation?! If so, how? If not, why?
(15) How can you keep a track of time during meditation?!
(16) How can the waywardness of mind be tamed?
(17) Why is the meditation on flame preferable to that on an object like a flower or a fruit?
(18) To the question, *koham* (who am I?), what answer does our breath give?

(19) Bhagawan Baba says, "*Dhyaana* (Meditation) is a discipline which no text-book can teach and no class can communicate. *Dhyaana* classes indeed! Those who handle them do not know what *dhyaana* is; those who attend them do not care to know." Discuss.

You sit in Meditation for ten minutes after the evening bhajan (devotional singing) session; so far, so good. But, let me ask, when you rise after the ten minutes and move about, do you see everyone in a clearer light as endowed with Divinity? If not, Meditation is a waste of time. Do you love more, do you talk less, do you serve others more earnestly? These are the signs of success in Meditation. Your progress must be authenticated by your character and behaviour. Meditation must transmute your attitude towards beings and things, else it is a hoax. Even a boulder will, through the action of sun and rain, heat and cold, disintegrate into mud and become food for a tree. Even the hardest heart can be softened so that the Divine can sprout therein.

– Sri Sathya Sai Baba

"The knower and the known are two different aspects of one Cosmic Consciousness."

M Kroy

8. ASPECTS OF MEDITATION – 2

A sound body houses a sound mind and a purified mind leads to the blossoming of the native Self or spiritual awakening. Spiritual evolution can be perceived as a three-stage process: Firstly, a sound and healthy body; secondly, a purified mind and enlightened intellect subservient to the spirit; and eventually, spiritual awakening and abidance in the spirit.

"The mind is prone to gathering experiences and storing them in memory", Says Baba. "It does not know the art of giving up. Nothing is cast away by the mind. It does not have even a short interval between one thought and the next. And in the continuous succession of thoughts there is no order or relationship. Meditation is the name for a period of rest we provide for the busy and wayward mind."

As long as man suffers from the delusion of doership, the impact of past actions, in the form of impression of the enjoyment of such actions, persists. These impressions are stored, and remain latent, in one's psyche, ready for recall given the right stimuli. Recollections of such past experiences are called *vaasanaas*. Such recollections are triggered by sensory perceptions. For example, the mere sight, indeed the very thought, of a mango may, by association, bring to mind the impression of sweetness which the experience of eating a mango even in the very distant past may have given. The *vaasanaas* influence the thought process, ie the mind; mind, in turn, plays the tune and the body acts out the role through the five senses of action (*karmendriyas*).

Influenced by the *vaasanaas*, the mind is thus prone to going down the memory lane and roaming about in the fields of joyful recollections of the past. The compelling attractions of, and the stimuli from, the world-of-objects outside, aided and abetted by the irresistible desires inside, to re-live and re-enjoy the past experiences, find the mind reaching out and engaging in sense activity once again. This causes the agitation of the mind. Detachment of the mind from the sense-objects as well as the relief from the consequent mental agitation, is essential to a successful session of meditation. Not only should an aspirant avoid the obstacles such as pride, conceit, mischief, the tendency to discover the faults of others, etc, on the path of meditation, warns Baba, he must also be ever vigilant never to lose his temper even over small things, for that will otherwise block his progress. On the other hand,"The aspirant must welcome gladly the announcement of his defects by any one." "He must, by inward observation, examine the mind and its contents and condition. By proper disciplinary habits, he should remove the accumulated dirt, little by little, systematically. The aspirant must minimise all discussion and argumentation, for this breeds a spirit of rivalry and leads one on to angry reprisals and vengeful fighting. Do not struggle to earn the esteem of the world. Do not feel humiliated or angry when the world does not recognise you or your merits. Learn this first and foremost if you are an aspirant for spiritual success. A sense of joy is necessary for concentration and meditation to progress."

In order to restore the quiescence of the mind, *Kaivalyopanishad* advises thus:

> "In a place without any disturbance, resting in comfortable posture, clean (externally) and pure (internally), head and body held erect in a line, with a mental attitude of detachment, exercising control over the senses, mentally saluting one's preceptor with reverence, meditate within the Lotus of the Heart, upon the Untainted, the Pure, the Pristine and the Blissful."

Mind is very powerful and single-minded. To harness its energies usefully and to make it more pliable and meditation-worthy, the attitude of reverence is absolutely vital. The attitude of reverence must combine within itself the four elements of love, respect, prayerfulness and humility. With such reverence, offer the following prayer (given by Baba Himself), as you sit down for meditation:–

> "O Lord! Take my love and let it flow
> in fullness of devotion to Thee.
> O Lord! Take my hands and let them
> work incessantly for Thee.
> O Lord! Take my soul and let it be
> merged in one with Thee.
> O Lord! Take my mind and thoughts
> and let them be in tune with Thee.
> O Lord! Take my everything and let
> me be an instrument of Thee."

Never doubt that the prayer will be answered. Remember the story of the *dervish* (mendicant) who was tempted by the devil to cease calling upon *Allah* on the ground that *Allah* never answered: 'Here am I'. In the words of the *Sufi* poet, Jalal-Uddin Rumi, Prophet Khazir appeared to the *dervish* in a vision with the following message from God:

> "Was it not I who summoned thee to My service?
> Was it not I who made thee busy with My Name?
> Thy calling 'Allah!' was My 'Here am I'."

Some helpful preliminaries, beneficial points of preparation and the different types of meditation as outlined by *Bhagawan* Baba are reproduced hereunder for easy reference.

PRELIMINARIES

Time :
Ideal time is between 3 am to 6 am, *Brahma-muhurtam* (divine, propitious period), otherwise any time during morning or evening will do. However, one must keep to a fixed time.

Seat :
Never sit on bare ground. Use either a wooden plank, little elevated (½" to 1") from ground, or a mat of *Darbha* grass or deer-skin, with thin white cloth spread on top. Such an arrangement acts as an insulator to ensure that the spiritual charge received during meditation is not earthed and lost.

Direction :
Magnetic force flows from South to North pole; Electrostatic force flows, and the rotation of earth takes place, from West to East. Facing towards North or East therefore relaxes mind and tones up the nerves more easily.

Posture :
Padmaasana (Lotus posture) or *sukhaasana* (easy posture) or any other "comfortable" posture. Do not force yourself to sit in the Lotus posture if it means putting yourself under strain. You may gradually progress towards it if you prefer it, otherwise it is not absolutely necessary. Do not make yourself too comfortable that you may drift off to sleep.

Hands :
In front, fingers in close contact with each other.
[Please note that keeping the hands in *Chin Mudra* (see Chapter 14) is likely to be a source of distraction during meditation.]

Eyes :
Half open or fully closed making sure that neither your vision wanders nor do you drift off to sleep. Swami has also said that, "There are seven Suns, emanating seven types of rays; that is the reason why you are advised to have half-closed eyes when you meditate on the Form of the Lord. Then there will be the first three rays trying to penetrate the upper eyelid and the last three, the lower eyelid; but the eye will receive only the fourth ray, the fourth colour."

Relaxation :
By means of mental message, relax the neck, the shoulders, the hands, the chest, the teeth, the stomach, the fingers, the back, the thighs, the knees, the calves and the feet.

PREPARATION :

Start :
With the chanting of 3 AUM's.

So-Ham :
Recite *So-Ham* silently for 1 to 3 minutes, *So* (He, Divinity) as you inhale and *Ham* (I, ego) as you exhale. He comes in with every breath and ego goes out. *So-Ham* also symbolises the fundamental unity, the One-ness of He and I.

Praanayama **(Breath-Control) :**
Praanayama is regarded as the best exercise for cleansing the body of its impurities. There are three steps: one breathes in through the left nostril, holds the breath for some time in the lungs and breathes out through the right nostril. Inhalation is described as *'poorakam'*, exhalation as *'rechakam'* and holding the breath as *'kumbhakam'*. *Praanayama* imparts life and vigour to every cell of the body and helps in the purification process (*naadi shuddhi*). However, *praanayama* is not a mere deep-breathing exercise, *praana* is the cosmic life principle. *Praanayama* is a spiritual exercise, while deep breathing is a physical exercise. *Praana* is the vital force, the energy, the vitality which pervades the entire universe. We establish our contact with the cosmic life-principle through *praanayama* and accumulate a store of vital force within ourselves. Baba says: "To breathe in all that is good is *'poorakam'*. To give up all that is bad is *'rechakam'*. To retain in the heart what is good is *'kumbhakam'*. The thought that 'I am verily *Brahman*' is *poorakam* (breathing in), holding that thought steady thereafter is *kumbhakam* (retaining the breath), and the negation of the phenomenal

God has a million names... a million forms. Select any name of His that appeals to you. Choose any form of His. Every day when you awaken to the call of the brightening East, recite the Name, meditate on the Form. Keep the Name and the Form as your companion, guide and guardian throughout the waking hours. When you retire for the night, offer grateful homage to God in that Form, with that Name - for being with you, by you, beside you, before you, behind you, all day long. Know that within the many forms and the many names, God is present in all of them. The inner being is, in reality, only One.

Sri Sathya Sai Baba

world by discarding it as ephemeral is *rechakam* (breathing out). This is the real course of *praanayama* for the enlightened, say the *Vedas*, whereas the ignorant turn it into a torture of the nose!

Relative time-proportions of breathing in, holding the breath and finally breathing out are 1:4:2; "two seconds long *'poorakam'* (inhaling), eight seconds long *'kumbhakam'* (holding the breath) and four seconds long *'rechakam'* (exhaling)." "*Praanayama* has to be practised carefully for three months; later, the duration of *poorakam, kumbhakam* and *rechakam* can be doubled. When six months are spent in this steady practice the activities of the senses are laid low. If practised with faith and feeling, *praanayama* will tame the agitations of the mind, otherwise it becomes mere physical exercise improving just physical health."

Note :
No thought of past events, no trace of anger or hatred, no memory of sorrow should be allowed to interfere. To counteract any intrusion by these, entertain thoughts which will feed the enthusiasm for meditation.

Japa Sahit Dhyaana (Name and Form Type)

- Offer silent, earnest, heartfelt prayer to the Lord for His Guidance and Grace.

- Recite silently the verse (*shloka*) on the glory of the Lord that most appeals to you.

- While so engaged, draw before the mind's eye the form which that name represents.

- When mind wanders away from the recital of the Name, take it on to the picture of the Form. Let it dwell either on that sweetness or this. Treated thus, it can be easily tamed.

- The imaginary picture drawn will get transmuted into the emotional picture dear to the heart and fixed in the memory.

- Finally, it will become the *saakshaatkaarachitra* (real presence), when the Lord assumes that form in order to fulfil your yearning.

- After 10 or 15 minutes in the initial stages and longer thereafter, reflect on the peace and bliss you had during meditation, ie, bring back into memory the joy you experienced. This will steady faith and increase earnestness.

- Then do not get up suddenly, nor start moving about resuming your avocations. Loosen limbs slowly, deliberately and gradually and then enter upon your usual duties.

Result :
Being able to see the God whom you adore, in every other person as intently as you see Him in yourself.

Note 1 :
Do not get discouraged that you are not able to concentrate for long from the very beginning.

Note 2 :
Dwell always on one Name of God, one personification of any one of His innumerable attributes of glory.

Jyoti Meditation (Meditation on the Flame)

- Most effective and most universal way.

- Offer a silent, earnest, heart felt prayer to the Lord for His Guidance and Grace.

- Keep a lamp with an open flame, steady and straight, or a candle in front. Look on the flame steadily for some time.

- Closing the eyes, try to feel the flame inside you, between your eyebrows.

- Let the flame slide down into the lotus of your (spiritual) heart, illuminating the path.

- When it enters the heart, imagine that the petals of the lotus open out one by one bathing every feeling and emotion in the light and so removing darkness from them. Then there is no space for darkness to hide.

- The light of the flame becomes wider and brighter.

- Let it pervade your limbs; now, those limbs can no more deal in dark, suspicious, wicked activities, because they have become the instruments of light and love.

- Let the light reach up to the tongue; falsehood vanishes from it.

- Let it rise up to the eyes and ears and destroy all dark desires that infest them leading into perverse sights and puerile conversation.

- Let the head be surcharged with Light and all wicked thoughts flee therefrom.

- Imagine that the light is brightening more and more in you, more and more intensely.

- Let the light radiate all around you in ever widening circles, reaching your loved-ones, your kith and kin, your companions, even your rivals, enemies, strangers, in fact, all living beings encompassing the entire world. Then all is light; Light is in you, you are in the Light.

- Since light illumines all senses everyday so deeply, so systematically, a time will soon come when you can no more relish dark and evil sights or yearn for dark and sinister tales or rave for low, harmful, deadening things, or approach places of ill-fame and injury, or frame evil designs against anyone at any time. Stay on in that thrill of witnessing that light everywhere.

- If you are adoring God in any form, now try to visualise that form in the all-pervasive light, for, God is Light, Light is God.

- Practise this meditation everyday regularly. At other times, repeat the name of God, any name fragrant with any of His many majesties, always taking care to be conscious of His might, mercy and munificence.

'SO-HAM' Meditation *(Ajapa* or *Hamsa Gayatri)*

- Before you start your meditation session, chant *'So-Ham'*, inhaling *So'* and exhaling *'Ham'*, inhaling through one nostril and exhaling through the other.

- *'So-Ham'* means 'He' is 'I' (myself); it identifies you with the infinite and expands your consciousness.

- Harmonize the breath and thought.

- The mood of relaxation produced by this *'Soham'* recital is a good pre-condition and is very conducive to a profitable session of meditation.

- In reality, with each breath, you are averring *'Soham'*, I am He. It is a fact which you have ignored so long. Believe it now.

- Watch your breath and meditate on that grand truth, slowly the 'I' and the 'He' will merge and there will be no more two, for *'Soham'* will get transformed into 'OM', the primal sound. That OM (AUM) is the Reality behind all this 'relative unreality'.

Remember that :

- "The fruit of meditation is the experience of *atmic* bliss.

- Patience is the only strength one needs.

- If one is engaged in counting up the rules, adding up the time spent and the expense incurred, such 'meditation' can belong only to the objective world; it can never come into the subjective, the spiritual field.

- Meditation should not be confused with the loss of body-consciousness.

- Meditation should be 'performed' enthusiastically, with full faith and care and strictly according to discipline.

- Bodily contact with others should be avoided. It should be recognised that there is a divine energy in the human body. When this divine energy comes into contact with another person, it is likely to receive the bad thoughts in the latter. If the other person is good, one may receive good thoughts from the contact. But one cannot decide who is good and who is bad. Hence, if one sits apart during meditation, one may experience highly elevating thoughts.

Dhaarana - Dhyaana - Samaadhi (Concentration - Meditation - Equipoise)

In one of His discourses, Baba has explained to students yet another way of how meditation can be done. It is as follows:

"The first step is *'Dhaarana'*. Twelve *'dhaaranas'* amount to one *'dhyaana'*. Twelve *'dhyaanas'* equal one *'samaadhi'*."

"*'Dhaarana'* is steady concentrated viewing of any object for twelve seconds. You have to look at any object, a flame, a picture or an idol for twelve seconds only with total concentration, without blinking the eyelids. This is *'Dhaarana'*."

"Practising *dhaarana* is a preparation for *dhyaana* (meditation). The duration of *dhyaana* is twelve *dhaaranas*. This means that *dhyaana* should last 12 x 12 = 144 seconds, that is, two minutes and twenty-four seconds. *Dhyaana* does not call for sitting in meditation for hours. Proper *dhyaana* need not last more than 2 minutes 24 seconds. It is only after *dhaarana* has been practised well that one can do *dhyaana* (meditation) well.

Twelve *dhyaanas* equal one *samaadhi*. This means 144x12 seconds, that is, 28 minutes and 48 seconds – very much less than an hour. If *samaadhi* is prolonged, it may prove fatal.

By continuing this practice of *dhaarana*, you develop the capacity to perform *dhyaana* for 2 minutes and 24 seconds. Continuing the practice of *dhyaana*, in this way, you develop the capacity to be in a state of *samaadhi* for 28 minutes and 48 seconds.

Samaadhi is not a state of unconsciousness or some other kind of consciousness. It is nothing of the kind. The correct meaning of *samaadhi* is *sama-dhi*, the state in which the intellect has achieved equanimity. Whether in pleasure or pain, in praise or blame, in gain or loss, in heat or cold, to be able to maintain an equal mind is *samaadhi*. That is the real fruit of meditation.

To maintain one's calmness and concentration during meditation, unaffected by any disturbing elements, *dhaarana* has to be practised. Through *dhaarana*, control of the senses is also achieved. Purity of mind is also secured. Through mental purity, the Divine is experienced.

There is also an internal method of practising *dhaarana*. When you close your eyes, a small dark spot appears before the inner eye. You may concentrate on this spot for 12 seconds without letting it move. By this practice, the power of meditation can be developed.

Through the powers of *dhaarana* (concentration), you can develop single-pointed contemplation, *dhyaana* (meditation), known in *Vedantic* parlance as *saalokyam*. This means concentrating your thought on what you desire, ie absorption in the thoughts of divinity. The practice of meditation leads to *saameepyam* (proximity to the Lord) which, in turn, leads to the next stage *saaroopyam* (experience of the vision of the Lord). This may be compared to the arrival of a river to merge in the ocean. At first the ocean repels the advance of the river. After repeated attempts of the river to merge in the ocean, the latter allows the river to pass under its waves. Spiritually, this process of merger of the *jivaatma* (individual) with the *paramaatma* (divine) is described as *saayujyam* (mergence in the divine).

The first stage in the process is *saalokyam* – continuous contemplation of the divine. Think about the Lord in whatever action you do. Then, you achieve *saameepyam* – nearness to the Lord. Coming nearer, develop closer relations with the divine. In due course, the state of *saaroopyam* is attained. The realisation that 'you and I are one' dawns. Then *saayujyam* – complete oneness with the divine, is experienced....."

Baba warns us not to become preoccupied with the (inessential) rituals, nor to get side tracked or lose bearings in the mechanics of the various types of meditation or any other spiritual exercise, but to remember always that the aim of all spiritual *sadhana* (exercise) is to achieve purity of heart and mind so that the divine love latent within us can surge into a perennial stream of unconditioned and unconditional flow. Meditation is not trying to achieve or become anything; it is simply an act of Being.

O Divine Mother Sai ! Bless me that I may remember You with my every breath.

QUESTIONS:

(1) Why should one not sit on bare ground for meditation?
(2) How can facing the right direction help us in meditation?
(3) What is wrong in meditating in the comfort of ones own bed?
(4) Is it possible to meditate with eyes fully open? Give reasons.
(5) Why is the period between 3am and 6am considered to be the ideal time for meditation?
(6) What is the principle of Name and Form type of meditation?
(7) What is meant by persistence of vision?
(8) What is the significance of using flame as a means of meditation?
(9) What is meant by *So-Ham*? What is its connection with mind and AUM?

(10) "We talk best when we are silent,
We see best when our eyes are closed,
We hear best when our ears are shut,
We think best when the mind is laid to rest!"
Discuss.
(11) Explain *dhaarana*, *dhyaana* and *samaadhi*. How are these used in the fourfold approach to the Divine?

Life is a pilgrimage, where man drags his feet along the rough and thorny road. With the name of God on his lips, he will have no thirst; with the form of God in his heart, he will feel no exhaustion. The company of the holy will inspire him to travel in hope and faith. The assurance that God is within call, that He is ever near, nor is He long in coming, will lend strength to his limbs and courage to his eye.

— *Sri Sathya Sai Baba*

> *"If you abide always in the Self, which is the substratum of all experience, you will find the world, of which alone you are aware, just as unreal as the world in which you lived in your dream."*
>
> *Maharshi Raman*

9. A DREAM WITHIN A DREAM

What is a **DREAM**? **D** - Desires, **R** - Repressed, **E** - Expression, **A** - Agitation and **M** - Mind; Repressed Desires seeking Expression through the Agitation of Mind. That expression, that projection is a dream.

Dream also implies that there is a reality. In fact, dream and reality are two relative terms. A dream can be identified as such only when we can delineate the reality. Only when we know both can the two be singled out and separated. Only when we experience the reality, will we be able to discard non-reality as a dream. Or, conversely, only if we are able to define what a dream is, can we infer what reality might be.

Truth or reality cannot be *Sat* (ever-existent) if it suffers from inconstancy. We cannot call a thing *Sat* merely because it is experienced and appears to have some pragmatic value. In dream we experience things which are valid but only as long as the dream lasts. As soon as we 'wake up', they disappear as though they never existed. Our experiences of the 'wakeful' state, likewise, which are meaningful to us while they last, disappear as soon as we enter into 'dream' or 'deep-sleep' state. The world of our so-called 'wakeful' experience is, in essence, of the same mould as our dream world. The dream experience appears unreal upon waking whereas the waking experience is absent in dream. Both, however, are non-existent in 'deep-sleep' which, in turn, is not experienced in either of the other two states. Mutual exclusivity of these states therefore brings into focus their limitation and confirms their inconstancy (ie unreality).

"One may have a dream that one is a child, that one attends school, makes friends, marries, becomes a father, has a career and so on – a sequence of events that covers, say, forty five years of one's wakeful life. The dream may have started at 3.15 am and be over by 3.17 am. In the two minutes of the waking time, the dreamer would have experienced events through the forty five years of dream time. When the waking state is transcended, it also is seen to be a dream, and a life time in the waking state has taken only a few moments in the transcendent state. The waking state is seen to be a dream and the dream state, therefore, a dream within a dream. The dream state is unreality in truth. The waking state is truth in unreality and the transcendent state is the truth in truth. The 'I' in the dream state is taken as the body, 'I' in the waking state as the mind and the 'I' in the transcendent state is God".

There are two essential differences between the so called 'dream' and the 'wakeful' states. Firstly, our dream is the projection of our mind, and the manifested world is the projection of the Cosmic Mind. Whilst man's dream is ephemeral and most of the time, chaotic, reflecting an incoherence in the nature of the repressed desires prompting it, the universe is an eternal dream of the Eternal Consciousness. Furthermore, this eternal dream, being a projection of the intelligent Cosmic Consciousness, it has beauty and harmony as its base and is governed by rational, intelligent laws whose discovery goes in the name of physics, chemistry, biology, astronomy and so on. Secondly, the time scales for the two states are different. For example, according to the *Atharvana Veda*, the life span of *Brahma* (the Creator) is : 311 040 000 000 000 years.

> 1 *Brahma* Day : 4 320 000 000 years
> 1 Second of *Brahma* time : 100 000 years

So, thousands of our life times represent only a fleeting moment of the cosmic time, just as a couple of minutes of the waking time could cover a life span in the dream time. The time scale is absolutely mind blowing. But consider this, if it were not so, how could the Creator wield simultaneous control over the entire cosmos?

A dream may be characterised by, or defined as, a state that is Fleeting, Apparent, Limited, Sense-based and Evanescent; in short a figment of one's imagination. Reality may, therefore, be inferred as being that 'state' which can be characterised by Timelessness, Refulgence, Universality and Eternity. Dream is F*A*L*S*E, reality is T*R*U*E.

In a dream, where do the faces and places, the conversations, the wiles and the smiles, the laughter and the tears, come from? When the dream is over, where do they go? Are these experiences brought into our mind from the outside in the first place and are they, then, driven out later? No, they are not. They are simply the projections of our conscience. Our dream mind projects itself into the manifold. It assumes the roles of both the subject and the object, the seer and the seen, the dream as well as the beholder of the dream. In effect, it is our dream mind saying:"I am one, I want to become the many." Just as the Lord says : " *Ekoham, bahusyaam*", "I am One, I became the many".

When we wake up from the dream, the dream merges with the beholder of the dream. The seer and the seen unite and coalesce into a single integrated consciousness once again, the manifold ceases to exist and disappears like a dream it really was. In effect, it is the dream mind proclaiming (to its projection) : you and I are one. Only when we thus transcend the boundary of the dream state, do we realise that while there appeared many, in reality there was only ONE. In much the same way, the manifested universe is the projection of the Divine or Omniwill, you and I providing the faces in His dream. It is in this context that Baba says to us : you and I are One. It does not mean that His body and our body are one but that the reality, the essence of 'you' is 'I' the *atma*, or 'you' are merely the projection of 'I'.

In the course of a dream, one would not believe what one saw as anything other than the reality. Because in that state, no other state is known and so that state appears to be the reality. It is only when we wake up from, ie, move out of, that state that we stumble upon the 'reality'. While in the dream state, we have no experience of the existence of any other state, in the wakeful state, however, we are marginally better off since we carry into it our experience and knowledge of a dream state. This provides the most important clue to the possibility that the present state could, potentially, also be a dream which could disappear as soon as we wake up from it.

Let us now examine the various aspects of the wakeful state. Take yesterday, for instance; how long did it last? A limited, finite period of time. Was it universal? No, while it was day here, it was night in some other part of the world. Can you recall it? No. Did it stay unmodified? No. So, if yesterday could not last, was not universal, was ever changing, it cannot fit the definition of reality. It can, at best, be referred to as a passing phase. An individual, likewise, is also forever changing until he dies. Since yesterday is typical of every other day past, present or future, and every face typical of every other face, we must conclude that life as we behold is no more than a passing phase, a dream. The same is also true of the phenomenal universe.

The word for the universe in *Sanskrit* is the two syllabled word *JAGAT*. *JA* means born and *GAT* means dead – a cycle of birth and death; here today gone tomorrow – a dream! A dream on a stupendous time scale in comparison with our own little dream may be, but a dream nevertheless.

Baba says: "Both the waking state and the dream state are of the nature of illusion; in both, we have the deep-seated, latent impressions (*vaasanaas*) operating. The manifested world (*jagat*) is as much a super-imposition on the reality (*Brahman*), as a series of pictures on the wall." One is a 'day-dream', the other a 'night-dream', that is all.

One might still argue that the dream state is unreal and the wakeful state real. But why look further? The answer is simple. We cannot be absolutely positive about the nature of reality until we have crossed the boundaries of the unreality or the dream. That is possible only when we step out of the changing, dream state into an unchanging state which is different from the dream. Only when we experience the state of reality which is unchanging, eternal and universal, will we be in a position to discard all else that falls short, as unreal, as a dream. And since we know that the manifested world is in a state of perpetual flux, it follows that it cannot be real in the absolute sense; it can only be a passing phase, a dream.

Let us consider another example: We look upon beloved Baba as God incarnate with a form and attributes. But have we experienced the formless, the attributeless majesty of the Divine Principle? If the answer is no, then there has to be a 'state' of awareness which has yet to come. By implication, therefore, we must still be in less than real, a dream state. The formless, attributeless, almighty Lord willed it so and we see Him in His dream on our planet earth with form and attributes in the form of Baba and when Baba wills it so, He appears to us in our little dream which is therefore a dream within a dream.

Does the manifested world exist by itself? Can it be perceived without the willing connivance of mind? In deep sleep state, there is no mind and there is no world. Only while 'awake' is there a mind as well as the world! This is the classic principle of the Invariable Concomitance, the unchanging coexistence. Mind and the world are coeval. As long as there is a mind, there is a world; when the mind is absent, so also is the world! The manifested world neither exists by itself nor is it conscious of its existence. It comes alive only through the mind. In other words, the world of matter parades in glory before ignorance but disappears before wise scrutiny. How can such a world be real in the absolute sense? Its 'reality' is only relative and not absolute.

A world that is ever-changing, that is not self-conscious that is dependent upon the testimony of the mind for its existence cannot be real. If we are to establish the truth and truth alone, then we have no alternative but to accept the world as a mere dream! For, if we look upon this changing world as the reality, we are then unlikely to find the unchanging reality. Take the example of a piece of rope seen as snake in the twilight. As long as we see the snake, we cannot see the rope as such. The non-existent snake assumes reality, whereas the reality, the rope, seems wholly non-existent. The minute we stop seeing the snake, the rope will be seen as the reality it actually is.

Mind figures prominently in all this. Let us examine its credentials. Is there awareness in the deep sleep state? No. Says who? Says the mind. But the mind is not active during the deep-sleep state. That being the case, of what value is the testimony of the mind regarding our existence or experience during the deep-sleep state, when it is itself non-existent? Seeking the testimony of the non-existent mind to prove our existence or to disprove our awareness during the deep-sleep state is, says Raman *Maharshi*, tantamount to calling the evidence of one's child to disprove one's birth! In reality, there is no faculty known as mind. Mind is only surmised, says *Tripura Rahasya*, for the location of the dream subject, the dream vision and the dream object. Its reality therefore is of the same mould as that of the dream.

In spite of all the pointers and all the logic pointing to it, why do we still find it hard to believe that the wakeful state is also a dream? The reason is that just as the dream mind does not permit us to doubt the reality of the dream state, the wakeful mind, likewise, does not allow us to doubt the reality of our wakeful experience. The mind, clearly, is an expert at marshalling its resources until it can see the scales of argument swaying in its own favour. A philosopher once posed the question: If a king in the waking world were to dream for twelve hours every day that he is a beggar, and if a beggar in the waking world, likewise, were to dream that he is a king, who is the king and who the beggar?

You may claim that the waking king is the real king. But that would be the pronouncement of the waking mind. Could we expect it to assert anything else ? The dream mind, likewise, could make an equally valid assertion in relation to the dream world. To establish the truth, however, we need the help of a judge. But the judge must not be partial to one side or the other. Besides, he must have the testimony of both the sides, both the parties to the dispute, right in front of him. Is it any wonder then that our waking mind which is biased towards the waking state, would have us believe that the wakeful state is the real state and not a dream? Just as in a dream, we cannot make a comparison between the dream and the waking states, so also in the 'wakeful' state do we find it difficult to make a comparison between the 'wakeful' state and the higher state of awareness. But, as we say now after 'waking' in regard to the dream world, so will we say, then,

The world we see around us cannot give us happiness. From moment to moment it is changing. The experiences the world gives us in the waking state get obliterated in the dream state, and those of the dream state cease when we wake up from the dream. The dream experiences are our creation. And so are the waking state experiences. What we see is nothing but our own creations. The vision experience of the world is but a projection of our mind and the reflection of our inner thoughts. As the thoughts, so the vision. The colour of the glasses you wear determines the colour in which things appear to you. If you wear red glasses, everything will appear red. If you wear green glasses, everything will appear green ...

The question arises - how can you be content, living in this illusory world, gathering and relying on illusory knowledge? Realise the Person beyond all illusion, who is the creator of this illusion, who is revealed in and through this illusion. Worldly knowledge is of the temporary, the particular, the finite, the individual; how can it reveal the Eternal, the Universal, the Infinite, the Absolute? The Vedas have the answer. They ask us to analyse our dream experience. Dreams are unreal; they are illusory. Yet, for the time we are dreaming, the experience is real and valid. Often, in these dreams, as a result of illusory experience itself, such extreme awareness is created...that the person dreaming awakens. What caused the awakening? The dream itself helped in the destruction of the dream. So too, in this wakeful dream - in the illusory world where every experience is deemed true and valid - some experience or divine axiom will awaken man into the Higher Awareness.

Sri Sathya Sai Baba

in regard to this 'wakeful' world when we wake up into the consciousness of the Absolute. Baba says: "You slept and so you dreamt. You slept the sleep of ignorance (*ajnaana*) and delusion (*moha*) and so you dreamt this world (*samsaara*). Awake and you will have no more dreams. When the dream is gone, the delusion also goes." "When you are immersed in deep sleep, what happens to your joys and sorrows, your profits and losses? They have no reality then, nor have they any later. At both times they are but the creation of your fancy. He who knows this secret will always exult in the joy of companionship with himself, the contemplation of his own reality. This is real permanent joy."

To conclude, what we commonly refer to as the wakeful state is also a kind of dream from which we must wake up into the *atmic* reality where there are no preferences and prejudices, no barriers of time, no you and I, but simply **One Truth, One Reality, One God**. To know that reality, we have no option but to see the manifested world, first, as a dream. Otherwise the reality will for ever remain obscure and elusive.

O Divine Mother Sai ! May all my dreams be centred upon Thee.

QUESTIONS:

(1) What is a dream? How can it be identified?
(2) What are the differences between the 'wakeful' state and the 'dream' state?
(3) Where do the faces and places in a 'dream' come from and where do they go upon 'waking'?
(4) It may be argued that the 'dream' state is unreal and the 'wakeful' state real, because the food of the 'dream' state cannot satisfy the hunger of the wakeful' state whereas the food of the 'wakeful' state can. Is this argument valid? Discuss.
(5) What is the Principle of Invariable Concomitance? Discuss.
(6) What is the nature of Truth or Reality and what causes it to be obscure?
(7) What is the part played by the mind?
(8) What is the difference between "sleep-waking" and "waking-sleep"?
(9) "There is full awareness in sleep and total ignorance in waking". Discuss.

*"Silence is as deep as eternity,
speech as shallow as time"*

Carlyle

10. SOUND OF SILENCE – 1

People imagine that they cannot be happy unless they are constantly in the company of others; loneliness is therefore perceived as a measure of unhappiness. A moment's reflection, however, would reveal that the root cause of unhappiness is not 'loneliness' but attachment to objects other than the Self; 'loneliness' being seen as the loss of attachment. Bliss, on the other hand, is native to one's Self and real happiness, therefore, can only be experienced when one is alone, communing with one's inner Self in silence.

Commingling of the finite and the infinite, ie, the mergence of our thinking mind with the Cosmic Mind, can come about only through the medium of silence. However, in our mad pursuit of the fleeting pleasures of the material life, we are so utterly lost in intense mental and physical activity that we have forgotten the way to tap the great unseen power of silence. With the blight of "noise-pollution" caused by the agitation of our mind let alone the constant drumming of the loud noises of the outside objective world, how can we hear the sound of silence, the language of the soul, the subtle voice of the spirit. Spiritual vision and deeper understanding of the Self are unfolded in the moments of silent reflection. In fact, silence, it is said, is the perennial flow of language. It is interrupted by speaking; when words cease, silence prevails once again.

The purpose of all human endeavour is to reach that end which is the very beginning, that timelessness which is the beginning of all time, that stillness which is the springboard of all flux and that silence which is the very threshold of all sound. It is in that timelessness, stillness and the depth of silence that the footsteps of God can be heard. There is a saying (in *Kashmiri*):

*"Tchopa chhai ropasenz
Karakhai ta sonasenz"*

"Silence by itself (ie in word) is only silvern; if observed (ie in deed), it is golden". Silence is neither getting away from the crowd, nor running away from the noisy part of life nor indeed getting lost in oblivion. One may hide away in the still depths of a forest and yet find no quiet if one's own mind is noisy. Practice of silence does not mean merely refraining from speech; it requires cessation of all mental activity.

In the days of yore, a spiritual aspirant joined a hermitage in the hope of receiving instruction in the secret knowledge from the master. The student served his master dutifully. However, he was all the time anxious to know when he would receive the instruction. Like a keen student, or so he thought, he put to his teacher one question persistently: "Revered Sir! When shall I receive the instruction?" Not a word passed from the lips of the teacher. Time rolled on but the teacher maintained silence to the utter chagrin of the student. Eventually, one day, the student plucked enough courage to ask him: "Revered master, I have been your student for such a long time and have served you dutifully, when will you be pleased to reveal to me the secret of life?" The teacher finally broke his silence and, with love and compassion in his eyes, replied: "My dear son, I have been instructing you all along but you have not been listening! What you are after is so secret that it cannot even be whispered, it can only be revealed in the language of silence". Even as the teacher was reprimanding him thus, he imparted to him three important lessons, namely:

(1) In his pursuit of 'information', he was overlooking an important aspect – his own transformation;
(2) Silence is a powerful and potent medium of communication;
(3) The secret of life or the highest truth can only be revealed through the medium of silence.

In a class room, if every student revelled in his own noise and blew his own trumpet, in the cacophony of those sounds how could the teacher be heard? It is only through silence that the instruction from the teacher can be received and understood. In much the same way, in the din and commotion stirred up by our thoughts and desires, we are not able to listen to the voice of the master within. Only when we are able to still our mind, subdue our thoughts and desires and quieten our agitation, will we be able to listen to the voice of silence within.

Vedanta declares that the *atma*, the Self, is not to be reached by too much talk; no, not by the highest intellect; no, not even by the study of the scriptures themselves, but through silence alone which has the power and potency all its own.

A sage sent his son out to learn about the secret of the universe. Some time later he returned to announce that he had mastered so many sciences. The sage was not impressed and sent him back. He returned a few years later having added a few more subjects to his list. But once again he was sent back. The next time the son returned, however, he was serene and calm, and his father, the sage greeted him thus: "Aye, today my son your face shines like a knower of *Brahman* (God). The lustre on your face and the language of your silence speak volumes; you are now a blessing to mankind".

What is the nature of this silence? How is it possible to listen to it? What is there to listen? Is silence, in fact, a name given to another form of sound? These are some of the questions deserving our consideration.

Baba has explained that there are three kinds of sounds. They are known as *Saamaanya*, *Varna* and *Mooka*. He has described them as follows:

- "*Saamaanya*" means ordinary. It is the sound associated with the objective world. It is the sound produced by falling, breaking and fusing or by the movement of any object. For instance the patter of rain, or the peeling of thunder, the gurgling of rivers, the sounds of digestion, the closing of eyelids over an eye or the dropping of dew on a tender petal of rose, will all produce this sound.

- "*Varna*" is the sound of the spoken world. (Vernacular in English). It is armed with a specific meaning and intention. It is the flow of the heartbeat of one into the heartbeat of another.

- "*Mooka*" is known as the sound of silence, or the sound produced by the primeval movement. It is the cosmic sound.

To understand this sound of silence, we must first try to understand the principle of relativity which is the basis of this manifested world. The existence of everything in the manifested world is relative; day and night, heat and cold, right and wrong, etc. Day is seen as such only because of the night which is there to compare it with, and so on. In other words, night is the datum against which day can be recognised and vice versa.

We all know that our planet earth rotates about its own axis and revolves around the sun. The cycle of day and night and the rotation of the seasons bear testimony to that fact. But, even if the sun does not move and is considered stationary in relation to the earth, it does move as a component part of the cosmos. Our planet, rather the solar system, trundles along in space in perpetual motion not by accident or in a haphazard manner, but in a precisely defined and ordered manner. (The awesome but benign power of the Cosmic Being who is at the helm of it all although demands not but surely deserves our reverence). Consider the example of a passenger walking from one end of the compartment to the other in a moving train. To a question as to whether the passenger is in motion, the obvious answer is: Yes. However, if he were to take his seat, would we say that he is at rest? The answer is: No. Since, although he is himself not moving, he is sharing the motion of the train. When the train comes to a halt at the station, we can finally say that the passenger is at rest: Or can we? Since even when stationary, the train is sharing the motion of the earth. So this argument goes on. What is clear, however, is the fact that whether or not we generate movement locally, the whole planet is, without a doubt, in perpetual motion. And this motion forms the threshold for measuring other local movements.

In much the same way, the sound as we know it also has a datum against which other modulations of sound are measured. This threshold of sound is commonly referred to as silence. Is this silence absolute or does it also represent a sound? We know that change is accompanied by movement and all movement causes vibration which in turn produces sound. Even our thoughts cause sound! If this were not so, how could we 'hear' our own thoughts? Hearing is related to sound. In a state of thoughtlessness, no thoughts are 'heard' – absence of thoughts, absence of sound the thoughts produce. But the minute we resume thinking, we again begin to hear our thoughts.

Since the whole universe is in a state of perpetual motion, there has to be a perpetual sound. So the so called silence indeed has a sound which forms the threshold for every other type of sound superimposed upon it. One could say that it is the thought of God or the cosmic thought. Since this threshold, ie, the Sound of Silence does not change from place to place, person to person or time to time, it can be so only if it is beyond the laws of time and space in which case it must be *sanathana*, ie, eternal and universal. If it is *sanathana*, it stands to reason that it must belong to the realm of the spirit which is also *sanathana*, rather than that of the body, which is not so. In other words, it must be in tune with the divine will. Projection of the divine will, it is said, became the vibrationary energy which, in turn, externalised Itself as the five primordial elements. Earth-Water-Fire-Air-Ether, or in scientific parlance, Solid-Liquid-Energy-Movement-Space. That is why these elements vibrate with Sound (of Silence). This sound is indeed our contact point with the Creator Himself. If the Creator be perceived as the Cosmic Being, then this Sound of Silence, verily, is His breath, His thought, His will. To summarise then, we have been able to establish three important facts about 'silence':

(1)   Silence, as we know it, has a sound.

(2) This sound of silence is *sanathana*.
(3) Sound of silence is the sound of creation, the breath of God, indeed God Himself.

Now, what name can we give this Sound of Silence? Since it represents God, we could as well call it by that name. But the word God means nothing to someone who does not know English. Similarly, calling it *Brahman* may not find favour with those who do not know *Sanskrit*. For the present, however, let us use the word God. But God has a universal, cosmic form and not a particular form. How can we summon Him, asks *Swami* Krishnaananda, by a particular name? We must only use a universal name befitting a universal form. But that presents a problem. He is not only smaller than the smallest, he is also bigger than the biggest (*anoraniyaan, mahatormahiyaan*). He is neither man, woman nor child, yet He is all these. He is neither here nor there, yet He is everywhere. How can that which is everywhere be designated by a language which belongs to a particular country or a person? What we require is a comprehensive language which can satisfactorily describe the comprehensive, all encompassing nature of God. But there is no comprehensive language; all languages are only local. There are many languages but there is no single language which can be applied to the whole world. Even if there were such a language, it would still be only a local language from the point of view of the vaster Cosmos. So, there is neither a universal language, nor can there ever be such a language describing all the attributes of God. However, this problem can be satisfactorily overcome if, instead of attempting to 'manufacture' a name which can never have more than a limited validity, the cosmic sound itself is used to represent Itself, ie, by the actual sound vibration itself. And that vibration is AUM! Incidentally, when one keeps one's ear close to an electric pole, Baba says, AUM can be heard.

AUM is referred to as *Naada* or *Shabda Brahma*, ie, Word of God, or simply the Word. There is a *Vedic* verse which proclaims:

> "*Prajapati vai idam agra aaseet*
> *Tasya Vaak dwitiya aaseet*
> *Vaak vai Paramam Brahma*"

Translation: "In the beginning, *Prajapati* (the Lord of all Creation) alone was; His Word was (or, came) next; the Word verily (was) the Supreme *Brahman*".

The same truth was later echoed in the New Testament. In the gospel according to St. John, it is said:

28.2.1992.

THE SOUND OF SILENCE

'I want peace' - so we all proclaim,
Peace that is lost can well be found;
Just mind disclaim and Self reclaim,
And tune in to Primordial Sound.

'I' is ego and 'want' - desire,
'I and mine' the trail ego-bound;
Cast ego 'n' desire in the fire,
And you'll hear that Primeval Sound.

Beyond virtue 'n' vice, pleasure 'n' pain,
With ire and fire no lomger bound,
Just light the Flame and chant the Name,
And breathe in 'n' out the So-Ham Sound.

When there's peace within the mind,
And you take the path inward-bound,
Leave shadows behind, Light you'll find,
All the way to the Source of Sound.

When there is peace within the home,
Peace 'n' joy will spread all around;
Leave 'wants' alone, make peace with Aum,
Just tune in to the Primal Sound.

When there is peace within the state,
Peace and joy will surely abound;
It's not too late, just give up hate,
And let us hear that Cosmic Sound.

When there is peace upon this earth,
Heavenly joy will then be found;
With man's new birth, on the happy earth,
There will resound that Silent Sound.

PKK

> "In the beginning was the Word,
> the Word was with God, and
> the Word was God".

Although both these expressions, the *Vedic* as well as the Biblical, carry the same meaning and point towards one and the same Truth, yet our innate linguistic or cultural loyalties may prompt us to show preference for the use of one or the other. Whilst this is perfectly acceptable, and we may call the Sound in a variety of different names and languages, it must be clearly understood that the Sound vibration itself stands uniquely as AUM and is therefore not open to preference, modification or change. The names might change but the Sound of Silence itself cannot. AUM is not just a *Sanskrit* word, it is simply the Cosmic Vibration as it actually sounds. Whether we call it *Pranava* or *Shabda Brahman* in *Sanskrit* or simply the Word in English, the Vibration itself, universally and uniquely, remains AUM. That is why it is said that *Brahman* is immanent and contained in AUM and, therefore invoking AUM is invoking the Supreme, and that AUM syllable alone is the true form of God. AUM not only denotes the name of God, it also connotes His form, majesty and munificence. Whereas other names change with the changing forms, AUM is the imperishable name and form.

AUM has three characteristics:

(1) It is the sound of creation – that is why it is reverentially called the Word of God.
(2) It is full of intelligent, self effulgent consciousness, ie, it is *Brahman* Himself. The words we utter carry specific meaning and, no doubt, have potency, yet they have no awareness of their own. The cosmic vibration AUM, on the other hand, is Cosmic Awareness itself.
(3) It exists by its own right. It is important to appreciate that, by chanting AUM, we do not create AUM.

AUM is a cosmic vibration. It is not an incantation devised by us or a sound created by us. When we chant AUM, we merely try to create within ourselves a vibration which is in sympathy with the cosmic vibration so that, for a time, we too are in tune with the cosmos and the totality known as God.

In other words, AUM represents not only the process as well as the power of creation, it is also the means of realising that power; when one dives deep into the depths of silence, one hears this cosmic sound. Baba says that to hear this sound, this whisper from supersoul to soul one has to approach as near as possible to the core of one's own being. "AUM not only permeates the whole universe, we also aver it with our every breath. Every time we breathe; we say *'Soham'*; *'So'* as we breathe in and *'Ham'* as we breathe out, ie, the unity of the internal and the external worlds. It is also known as *Ajapa or Hamsa Gayatri*. The apparent duality is projected by the mind. When the mind and the senses are defunctionalised, duality disappears; *Sa* (He) and *ha* (I) both fade away transforming *Soham* into OM – one Truth."

Our education begins with silence and it must end in silence. What happens in between is simply digression. This silence is the vibration AUM. Realising It is as close as we can expect to get to His grandeur, glory and majesty. Experiencing It is the challenge, the supreme prize, the ultimate discovery. This gauntlet is thrown down at us with every birth. Are we ready to take up the challenge? Mum , or more appropriately AUM, is THE WORD!

O Divine Mother Sai! Teach me how to hold my noisy mind quiet that I may converse with my-Self in S(a)ilence.

QUESTIONS:

(1) Define silence. What is its significance?
(2) "Beware the fool whose volume of words is as that of ten men–a hundred arrows shot and each one wide of the target". Discuss.
(3) "Every sound that breaks the silence only makes it more profound". Discuss.
(4) "To be alone with silence is to be alone with God". Discuss.
(5) How many types of sounds are there? Explain with examples.
(6) What is the connection between relativity and sound?
(7) "Thoughts leave a signature in sound." Discuss.
(8) Discuss the three important aspects of Sound (of Silence).
(9) What is the most important name that can be given to the Sound of Silence and in what language? Discuss.
(10) Discuss the characteristics of AUM.
(11) What is the difference between chanting of AUM and the cosmic vibration AUM?
(12) It is said that the five primordial elements reverberate with the cosmic vibration of AUM and since man is a product of these elements, he too must be averring AUM. Explain.

*"Listen to the Primeval Pranava, AUM,
resounding in your heart as well as
in the heart of the Universe."*

Sri Sathya Sai Baba

11. SOUND OF SILENCE – 2

It is said that in the timeless beginning, *Brahman* (God) alone was. It was of the nature of supreme silence. Out of the supreme silence emanated the primal sound when the dawn of Creative Will stirred the formless into activity – the sound aspect and expression of God. Aum-*kaara* or *Pranava* is known as the primal, primordial or primeval sound, ie, the sound existing from the beginning of creation.

Pranu means to vibrate; *pranava* also means that which runs through *praana* (life) or pervades all life. It is the essence of the Life-Principle. It is the vital vibration that fills the universe and is subtle sound of our very breath. All the five primordial elements – earth, water, fire, air and space, vibrate with this sound.

The whole creation has emerged out of the supreme *Brahman*, the *Sat* (Existence) – *Chit* (Awareness) – *Aananda* (Bliss) Consciousness, more or less in the same manner as the dream world emerges out of our own mental consciousness. This emergence, '*sphota*' or outburst, it is said, could not be without a sound comparable to that of an "explosion" of a cracker or an atomic-bomb which goes out as "dhom ...". Cruder the instrument, guttural the sound; finer the instrument, sweeter the vibration. It is conceivable that since this outburst was of a subtle consciousness, the sound was devoid of the hard guttural "dh" and was only in the nature of soft and sweet vibration "AUM".

The "emergence" of the manifested world is an ever continuing process and so too, therefore, is the cosmic vibration of "AUM". "AUM" being a sound wave with intelligent divine consciousness, it has the power to keep our own consciousness in tune with the divine. That is why *yogis* incessantly meditate on "AUM". All the *Vedas* and the *Upanishads* are replete with verses extolling the significance and importance of "AUM", as for example: "AUM *iti aikaaksharam Brahma*" (AUM that one imperishable word is *Brahman*); "*Tasya vaachakah pranavaha*" (His name is *Pranava*), etc. "AUM" is the origin of Creation. It is the source, the sustenance and the strength. It is the life of every being. Just as air forced through the reeds of a harmonium produces various notes, AUM is at the root of all the sounds in all the worlds. The ever vibrant *anaahata* (ever new) sound in the *sushumna naadi* which our gross hearing faculty cannot hear is said to be AUM. *Sushumna naadi* is situated in the spinal cord; it is the ethereal cord of the subtle body.

"AUM" is composed of three syllables (*padas*), A (Ah), U (Oo) and M (Ma), the *ardhamaatra* – the half syllable represented by the crescent, and the dot (*bindu*). A, U and M stand for the creation, preservation and dissolution, the past, present and future and the gross, the subtle and the causal aspects of the universe. 'A' is connected with awareness or wakeful (*jaagrat*) state; 'U' is somewhat subtle and is connected with idea and has some relationship with the dream (*swapna*) state. 'M' is causal and is connected with the deep-sleep (*sushupti*) state. The *ardhamaatra*, the half syllable, represents the continuity of the triple processes which keep the creation going. The *bindu*, dot, symbolises the *jiva* (individual soul).

Baba has also explained the significance of the three constituents, *Akaara*, *Ukaara* and *Makaara* (ie the three syllables - A, U & M) as follows : "*Akaara* represents the vital principle (*Praana* - *tattwa*); *Ukaara* represents the mind; *Makaara* represents the body. AUM-*kaara* is thus the unified expression of the *atma*, the mind and the body."

The cosmos emerged from *Akaara*. It is the life-force (*praana*). The mind principle came from *Ukaara*. The body emerged from *Makaara*. The *atma*, the mind and the body which emanated from the three syllables - 'A', 'U' and 'M', permeate the sun, the firmament and the entire universe. AUM-*kaara* is the essential basis for the entire creation."

About the three forms of the AUM-*kaara* principle - *Naada*, *Bindu* and *Kalaa*, Baba says : "'*Naada*' is the sound that comes from the life-breath. This means that AUM-*kaara* is associated with the sound coming from the life-breath. The five kinds of life-breath, ie, *praana*, *apaana*, *samaana*, *udaana* and *vyaana*, are expressions of the life-principle. These five represent the five basic elements (*pancha bhootas*)."

" '*Bindu*' is the unified form of the *atma*, the mind and the body. '*Kalaa*' is the reflected image of the Omni-self (*Paramaatma*) through the intellect (*buddhi*). The triple principle - *Naada*, *Bindu*, *Kalaa* - permeates the entire universe."

Every name has a key word. Based on this, 'A' is believed to connote *Brahma*, 'U' *Vishnu* and 'M' *Maheshwara*. In the word *Brahma* the last letter A, in *Vishnu* the last letter U and in *Maheshwara*, the first letter M are said to be the key letters. "AUM" thus encompasses the triple aspect of godhead

When troubles come, look beyond the mountains to the blue skies. See that you are only witnessing My play. See that your life is as temporary as the passing clouds. Your coming and going is just part of the performance.

Take God alone seriously, and play the parts you are given by Me with love. I will grieve should you misunderstand your roles. You are the Spirit within you; you are your blessed Self. My Kingdom that is within you is your real home.

Oh, how I love you. How I care for you. Come! Rejoice with Me. You are ever dear to Me.

Sri Sathya Sai Baba

as well as their respective energy aspects. Thus it can be understood that there can never be a name or concept of God outside the fold of Aum-*kaara*. In fact AUM is the one expression which equally applies to all names and concepts of God. In other words, all forms of God respond when AUM is chanted.

We mostly lead our lives in the world experiencing the three states of consciousness, ie, 'wakeful', 'dream' and the 'deep-sleep' states, represented by 'A', 'U' and 'M'. The continued vibration implied by the half-syllable signifies that the infinite supreme consciousness illumines each of the three earlier states of consciousness. Recitation of AUM must peter into silence, the *ashabda* or the soundless state, where the sound of AUM rings without being aloud, vibrating in our ears even when we have closed our lips. This immeasurable, letterless resonance, the rich sound of silence, is represented by what is called *amaatra* AUM, and is said to signify the Self or *atma* which is transcendental or beyond the three stages of consciousness. It is deeper and beyond the three bodies – the gross, the subtle and the causal, and is the very core, the essence of our reality; it is the basis and the substratum of our very being.

The *amaatra* AUM signifies the *Turiya* or the Beyond State, wherein we abide in our Self, to the exclusion of everything else. It is said to be just Existence, pure Awareness and the supreme state of Bliss. When we transcend ignorance by going beyond 'A' the waking state, beyond 'U' the dream state and beyond 'M' the deep-sleep state and then trail into the lingering resonance of *amaatra* AUM and delve into the silence of our inner personality, we then touch the source of our being and obtain a glimpse of the divine part of the human being – the divine soul.

Mandukya Upanishad begins by describing AUM as follows:–

> "*Aum–ity–etad–aksharam–idam sarvam,*
> *Tasyopa–vyaakhyaanam, bhutam bhavat–bhavishyad–iti*
> *Sarvam–Aumkaara eva; yat–chaanyat trikaalaateetam*
> *Tad–apyomkaara eva.*"

Translation: "AUM is imperishable, and it is 'all this'. Everything else, whatever be of the past, present or future, is simply like an exposition, explanation or commentary on the meaning of this great Truth – the imperishable AUM. By 'all' is meant everything without reservation; whatever is visible or cognisable, whatever can come within the purview of sense-perception, inference or verbal testimony, whatever can be comprehended under the single term, creation, – all this is AUM. All that was in the past, all that is now in the present, and all that will be in the future, all this is AUM. Not merely this; that which is beyond time, also, is AUM".

AUM has two-fold nature, the temporal and the transcendental: it is *shabda* (sound) as well as *shabdaateeta* (beyond sound). It is constituted of A, U, M, representing all creation; but it also transcends the distinctions of A, U, and M, which is represented by the soundless form of AUM. That which is the past, present and the future is the temporal comprehension of the gamut of AUM, and that which transcends time is the eternal nature of AUM. AUM, therefore, not only represents the name and form, it also connotes the nameless, the formless, Consciousness. The first *akshara* or alphabet taught to children in India used to be AUM. How very apt! *Akshara*, besides being an alphabet, also means *a-kshara*, without death, imperishable, the supreme truth or God.

For the eight attributes of AUM, see Chapter 21 under sub-heading Eight (8).

Chanting of AUM-*kaara*:

- In the chanting of AUM, 'A' emerges from the throat (originating in the region of the navel), 'U' rolls over the tongue and the 'M' ends on the lips. AUM is thus the sum and substance of all the words that can emanate from the human throat. Baba has suggested the following steps for chanting AUM-*kaara*:

- Let the tongue lie relaxed on the floor of the mouth.

- Take a deep breath and while holding the teeth and the lips slightly apart, permit the 'A' sound to formulate and vibrate in the throat. Feel the vibrations in the throat.

- Let the sound rise up spontaneously and as it enters the space behind the tongue (oropharynx), the 'A' sound should have changed, imperceptibly, into an 'O' sound. As the sound rolls over the tongue, the vibrations are felt in the mouth and the lips should very gradually begin to close.

- As the space between the lips becomes narrower and narrower, the sound again changes, imperceptibly, from an 'O' into a 'U' sound.

- Finally, with the meeting of the lips, the sound vibrates as 'M' and the vibrations can be felt not only in the mouth and the lips, but in the nose, around the eyes and throughout the skull also.

- With the meeting of the lips and the merging of the 'U' sound into the AUM-*kaar* reaches its highest peak of volume and gradually the descent begins with the 'M' sound.

- During the descent, the 'M' sound gradually tapers off and merges with silence.

- AUM must be pronounced as slowly as possible, rising in a crescendo until it reaches its peak at 'M'. Then it must take a curve at 'M' and descend as slowly as it rose, taking as much time as it took to ascend it must gradually disappear into the silence reverberating in the cavity of the heart.

- Do not take it in two stages, thinking that your breath will not hold so long.

- Let the silence coincide with the pause between two breathing cycles and prolong it as long as possible without discomfort.

- With the cessation of breath, there is cessation of thought, and a limpid calm steals over the mind. Enjoy it, relish it, for it is peace that passeth understanding.

- Let the next cycle of AUM-*kaara* be chanted within this pool of tranquillity which will augment it further, until the mind is completely immersed in it. This is the threshold of the residence of the Inner Self, the real *Prashanti* temple.

The ascent, reaching the peak, and the descent during the chanting of AUM can be likened to the approach of an aeroplane from a distance, attaining the full volume of sound as it passes directly overhead and then gradually tapering off as it flies away, eventually petering into silence. It is only when the sound 'A' joins 'U' and the sound 'U' joins 'M', that we get the complete sound of AUM. It is only when the gross, the subtle and the causal aspects of body, or 'waking', 'dream' and 'deep-sleep' states combine that we get the glimpse of the divine soul.

The Modes of AUM-*kaara* chanting:

In the *japa*, continuous chanting of any *mantra* (sacred formula), the incantation passes through four stages of the sound process. These are: *Vaikhari, Madhyama, Pashyanti* and *Paraa*. With each successive mode of chanting, the potency of recitation and the benefit derived, it is said, increase exponentially.

- ***Vaikhari**:* This is the first stage of the sound process; it involves loud incantation with the sound proceeding from the mouth. One repeats AUM in a loud voice so that the mind gets forcibly concentrated on the sound. This is best suited for the early stages until the mind gets habituated to the recitation.

- ***Madhyama**:* This is the second stage where the sound of incantation is not heard, but the lips move while repeating the *mantra*. It is the middle stage between sound and soundlessness. In this stage, the sound stems from the larynx but is hardly emitted from the lips.

- ***Pashyanti**:* This is the third stage where all is soundless. There is no utterance of the word overt or covert, but the recitation of the *mantra* still continues in the mind without an effort. In this stage, the conscious process of incantation comes to a stand-still, recitation becomes a part and parcel of one's being and one perceives and experiences the *mantra* involuntarily. The whole process is from the conscious to the unconscious or subconscious, from the voluntary to the involuntary, from the gross to the subtle.

- ***Paraa**:* The fourth stage is reached when the *mantra* itself is forgotten and only its impact remains within the consciousness. This is the *paraa* stage where every reference to the recitation is set aside and the consciousness reaches its transcendent, its own inherent nature. *Paraa* means far, distant, transcendent. This is the *Turiya* or the Beyond 'state' where there is nothing but bliss, happiness and upsurging waves of joy.

AUM is the sacred, perennial sound, all other sounds in the universe being only the modulations of AUM. To keep our consciousness in tune with the divine consciousness, we must use the right frequency, the frequency of AUM – repeating and meditating on AUM all the time. " The chanting will, in due course, then crystallize into a habit within our mind so that even in our sleep and unconscious moments, it will go on chanting AUM. The chanting thus should crystallize into our very nature, like our inhalation and exhalation, a regular and unceasing process."

O Divine Mother Sai! May my every single breath be in tune with the Cosmic Vibration Aum.

QUESTIONS:

(1) What is the connection between AUM and Creation? Discuss.
(2) Explain the composition of AUM and the relationship with the different states of awareness and time.
(3) Explain the significance of *amaatra* AUM.
(4) Discuss the temporal and the eternal aspects of AUM.
(5) Why is AUM referred to as *akshara*?
(6) AUM is said to be the sum and substance of all the *Vedas* and that all forms of God respond when AUM is chanted, why?
(7) Demonstrate the correct way of AUM-*kaara* chanting.
(8) Describe the various modes of AUM-*kaara* chanting. Which one do you think is the most potent mode and why?
(9) AUM is said to be the Sound of Creation and since Creation is a continuous process, AUM must be resounding in the universe all the time. Why do we find it difficult to hear it? What do we need to do to hear this Cosmic Vibration?

Detachment, Faith and Love - these are the pillars on which Peace rests. Of these, Faith is crucial. For, without it, sadhana (spiritual practice) is an empty rite. Detachment alone can make sadhana effective, and Love leads quickly to God. Faith feeds the agony of separation from God; Detachment canalizes it along the path of God; Love lights the way. God will grant you what you need and deserve; there is no need to ask, no reason to grumble. Be content, be grateful whatever happens, whenever it happens. Nothing can happen against His Will.
— Sri Sathya Sai Baba

"The Perennial Philosophy and its ethical corollaries constitute a highest common factor, present in all the major religions of the world ... It is only in the act of contemplation, when words and even personality are transcended, that the pure state of the Perennial Philosophy can actually be known."

Aldous Huxley

12. SANATHANA DHARMA

"Aikam sat viprah bahuda vadanti" is the *Vedic* dictum, which means that "Truth is One, the wise call it by many names." Attainment of that Truth is the goal of all human endeavour; various religious faiths are but different pathways leading to that goal. The fact that there is no underlying conflict between the various faiths in spite of the apparent differences is beyond doubt since the catholicity of their fundamental teachings seeks only to promote the brotherhood of man under the fatherhood of one Almighty God.

Baba says:

> **"There was no one to know who I am, until I created the Universe at my pleasure with one Word. Immediately, mountains rose up and rivers started flowing. The sun, moon and stars sprang from nowhere to prove my existence. Came beasts and birds, flying, speaking, hearing, and mankind too, and My knowledge was placed in his mind."**

The whole creation, it is claimed, is no more than a resolve in the mind of God (Cosmic Mind). When He has a desire for Creation, the whole universe springs up in no time at His will. Unfortunately, conditioned by the limitation of our mind, we often find it difficult to comprehend how something so material and of the scale and size of the physical universe, could be created in a trice by merely wishing so. However, a little reflection would reveal that there exists a parallel in our every day life. During sleep, the whole dream world, with all its multiplicity, is brought into being in an instant by a mere wish of the individual dream mind. Just as in the 'dream' state, there is no doubting the experiences of the dream world as anything but real, so also every bit of the 'wakeful' world appears to be real in the 'wakeful' state. The dream mind projects itself into the faces and places it creates in its dream and therefore lives the dream experience through them. The Cosmic Mind, likewise, projects Itself Will-fully and becomes the

many; having created the many, It then enters into all of them. Thus, God, it is said, created man in His own image, and for man's successful odyssey through the space-time continuum, He deposited into his care the knowledge about Himself and His creation.

This knowledge was revealed to man at the very beginning of time which is why it is known as the Ancient Wisdom, and since its essential message is timeless and unchanging, it is also referred to as the perennial philosophy. The single word in *Sanskrit* describing the universal, eternal and unchanging nature of this ancient wisdom, is *Sanathana*. Since God is *Sanathana*, so also must be the knowledge about Him that man was made privy to. The code of conduct in thought, word and deed, the spiritual discipline necessary to realise that unchanging truth is *Sanathana Dharma*.

Far from being thrown in, helplessly, at the deep end, man was, from the very dawn of creation, lovingly equipped with the armour and equipment of *Sanathana Dharma* to enable him to realise his destiny. Nevertheless, the problem of how to integrate his intelligence and his inner urges for fullness, freedom and love, and uplift himself, has dogged man at every time and in every clime. "The Grecian said, 'Man! Know thyself'; the Roman said, 'Man! rule yourself'; the Chinese said, 'Man! Better yourself'; the Hindu says, 'Man! unveil yourself'; the Muslim said, 'Man! Submit yourself'; the Psychologist says, 'Man! Be yourself'; the Psychiatrist says, 'Man! Cure yourself'; but God says, 'Trust Me. Without Me, you can do nothing.' With the bounteous Lord, we can win everything."

However, from time to time, when man lets go of the spiritual disciplines and strays away from the God-ward path leading to his own moral decline and disharmony in the world at large there, inevitably, arises the need to remind and re-educate him about the true goal in life. Advent of *avataars*, great spiritual masters or prophets fulfilled this need through their teachings. Depending upon the nature, size and severity of the problems of the various times in the history of mankind, came *avataars* like Rama and Krishna, great spiritual masters like the Buddha and the Christ and prophets like Moses and Mohammed, etc. Thus came into being different religious faiths at different times. Let it be clearly understood, however, that the Masters of the spirit did not come with the purpose of establishing new religions as such but they came only in answer to the specific needs of the times and places, and simply to restate the purpose of life on earth and to rekindle in man the love of God through the love of his fellow man so that mankind may live in peace and harmony.

Although the times at which the masters came and the languages they discoursed in were different and the people they taught were of different colours and temperaments, yet the essence of their messages was the same – redemption of man. Can anyone claim that what Rama and Krishna taught many millennia ago, or what Jesus Christ and other masters of the spirit taught in the relatively recent past, is no longer relevant today and will not be so in the future? Certainly not! If it is true and valid now as it was then and will also be so hereafter then, clearly, what they upheld and taught cannot be outside the ambit of *Sanathana Dharma*. Within that broad context, it stands to reason that, given the specific need at any given time, only a certain facet of the Truth in preference to other facets and appropriate to that need, would have been emphasised at that time. This, although not so intended, appears to have contributed to the apparent plurality of faiths in existence today. However, the mistake lies in assuming that the various faiths are in conflict and mutually exclusive and that any one faith, on its own, represents the Truth in totality. In fact, even a little understanding of the major religions would go a long way in removing the psychological barriers between one's own religion and that of others by realising the profundity of *Swami* Vivekananda's statement that : "All religions from the lowest fetishism to the highest Absolutism or *Advaita* are but so many attempts of the inner mind to grasp and reach the Infinite or God".

Baba says: "Many blind people are touching this tremendously broad *Sanathana Dharma* and they are describing it as consisting of only that which they are able to comprehend. Those who follow *Vaidika* (of *Veda*) *Dharma*, those who follow Jainism, those who follow Christianity, those who follow Islam and so on, all of them describe that part of *Sanathana Dharma* which is appropriate to their respective religions. *Sanathana Dharma* in its entirety is not being seen and described by any one of them. Each one of them is describing only a fragment. We need not discuss whether what each one of them is saying is true or untrue. There is no doubt that they are describing accurately what they have experienced and what they have chosen to describe. But each one is describing only a part of *Sanathana Dharma*. No one is describing the totality of it. Therefore if you want to understand and establish the total picture of *Sanathana Dharma*, what you have to do is to make a synthesis of the essence of all religions. When we are able to bring and put together the ideas of everyone, the moral laws supported by all religions and the truth that is in all religions, we will have a picture of *Sanathana Dharma*."

Unfortunately, the ignorant and the fanatical, who have neither the temperament to study and understand other religious faiths properly, nor indeed the ability to grasp the fundamental teachings of their own, through their selfishness and bigotry, grotesquely distort simple statements of Truth, exaggerating and misinterpreting their apparent differences. Superstition and scepticism born out of such blind faith naturally results in making one faith appear markedly different from the other. Is there any wonder that the places of worship have lost their appeal as the citadels of spiritual power and regeneration which they were meant to be? Their strength and character are no longer measured by the sanctity and the potency of their uplifting and ennobling vibrations but by the robustness of the structure and the beauty of the architecture. And so, enormous resources are solicited and committed for the upkeep of the empty shells while the plight of the spirit of man goes unheeded.

To seek to limit the universality of God's benevolence to a "chosen few" is tantamount to placing the rest of His Creation outside the reach of His Grace and relegating them to perdition. Those who find it difficult to interpret the catholicity of God's love beyond the narrow confines of denominational preferences and prejudices, says Dr Gokak, also find the concept of His Infinite Presence in its unmitigated splendour and His unconditional love towards one and all far too overwhelming and therefore beyond comprehension. As he remarks: "God is not a Pope or Super Archbishop to be annexed exclusively to this church or that or to Christianity as a whole..... The Holy Spirit is not a bottle of smelling salts in the exclusive pockets of Christians! It is a universal, not a denominational, reality." What the Hindus call *atma*, the Muslims *rooh*, and the Christians the holy spirit, are merely different names describing the same thing. Whatever the name we go by, whatever the professed faith or the type of the scripture read, "all that the holy spirit is interested in knowing is whether a man's heart is pure and whether it is dedicated to God."

Aldous Huxley reminds us that the Perennial Wisdom (*Sanathana Dharma*) is not in conflict with any religion. On the contrary, the essence of every religious thought and principle finds full expression and total fulfilment within the *Sanathana Dharma*. "It is perfectly possible for people to remain good Christians, Hindus, Buddhists or Muslims and yet be united in full agreement on the basic doctrines of the Perennial Philosophy."

Unfortunately, the language in which these doctrines were first written often becomes the excuse for ascribing a certain sociological and religious bias on the doctrines so formulated. However, the peerless sublimity of *Sanathana Dharma* can be appreciated only if the subject is approached in the spirit of a true seeker, focussing attention on the essence alone and resisting all temptation to give in to the linguistic or socio-cultural prejudices.

It is an inherent characteristic of matter, both organic and inorganic, to be in a perpetual state of flux. The physical universe being composed of matter is subject to the laws of time, space and causation and is therefore continuously changing. Physical body being a part of the physical universe is, likewise, changing and subject to the same laws. Furthermore, like all matter, thoughts are also born, they grow and they die. Thus, both the physical body as well as the mind belong to the physical universe and must therefore obey its laws.

Form is the result of combination of force and matter. However, all combinations must dissolve and whatever has form must, sooner or later, break up and disintegrate. A doubt may arise: If mind is matter and matter is inert (*jada*), how is it possible for the mind to feel and think? The answer is that, although it may appear so, it is not the mind that feels or thinks, because it is not intelligent. On a cassette may be recorded an exposition of the *Vedas* which, when played, we may be able to listen to and benefit from; but even so, can we credit the inert cassette itself with the intelligence and the wisdom enshrined in the exposition? Can a pen claim the credit for writing magnum opus or a knife for performing life-saving surgery? Obviously not. Just as switching the current on makes the exposition come alive and the cassette sound intelligent, so also when the shining splendour of the *atma* (soul) is reflected in the intellect (*buddhi*) which in turn is reflected in the mind (*manas*), the mind appears to behave as if it were intelligence itself. *Atma* (the life-force) may activate the thought, it cannot be the thought itself, it may activate the body, it surely cannot be the body itself, just as the current activates the cassette but cannot itself be the cassette. So, the body, which is no more intelligent than a piece of meat in a butcher's shop, cannot be the *atma*. *Atma* is of the nature of Eternal Existence (*Sat*), Total Awareness (*Chit*), and Absolute Bliss (*Aananda*).

Atma constitutes the unchanging spiritual base for the physical personality of man. It is therefore not subject to the laws of time, space and causation. Bible says that matter came into existence when 'the Spirit of God moved.' Matter comprises particles and particles imply movement. Movement, in turn, is possible only where there exists a potential difference or gradient. In the case of *atma*, however, there is complete absence of gradients, ie, higher and lower, more and less, here and there, now and then, etc, and therefore complete absence of movement. If *atma* can exist in total stillness, it cannot be composed of particles because particles are inherently mobile. And if it is not composed of particles, it clearly cannot be disintegrated or destroyed. *Atma* must therefore be indivisible and indestructible. For the same reason, it must also be without a beginning and therefore without an end, since what has a beginning must also have an end.

an inherent characteristic of matter, both organic and inorganic, to be in a perpetual state of flux. The physical universe being composed of matter is subject to the laws of time, space and causation and is therefore continuously changing. Physical body being a part of the physical universe is, likewise, changing and subject to the same laws. Furthermore, like all matter, thoughts are also born, they grow and they die. Thus, both the physical body as well as the mind belong to the physical universe and must therefore obey its laws.

Form is the result of combination of force and matter. However, all combinations must dissolve and whatever has form must, sooner or later, break up and disintegrate. A doubt may arise: If mind is matter and matter is inert (*jada*), how is it possible for the mind to feel and think? The answer is that, although it may appear so, it is not the mind that feels or thinks, because it is not intelligent. On a cassette may be recorded an exposition of the *Vedas* which, when played, we may be able to listen to and benefit from; but even so, can we credit the inert cassette itself with the intelligence and the wisdom enshrined in the exposition? Can a pen claim the credit for writing magnum opus or a knife for performing life-saving surgery? Obviously not. Just as switching the current on makes the exposition come alive and the cassette sound intelligent, so also when the shining splendour of the *atma* (soul) is reflected in the intellect (*buddhi*) which in turn is reflected in the mind (*manas*), the mind appears to behave as if it were intelligence itself. *Atma* (the life-force) may activate the thought, it cannot be the thought itself, it may activate the body, it surely cannot be the body itself, just as the current activates the cassette but cannot itself be the cassette. So, the body, which is no more intelligent than a piece of meat in a butcher's shop, cannot be the *atma*. *Atma* is of the nature of Eternal Existence (*Sat*), Total Awareness (*Chit*), and Absolute Bliss (*Aananda*).

Atma constitutes the unchanging spiritual base for the physical personality of man. It is therefore not subject to the laws of time, space and causation. Bible says that matter came into existence when 'the Spirit of God moved.' Matter comprises particles and particles imply movement. Movement, in turn, is possible only where there exists a potential difference or gradient. In the case of *atma*, however, there is complete absence of gradients, ie, higher and lower, more and less, here and there, now and then, etc, and therefore complete absence of movement. If *atma* can exist in total stillness, it cannot be composed of particles because particles are inherently mobile. And if it is not composed of particles, it clearly cannot be disintegrated or destroyed. *Atma* must therefore be indivisible and indestructible. For the same reason, it must also be without a beginning and therefore without an end, since what has a beginning must also have an end.

"Remove Ego (false identification of the Self with the body-mind complex), have vision of *atma*, the Lord, and merge in the bliss of *atma*". This, Baba says, is the essential duty of man or *Sanathana Dharma*.

Sanathana Dharma, essentially, teaches us about *atma*, the essential man, the Ultimate Truth, and shows us the way to immortality. However, in order to attain the truth, it not only identifies the spiritual goal but also lays down a code of temporal discipline in the day-to-day life for man to so conduct himself in the life's journey as to live in peace and harmony. It is the universal highway to God. *Dharma* followed by the sun, moon, etc, for the welfare of all life without any self-interest, preferences or prejudices, is an example of such *dharma*. Without such *dharma*, Baba says, the cosmos would turn into chaos. The code of conduct which will bring about the realisation of *atma* and the oneness of mankind maintaining peace and harmony must truly be *Sanathana Dharma*.

On a more fundamental level, the absolute oneness or unity is expressed most eloquently by the *Vedic* statement: "*Etad vai tatt*", This (Universe) verily is that (God).

In his exposition on the *Mandukya Upanishad, Swami* Krishnananda explains that the reconciliation of the two suggestive terms, 'this' and 'that', is brought about by the use of the principle known as "characterization by division and elimination of redundants" (*Bhaaga–Tyaaga–Lakshana*). The famous example usually cited to illustrate this principle is that of a person who may have been seen in a distant place sometime in the past but is seen in a nearby place now. "*Soyam Devadattah*" – "This" is "that" Devadatta. The pronouns 'this' and 'that' do not refer to two different objects or persons but merely reflect the displacement in time and space for the same person. The reconciliation of 'this' and 'that' is achieved not by contriving a unification of their distinct meanings but by the unity and singularity of the object (the person) they refer to. Temporal and spatial differences are thus discarded as redundants for the sake of recognising the unity of the person who is same always, then as well as now; there as well as here.

Similar method of reasoning is employed in comprehending the statements such as "*Sarvam hyetad Brahma*" (All this is God) and "*Ayam atma Brahma*" (This atma is God). This universe which appears to be proximate to our senses is that *Brahman* (God) which seems to be distant, and this personality of ours which appears to be so close is, likewise, reconcilable with that Absolute which appears to be so far from our reach.

A multitudinous variety seems to be identified with a single entity. But how can diversity or variety be equated with or seen as unity or singularity? The manifold variety implies differentiation. Consider the example of a child born on, say, 2 January 1900 and given the name John. John passes away on 1 January 1975. Thus the form known as John did not exist on 1 January 1900, nor did it continue to exist beyond 1 January 1975; its appearance lasted for the intervening period of 75 years only. Clearly, had there been no passage of time from the first to the second of January 1900, the form John would not have materialised or come into existence at all. Put another way, if it were possible to reverse the time from 1 January 1975 back to 1 January 1900 and hold it there, there would have been no birth of John and so also no death. The appearance of John is, therefore, directly related to and the projection of time. Birth of the body, its growth, degeneration and death, all these changes happen only with the passage of time; stop the passage of time, ie, remove the dimension of time, and the changes accompanying it will also cease. Thus, form, differentiation, definition, all these are the characteristics of, and projected by, time and space. Because of the perception of specific characteristics we begin to distinguish one set of characteristics from another and so, we have the variety, the manifold. However, this differentiation cannot be essential to the argument since the differences in the names and forms, the structural distinctions are redundant in the sense that they persist only as long as there is time and space. The essential *Brahman* (God) cannot be identified with the redundant attributes. So, all things are essentially one, although they may appear to be structurally different. Remove the characteristics and there will be no distinguishing names and forms. In other words, when the difference of space and the barrier of time are transcended, there is then the dissolution of the distinguishing characteristics and therefore no illusion of variety. What remains then is *Brahman* (God) alone.

The same conclusion can also be arrived at by a different process of reasoning. The world is referred to as the name-form-complex (*naama-roopa-prapancha*), the structural differences being the result of the interference of space and time in existence. The characteristics of *Brahman*, on the other hand, are described as *asti* (it is, it exists), *bhaati* (it shines) and *priyam* (it brings joy). With a little bit of reflection, it can be established that these three permeate and underlie every name and form. In all our activities in the phenomenal world, if the desired consequences do not follow from our contact with the other objects of name and form, we no longer want them; the objects we once claim to have loved could even invoke indifference, and our desires could turn into aversions. It is clear then that our contact with other objects is not for the sake of name and form but for the desired consequence we expect that they might bring about in us.

We want perpetual existence; we do not welcome death. This is prompted by the sense of *astittwa* (is-ness, existence) in us. The insatiable thirst for knowledge of the knower, is the urge of *bhaati* (effulgence, shining splendour) in us, and the yearning for happiness, delight, satisfaction, rather than pain, and seeking and experiencing that source of bliss *Brahman* (God), is due to the *priyam* (the attraction, the charm). So, it is this three-fold blend of *Sat-Chit-Aananda* (Existence, Awareness, Bliss) ever pulsating, even through the name and form, that we perpetually seek. In other words, we seek the underlying essence in the appearance, absolute in the relative, ie, *Brahman* (God) in all creation. So, "this" name and form complex, the manifested universe is, ultimately, "that" *Brahman* (God). This unity can be established by the recognition of *Asti, Bhaati* and *Priyam* or *Sat-Chit-Aananda* subsisting in name and form just as gold does in the ornaments. The shape of an ornament is not a contradiction to the existence of gold in it; whatever be the structural difference of the ornaments, gold is the common essence of all of them. It can be said, without any contradiction, that all ornaments are gold. Likewise, all "this" is *Brahman*; the structural diversity should not blur the recognition of the one essence permeating it. The variety therefore does not negate the essence; the variety also is the essence. In the case of this vast universe of variety therefore, says *Swami* Krishnananda, we need not be intrigued as to how 'this' can be unified with 'that', how the proximate can be the same as the remote. Reasoning on these lines, it is thus possible to resolve the dichotomy of 'that' and 'this', of 'Creator' and 'Creation', of 'energy' and 'matter', in one grand unity.

On *Sanathana Dharma*, verse 138, chapter 4 of the *Manu Smriti* states:

> "*Satyam brooyaat priyam brooyaat,*
> *Na brooyaat satyam a-priyam;*
> *Priyam cha naanrtm brooyaat,*
> *Aisha dharmah sanatanah.*"

Translation: "Speak the Truth, but speak it with Love. It is not enough to speak the Truth if not spoken with Love; nor is it enough to speak with Love that which is untrue. This is *Sanathana Dharma* (the Ancient Wisdom, the Perennial Philosophy)."

The first aspect emphasised in the above verse is to speak the Truth. The Truth referred to here is that which declares the immanence and permanence of the Self, the *atma* and, by implication, brings into focus the illusory existence and evanescence of the phenomenal world; in other words the Truth that is enshrined in the following four supreme statements (*Mahavaakyas*):

- *"Prajnaanam Brahma"* – *Brahman* (God) is the Pure, Self-effulgent consciousness, the constant integrated Awareness;
- *"Ayam Atma Brahma"* – The soul, the life-force in every individual is that *Brahman* (God);
- *"Tattwamasi"* – Thou art That (Consciousness Itself);
- *"Aham Brahmaasmi"* – I am *Brahman* (God).

Truth, by definition, is that which exists and stands by itself. It needs no external support or prop to lean on. It shines in its own splendour. Whether one believes in it or not, one cannot wish it away, nor make it disappear. As Ramakrishna *Paramhamsa* says: "You see many stars at night in the sky but not when the sun rises. Can you therefore say that there are no stars in the heavens during the day? Oh man, because you cannot find God in the days of your ignorance, say not that there is no God."

Truth is neither subject to growth nor to diminution; it is unchanging. In fact, Truth by virtue of its eternal, universal and unchanging (ie *sanathana*) nature has, at its disposal, all eternity for people to come round to recognising it. It has therefore no need to impose nor force itself upon those who may, through their ignorance, find themselves unable to accept it. That is the reason why the second aspect of the verse emphasises that Truth may be proclaimed, but only with Love. The clear implication is that it must never be forced upon others at the point of sword because one's own Self is the Truth and one will, eventually, discover it for oneself in one's own time, at one's own pace and by learning through one's own mistakes.

To conclude, *Sanathana Dharma* is not a code of conduct laid down by man; nor does it represent a religious doctrine. If indeed it were so, it could not be eternal and universal (*sanathana*). Just as it is not possible to formulate a law or code of conduct that is inviolate, for an object which is subject to change, so also it is not possible to subject to a changing law that which is timeless and unchanging (*sanathana*). As man evolves with time, his thinking and outlook are also modified. Man-made doctrine can therefore never be universal; it can at best hope to satisfy a limited local need at a specific time. Likewise, a universal and eternal doctrine can never be man-made. It is beyond the capability of man, himself subject to change, to lay down a code of conduct (*dharma*) that is *sanathana*. Such authority can only rest with the Lord Himself and no one else.

Sanathana Dharma, the Ancient Wisdom, the Perennial Philosophy, transcends the bounds of religion and race; it is divine wisdom addressed to mankind for all times and climes, in order to help human beings face and solve the ever-present problems of birth and death, of pain, suffering, fear, bondage, love and hate. It enables man to liberate himself from all limiting factors and reach the state of perfect inner balance, inner stability and mental poise, complete freedom from grief, fear and anxiety. *Sanathana Dharma* is thus the communication of Truth from God to Man – nothing less, nothing more!

O Divine Mother Sai! Deliver me from ignorance and grant me true faith.

QUESTIONS:

(1) If Truth is One, why should the wise call it by many names?
(2) What is the meaning of *Sanathana Dharma* and what other names is it known by and why?
(3) What is the connection between *Sanathana Dharma* and the teachings of various religions?
(4) What are the characteristics of matter? What is the relationship between thought, mind and matter?
(5) Is mind inert (*jada*) or intelligent? How does it operate?
(6) What are the characteristics of *atma*? Why is it said to be indestructible?
(7) Explain how "this" (universe) can be reconciled with "that" (God).
(8) What is the influence of time and space on the phenomenal world?
(9) How is *Sanathana Dharma* defined in the *Manu Smriti*? How would you interpret it?
(10) Who is the giver of *Sanathana Dharma*? What is the connection of *Sanathana Dharma* with Hinduism?

> *You may say that progress is possible only through My Grace, but though My Heart is soft as butter, it melts only when there is some warmth in your prayer. Unless you make some disciplined effort, some sadhana (spiritual practice), Grace cannot descend on you. The yearning, the agony of unfulfilled aim, that is the warmth that melts My Heart. That is the anguish that wins Grace.*
> *– Sri Sathya Sai Baba*

> *"A little consideration of what takes place around us every day must show us that a higher law than that of our will regulates events."*
>
> *Emerson*

13. LAW OF KARMA

Why is it that children begotten of the same parents are seldom alike in their temperaments? Why is one man honest, intelligent but barely able to eke out an existence, whereas another dishonest, dimwit but living in the lap of luxury? Why is 'A' rich but restless and wanting, and 'B' poor but happy and contented? Why is a son's life cut off in his prime whereas the father totters to a ripe old age? Why does 'X', a good person, meet a tragic death, and 'Y', a vile person, die peacefully?

Luck of the draw, pre-destination, accident or arbitrary selection? None of these, proclaims the Law of *Karma*! If it were any of these, what then would be the criterion that determined why one should be born disadvantaged and doomed to a life of destitution and misery, and the other qualify for a life of comfort and happiness? When children are begotten, do their parents predetermine on whom they wish prosperity and happiness and on whom misery and privation? Is it not a fact that they would rather wish for and provide, in so far as it could lie in their hands, equal opportunities to all of them? A wicked man having a virtuous son and a virtuous person giving birth to a wicked son are phenomena which are not without reason, although the reason itself may not be directly apparent. In the divine plan, nothing happens without a proper reason.

Karma connotes activity – activity in thought, word or deed. *Karma* does not stop with the completion of a particular act; in fact, activity that produces an effect which, in turn, has the potential to bind one into further activity, is called *karma*. Thus the Law of *Karma* means the Law of Causation, of the inevitable cause and consequence and of deed and destiny. "Mysterious, indeed, is the nature or cause of *karma*" ("... *Gahana karmano gatih*"), says Lord Krishna in the *Bhagavad Geeta*. What is the mechanism of *karma* as it operates in man?

Most outwardly, action is performed by the body through the five senses of action (*karmendriyas*), ie, hands, legs, tongue and the organs of procreation and excretion. This is done in the 'light' of the five senses of perception (*jnaanendriyas*), ie, sight, sound, smell, touch and taste; the instructions for action are issued from the inner senses (*antahkarana*) which become *manas* or mind when it thinks, *chitta* when it deliberates, *buddhi* or intellect when it decides, *ahamkaara* or ego when assuming doership or experiencing the reaction. These are the different roles played, or the different caps worn, by the *antahkarana*. The consciousness-cum-energy (*chetna*) for both the performance of actions as well as the experiencing of the reactions comes from the three attributes (*gunas*), *sattwa* (harmony), *rajas* (activity) and *tamas* (inertia). To begin with *sattwa* illumines the *antahkarana*, so that it becomes capable of cognizing or comprehending the world outside; *rajas* then sends out the ego by making it a thirst for happiness, which is experienced through touch, taste, form, sound and smell; *tamas* casts a spell over the *antahkarana* and makes one forget one's ever blissful reality, so that the ego dashes forth outside to experience the sense-happiness. The three attributes thus set the human machine into operation. All acts, whether physical or mental, are performed either to experience happiness or to acquire the means to happiness, to ward off unhappiness or, to overcome impediments to happiness. These actions bring in fruits thereof which can generate further action and thus keep one continuously moving in the cycle of birth-and-death, until one becomes a spiritual aspirant and attempts to liberate oneself from the vicious circle.

The Law of *Karma* is a unique, characteristic feature and a fundamental tenet of *Sanathana Dharma*, the Perennial Code. There is at the very beginning, says Baba, a cause, a reason, for which there is bound to be a consequence, an effect. Man is thus endowed with various faculties which enable him to perform his *karma*. Even as he carries out his *karma*, the fruit thereof determines the very type of life he will be endowed with at a future date. "As a man sows, so shall he reap." Every thought, word and deed is weighed, as it were, in the scales of eternal justice. Just as the Law of Cause and Effect works in the physical world, the Law of *Karma* works in the moral sphere. According to it, happiness or misery is merely a consequence of our own *karma* and, to that extent therefore, our own creation. It is not possible to escape from the consequences of what one does. Whatever action we perform, be it good or bad, whether knowingly or unknowingly, we will, one day, have to face up to the fruit which comes thereof. "But that is non-sense", we hear some say. "What heinous crime could a new born child have committed to be born deformed? No! We do not need to turn to this oriental philosophy of *karma* to explain away the plight of the child. There is a perfectly logical explanation; the parents of the child took drugs and so the child was born deformed. As simple as that!" Or, is it?

Well, not quite! Why should the consequences of the parents' misdemeanours or sins, over which the child had no control or say, be visited upon the 'innocent' child? Why should it be subjected to a handicap and denied an even chance in life? Why this particular child, why not the other? Why should a person who has committed a murder go free on account of a mere technicality or insufficiency of evidence? How are we to answer these and myriad other questions and how are we to reconcile these seeming inequalities and injustices with a just and compassionate Lord?

'Child is the father of man' claims modern psychology. What we have shaped into is, to a large extent, the outcome of the experiences we underwent in our formative years. The circumstances of our youth and the buffeting we receive in those wild years of our early life, says Gautam Sen, mould us and help form the basis of our character. "If that base was sound and strong, so are we now; if not, that weakness would also be all too apparent in our character now. And yet, however hard we may try, are we able to recapture those formative occurrences of our now-nebulous childhood? Obviously not; they have sunk deep beneath the mind's surface into the layers of our subconscious. Nevertheless, like the submerged nine-tenths of an iceberg, they are very much real. They are indeed, the most substantial portion of our psychological make-up."

Similarly, according to the Law of *Karma*, the nature we are born with is an extension, as it were, of the type of personality we died with in our previous life – for *karma* suggests rebirth. When Glanvil, the chaplin to King Charles II of England declared: "The soul came prejudiced into this body with some implicit notions that it learned in another.", he was clearly petitioning for the adoption of the doctrine of reincarnation. "... If I fail to pass those examinations in life which can only be taken while I dwell in a physical body", declared Dr Leslie Weatherhead, a former president of the Methodist conference of Great Britain, "Shall I not have to come back and take them again?" Whatever we enjoy and suffer are the consequences of our own actions in the past lives. We carry with us our own past. The mental and moral tendencies that we acquire in a particular life as a result of our past actions, work themselves out in appropriate surroundings in the next birth. In *De Principiis*, his major work and the first systematic theology of Christianity, Origen, the acclaimed prince of Christian learning in the third century and the most prominent of church fathers, declared :

> "Every soul ... comes into world strengthened by the victories or weakened by the defeats of its previous life. Its place in this world as a vessel appointed to honour or dishonour, is determined by its previous merits or demerits. Its work in this world determines its place in the world which is to follow this."

And you judges who would be just,
What judgment pronounce you upon him who though honest in the flesh yet is a thief in spirit?
What penalty lay you upon him who slays in the flesh yet is himself slain in the spirit?
And how prsecute you him who in action is a deceiver and an opressor,
Yet who also is aggrieved and outraged?
And how shall you punish those whose remorse is already greater than their misdeeds?
Is not remorse the justice which is administered by that very law which you would fain serve?
Yet you cannot lay the remorse upon the innocent nor lift it from the heart of the guilty.
Unbidden shall it call in the night, that men may wake and gaze upon themselves.
And you who would understand justice, how shall you unless you look upon all deeds in the fulness of light?
Only then shall you know that the erect and the fallen are but one man standing in twilight between the night of his pigmy-self and the day of his god-self,
And that the corner-stone of the temple is not higher than the lowest stone in its foundation.

"The Prophet" by Kahlil Gibran

The principle of reincarnation or rebirth, as a corollary to the Law of *Karma* makes it possible to ensure that even if the murderer escapes 'justice' in the court of man, he is not able to do so in the court of the Almighty Lord and that the justice dispensed catches up with him however many life times it may take and that he receives his just deserts befitting the crime, at the appropriate time. This, of course, presupposes a fundamental act of faith in the absolute fairness and justice of the Lord which, when we behold the breathtaking handiwork of the Lord, the order, the harmony and the beauty of Creation, and the precision in its operation, is clearly not hard to come by.

What is 'deep-sleep' state if not a state of partial death? In the 'deep-sleep' state, the mind and the senses are defunct and so, to all intents and purposes, 'deep-sleep' states can be seen as interludes of partial death between the successive 'wakeful' or dream states. Although the 'deep-sleep' state is a period of complete cessation of the day-to-day activity, neither is the individual identity, nor indeed the continuity of thought, lost through it. In fact, the continuity across the divide from one day to the next is maintained in toto.

In the case of the murderer, the retribution does not have to come the same day the crime was committed. But whether it comes the very next day, five months or five years later, the intervening periods of partial death, however many they may be, do not obliterate the memories or records of the case and the judgement, such as it may be, will come at a time of its own choosing. As long as the death is partial and some aspect of the human personality continues to exist, the identity of the subject and the memories are not erased but carried forward in time in tact. In much the same way, the death of the physical body is also only a partial death, since the continuity of the subject and the store of deep-seated memories are maintained in tact, in this instance by the continuity of the 'causal' body which transcends the death of the physical body. In fact, for man, rebirth cannot cease as long as the very cause for the birth or the 'causal' body is not completely extinguished. Body is a carrier for desires and a medium for their fulfilment; as long as the desires persist and outlast the body, transmigration of soul from one body to the next has to go on. There is thus compelling evidence pointing towards the continuity of life beyond death, the principle of rebirth, providing the only acceptable framework for a deeper and a truer understanding of life within which all pieces of the puzzle fall neatly into place.

The body-mind complex suffers from the duality of pain and pleasure. The soul, on the other hand, being immortal remains unaffected by the vicissitudes of life. As our identity with the immortal soul grows stronger, our emphasis on the physical aspects of our life diminishes in proportion.

With this our threshold of pain rises and so the physical suffering assumes progressively less importance. In this way, we go on evolving as we carry on paying our *kaarmic* debt, life after life, until it is fully discharged and the soul obtains permanent release or liberation (*mokhsha*). Thus nothing in life is arbitrary.

A new-born child, however innocent and helpless it might appear at birth, nevertheless carries with it, like everyone else, its own catalogue of past *karma*, a balance sheet of good and bad actions. Baba says: "Every child arrives into the world, bearing the burden of unrequited consequences accumulated in previous lives... It is born in this world in order to experience the beneficence and malignant consequences, that are the products of its own acts in the past lives..." And whatever the manner of suffering it may have to undergo at any time in the discharge of its *kaarmic* debt, it can be safely assumed that the deformity at birth could never be any more of a pay-off than would have been warranted by the specific nature of its actions in the past life or lives; the family the child is born into merely provides the appropriate environment and the drug addiction of the parents merely the convenient pretext. We must also bear in mind the possibility that, for a perfect balancing of accounts, one life time may not be sufficient. The day of reckoning will come when all the ingredients are present and the stage is set down to the last detail; this may happen in the same life time, the next life time or many life times later. In fact *Kenopanishad* emphasises the fact that the results of good or bad actions are not like the milk that one may get immediately as one draws it from the udder of a milch cow, but rather like the fruits that one gets from a tree long after the seed is planted.

After the epic *Mahabharata* war, in which he lost all his 100 sons, Dritrashtra, it is said, asked Lord Krishna why it was that he was not spared the life of even a single son who would perform the last rites for him when the time came. Lord Krishna, it seems, enlightened him thus: "Nothing that happens in this phenomenal world is without a cause; loss of all your sons, therefore, also has a cause. A barbaric action committed by you in the very distant past has drawn the type of consequence that you find so distressing. Listen! Fifty life times ago, you were a hunter. On one occasion, you were responsible for trapping under your burning net a pair of birds together with their entire brood of 100 young ones. The pair struggled hard and somehow managed to set themselves free but were, in the process, blinded by the smoke. Their young ones, however, were not so lucky; they could not struggle free and were burnt alive. It took fifty life times for you to earn and accumulate enough merit to get 100 sons in this life time. And now, the circumstances are right in every detail, the blind parents, 100 sons, etc, for the debt incurred by you to be paid off." This clearly illustrates that, however many life times it might take, there is always a balancing of the accounts. There can therefore be no reason for elation just because our bad actions may not have borne us bad fruit immediately, for we are sure to experience it sooner or later.

This however, raises a question: granted that in working out one's *kaarmic* debt, one has to suffer, but what reason can there be for the other members of the family to be drawn into suffering as well? The answer, according to the Law of *Karma*, is that the extent to which other members of the family are likely to get drawn into the suffering as well is unlikely to be any more than is their due in their own right, ie, in proportion to their own respective *kaarmic* debts.

The reason why a child is born of a particular set of parents is, according to the Law of *Karma*, neither by random selection, nor by accident; the child may have an outstanding debt towards the parents from a previous birth, or the parents may be under a past *kaarmic* obligation towards the child, so that the parties are thrown 'together' because of the mutuality of their *kaarmic* debts. However, even in the absence of any such mutuality of debt, it is possible for the parties to come together because of the very nature of their respective *kaarmic* debts. For example, a certain child may be ordained by its *karma* to be born a cripple in its present life; it is likely to be born to parents whose own *karmas* dictate that they undergo the sorrow and hardship of raising a crippled child. So, it is not the *karma* of one that has brought suffering and hardship upon the other, but simply that their respective *karmas* are so perfectly matched that they are best able to work these out through the parent-child relationship under which, therefore, they are brought together. Similarly, a certain couple's *karma* may ordain that they are to suffer the loss of their child at an early age. There may also be a child whose own *karma* dictates that its own sojourn on earth is very brief. So, this child could be born to that couple.

The *kaarmic* theory thus dispenses with the possibility of any chance or arbitrariness in human life and emphasises the essentially causal character of all existence. However, because of our predispositions and ignorance, we often pour scorn over the Law of *Karma* in the mistaken belief that it offers a license for 'tyranny by divine sanction.' In other words, to some, it is seen to suggest that a half-starved, naked and miserable person must have been pretty depraved and evil in his previous lives to have deserved the fate he finds himself in, and that he has therefore no right either to grumble at his plight or to act in a way that would alleviate his suffering and improve his lot, since doing so could be seen to construe as a challenge to the divine law!

This leads to the further claim that if all is predestined, why bother with action at all? But this is sheer ignorance. In the *Bhagavad Geeta*, man is referred to as *karmajaa* that is to say, born through *karma* propelled by desires in the previous lives. *Karma* is responsible for birth. The root cause of one's present happiness or misery can therefore be traced back to one's thoughts, words or deeds, ie, *karma* in the past incarnation. "*Karma* is really the creator for man, and the Law of *Karma*, far from being an odious, oriental absurdity advocating fatalism and giving legitimacy to submissive indolence, in fact underlines the importance of personal responsibility and asserts that nobody can get anything unless he earns it. A clear distinction, however, needs to be made between the action, which is the result of one's 'free' will over which therefore one has 'full' control, and the consequences of that action, over which one has no control." As Baba says:

**"It is but meet that man should strive,
Though success and failure be God ordained."**

A person has the freedom of will to shoot an arrow or to refrain from doing so; but once shot, he can neither recall the arrow nor in any way alter the consequence that his action may have set into motion. If the arrow falls harmlessly without causing any damage, he may go free, but if it causes an injury, he could expect to be severely dealt with.

However, there is no use pining for what could have been, nor speculating about what might be. What has passed is past and inaccessible; it cannot be re-lived or altered. What the future holds, one cannot know with any certainty. In fact that uncertainty is the only certainty about life. By brooding over the past and speculating about the future, Baba says, man is failing in his duties in the present. This is the cause of his misery. The important time, therefore, is the present; the moment is now. We must learn to live in the present, without harping on the past or worrying about the future, but not in a manner that might suggest that the purpose of life is to "eat, drink and be merry, for who knows what tomorrow might bring." On the contrary, we must be ever alive to the fact that it could be through our actions now that we may be drafting the script for the future pages of our destiny. "Whatever seeds you have sown by your actions," says Baba "those same seeds will mature and return to you a harvest made up of the consequences of your actions. If the seeds belong to one variety, you cannot expect to get back a different kind of harvest. Whatever acts you have indulged in, the appropriate fruits thereof will be given to you in the form of a garland which is hung around your neck.... That garland, given to you by the Creator, will adorn your neck although it will not be seen by physical eyes...." The way we act today is repackaged and returned to us as our fate tomorrow and so what is in our hands today will be out of our hands tomorrow. In other words, we are the architects of our fate today, tomorrow we become its slaves!

Having the "freedom" of thought and action, and exercising that choice, is it not fit and proper that we should be held accountable for the choice we freely make, and that we should have to accept ownership of the consequences directly resulting from that choice? Anything less, would surely be most unfair and illogical. For instance, how can we blame God for letting the spittle fall down on our face if we choose to spit heavenwards in the first instance? An immutable Law of Cause and Consequence, therefore, not only sharpens our sense of responsibility, but it also gives us opportunities to learn through our mistakes. Furthermore, through it we are assured that not even the most 'unlucky', the deformed and the destitute are likely to be consigned to an only life of doom and gloom without ever a chance of improvement or being able to live a normal life like others. On the other hand, the doctrine of rebirth intrinsic to this law guarantees other chances and holds out hope for a better future life for all without exception, through improved efforts in the present life. Clearly, the Law of *Karma* is a law of positive effort and not one of defeatism and despondency, a doctrine of hope and not merely of a logical dispensation of the consequences of virtue and sin. It holds out hope even for the man of stagnant awareness that progress has not slipped beyond his reach and that he can yet evolve in the next life if not in this one. In fact one cannot help but marvel at the unmistakable logic and the peerless sublimity of the doctrine. But then the perfection of all divine laws is always breathtakingly precise.

If action be in the hands of man, one might ask, why not also the consequence? This could be conceivable if one's actions (*karma*) and their consequences involved none other than one's own self, in which case the action could be judged and the fruit dispensed in accordance with one's own yardstick whatever its quality. However, our thoughts, words and deeds, inevitably, have an interaction with those of the other people who have their own perceptions of what is right and what is wrong, and their own scales of justice. Given such extremely complex interplay, satisfying all the constraints and boundary conditions fairly, without the sway of personal preferences and prejudices, is beyond the ken of man. That is the reason why, for the law to operate fairly, the consequence cannot come other than by divine dispensation.

It is said that even if only a fragment of God's grace is secured, a great deal can be accomplished. But without divine grace, nothing can be achieved. However, human effort is essential. If it does not want to fly, Baba says, even an eagle will not get off the ground. "But an ant that wants to move along can cover miles in due course. Effort is in human hands; success or failure rests with the Divine." Granted therefore that we have no direct control over the consequences of our actions, one thing however is clear: what we commonly refer to as 'fate' has a beginning, a cause; that cause is *karma*. But action cannot be without 'free will', says Raman *Maharshi*, and so, 'free will' is the root cause. By 'free will', therefore, can even fate be conquered. As *Swami* Vivekananda says, "Our *karma* determines what we are and what we can assimilate. We are responsible for what we are, and whatever we wish ourselves to be, we have the power to make ourselves. If what we are now has been the result of our past actions, it certainly follows that whatever we wish to be in the future can be shaped by our present action."

In answer to a question why some people must suffer so much and for so long, Baba has said: "Those who suffer have my Grace. Only through suffering will such people be persuaded to turn inwards and make the inquiry. And without turning inwards and making inquiry, they can never escape the misery (brought upon by their own actions in the first place)." As the Bible says, "Blessed are those that grieve for they shall be consoled...." There is, of course, the other aspect that, by concentrating the dose of suffering, the adverse effect of *karma* can be accelerated and the debt cleared sooner and quicker, thus bringing forward better times. That is why the suffering is perceived as His Grace. Besides, the extent of suffering dispensed can never conceivably be out of proportion to one's capacity to endure it; for, of what use would it be to take a person to court to recover monies due, if the person goes bankrupt and is therefore unable to pay? As Prophet Mohammed said: "On no soul does *Allah* place a burden greater than it can bear. It gets every good that it earns, and it suffers every ill that it earns."

The Law of *Karma* is based on justice and fairness and it holds out equality of opportunity for all. The wonderful thing is that although the consequences we face come strictly in accordance with the divine dispensation, the key to what shape or form that dispensation takes is rooted in the very choice of action and, to that extent therefore, rests in the hands of the person himself. As Baba says: "Sow a thought, reap a tendency; sow a tendency, reap a habit; sow a habit, reap a character; sow your character and reap your destiny; therefore you are the master of your destiny." Eulogizing the human potential in his poetic vein, Iqbal, a poet philosopher, once remarked (in *Urdu*) :

> *"Khudi ko kar buland itnaa ki har taqdeer say pahilay,*
> *Khudaa bunday say khud poochhay bataa teri razaa kya hai"*

Translation: "Raise your consciousness to such (sublime) heights that before your fate is decided, the Lord Himself may (feel disposed to) ask you how you wish it to be written."

"Thought", it is said, "is another name for fate"; what a man thinks, that he becomes

> "We build our future thought by thought
> For Good or Bad and know it not,
> Thought is another name for fate;
> Choose, then, thy destiny, and wait.
> Mind is the master of its sphere;
> Be calm, be steadfast and sincere;
> Fear is the only foe to fear.
> Let the God in thee rise and say
> To adverse circumstance – 'Obey'
> And thy dear wish shall have its way."

"If you think impure thoughts and harbour debasing immorality," say *Swami Ram Tirth*, "with the fulfilment of these selfish wishes, heart-breaking affliction, excruciating suffering and distracting sorrow shall be forced upon you into the bargain." "Grief shall prey upon your soul. The fool thinks he enjoys sensuous pleasures, but knows not that in an impure thought or deed his very vitality is bought, sold, and consumed. The Law of *Karma* retaliates and baffles you when you want to abuse it for selfish ends..."

It is at times argued that the notion of retribution does not quite fit in with the idea of a benevolent and compassionate Lord. "Do you think I would confront you with pain," asks Baba, "were there not a reason for it?" "Open your heart to pain as you do now for pleasure, for it is my Will, wrought by Me for your own good. Welcome it as a challenge. Turn within and derive the strength to bear it and benefit by it. It is all My plan to drive you by the pangs of unfulfilled need, to listen to My voice which, when heard, dissolves the ego and the mind with it."

"It is like baking a cake. I stir, I knead, I pound, I twist, I bake you. I draw you in tears, I scorch you in sobs. I make you sweet and crisp, an offering worthy of God. I have come to reform you. I won't leave you until I do that. Even if you stray away before you become a successful *sadhaka* (spiritual aspirant), I will hold on to you. You cannot escape Me."

Such then is the unbounded love and compassion of the Lord towards us. So, we must clearly understand that, firstly, the type of the retribution meted out is dictated by the very nature of one's own action and not any sadistic wish on the part of the Lord. Secondly, the retribution is dispensed with the sole purpose of bringing about the desired correction or improvement and is, therefore, in the best interests of the person concerned, even if he is unable to perceive it in that light at the time. Thirdly, the Law of *Karma* does not, in any case, take away from man the mercy of the Lord. Although even the mercy of the Lord, it could be argued, would also come only as a consequence of the penitential action of the subject.

From the discussion thus far, it is clear that every thought, word and deed, ie, every *karma*, gives rise to a commensurate consequence which seeks out an appropriate slot in the space-time-causation continuum when the conditions are favourable in every detail for a perfect balancing out. This is the basis of the Law of *Karma*. Its other features may be summarised as follows:

- The Law is eternal and universal (*sanathana*)
- The Law recognises no excuse;
- The Law is absolutely just;
- The Law is Divine.

According to the Law of Causation, *Karma* has been divided into three parts: (1) **Praarabdha Karma,** (2) **Sanchita Karma,** (3) **Aagaami Karma.**

Praarabdha karma is that part of man's past accumulated *karma* which has already begun to bear fruit in his present life. It cannot be avoided. This *karma* is like an arrow that the archer has already discharged. He cannot recall it. Therefore, he must take its consequences. It is said that, usually, God does not interfere with it until it has run its full course.

Sanchita karma is the name given to the balance of the past accumulated *karma* of man not worked out in this life but carried on to the next. However, it does determine his present character and innate tendencies. It is said that *sanchita karma* can be expiated through penance and totally destroyed by wisdom (*Jnaana*).

The present actions which accumulate into *kaarmic* effects for manifestation in the future are termed ***Aagaami karma.*** It is what we are sowing now for us to reap the fruits of in future. *Aagaami karma* is entirely in our hands.

Baba explains the three types of *karma* with the following analogy. He says that *sanchita karma* is like the granary holding the total accumulated grain stock. *Praarabdha karma* is the quantity of food grains taken out of the granary for our current use. *Aagaami karma* is like the new stock that we will be getting after the harvest.

The ready grace of God consists in preventing the aggravation of this *aagaami karma*. An aspect of this is to save us from the vicious circle of our present actions, which again is a result of the influence of *praarabdha karma*. The exceptional cases where all *kaarmic* effects, including that of *praarabdha*, are effaced are attributed to "Special Grace!"

Baba says: "....The Law of *Karma* is not an iron law. By dedication, by purification which invites benediction, its effect can be modified and terror assuaged. Do not despair; do not lose heart." According to Him, generally, His (usual) Grace will protect one from the ravages of past *karma* just as a bottled medicine loses its potency after the date of expiry, though outwardly it continues to look the same. Grace is like morphine, the pain is not felt, though you go through it. Grace takes away the malignity of the *karma* which you have to undergo. The special Grace is one where the visual appearance of the medicine also is changed to one's liking, ie, the consequences are completely wiped out.

From what has been discussed so far, it is clear that all work is bondage. Under the Law of *Karma*, all actions bring back reactions in the form of happiness or unhappiness which, in turn, put man into the cycle of birth and death. Once an action is done, the "doer" has to reap the fruit thereof over which he has no control to modify or escape from. However, the Law of *Karma* does not bind us if we renounce "doership", take refuge in God and act in concert with Him in everything that we do. Creation is a manifestation of the Cosmic Will and so all that goes on in this creation can only be for the pleasure of God. In whatever we do, Baba says, if we feel inspired thus, it is bound to reach God. So, the motive uppermost in our mind should be that whatever action is being done, it is done as an act of worship to the Lord. Without assuming "doership" or craving for the fruits and doing everything as an act of worship to God, we escape from the bonds of *karma*. This kind of action is called *nishkaama* (without attachment) *karma* or "holy indifference" according to the christian theology. It is also called *Karma Yoga*. To develop the right attitude towards action, *Swami* Vivekananda helps us with the following explanation: "When you give something to a man and expect nothing... his ingratitude will not tell upon you, because you never expected anything, never thought you had any right to anything in the way of a return. You gave him what he deserved; his own *karma* got it for him; your *karma* made you the carrier thereof. Why should you be proud of having given away something? You are the porter that carried the... gift, and the world deserved it by its own *karma*. Where then is the reason for pride in you?"

Karma Yoga does not demand renouncing the action but only the fruit thereof. An action will not bind one if, in its performance, both the conceit of "doership" and the sense of enjoyment of the desired results are wholly renounced. *Karma Yoga* therefore calls for cultivating an attitude of non-attachment, both overt and covert, with the action. This is illustrated by the story of the two monks who were walking down a road when they came across a pool of water. There was a beautiful woman on the other side, wanting to cross over but helplessly looking at the pool. The monks waded through the water and one of them, on seeing the plight of the woman, volunteered to lend her a helping hand. Actually, it was a little more than just a helping hand, for he lifted her up bodily and carried her across the water. That done, the two monks resumed their journey. Later, one of the monks remarked, "Being a monk, didn't you feel ashamed holding that woman?" His companion answered: "It is true that I carried the woman across. But that is where I left her, while you have been holding on to her all this while!" For the one who carried the woman, because of his attitude of detachment, the deed done essentially amounted to inaction in action (*akarma*), whereas for the other, his attitude, in spite of the fact that he did not perform the deed, typified action in inaction. Verse 18, fourth canto of the *Bhagavad Geeta* (The Song Celestial), reads:

"Karmanyakarma yah pashyed akarmani cha karma yah;
Sa buddhimaan manushyeshu sa yuktah kritsnakarmakrit."

Translation: "He who seeth inaction in action and action in inaction, he is wise among men, he is a *yogi* and performer of all actions."

It is the idea of "I am the doer", that is the binding factor. When a man gives up such feelings in his action, that action can be construed as no action at all. This is inaction in action (*akarma*). But if a man sits quietly and thinks that he is the "doer", he is ever doing action and getting bound. This is action in inaction. It is the identification with the body that promotes the "I-am-the-doer" sense. "As long as one suffers from egoism (attachment to the body), one's intelligence will not shine", says Baba. "Only when man gets rid of the body-consciousness, will he be fit to achieve liberation." The difference between a fatalist and a *nishkaama karma yogi* (doer of non-attached action) is that the former simply does not care but passively awaits what is coming to him whereas the latter is ever active. Fatalists, whose pleasures are tinged with anxiety and defeats embittered by regret, are apt to run away from life by drowning their sorrows in drink or drugs. A *nishkaama karma yogi*, on the other hand, is the most conscientious of men; he does not run away from life but accepts it fully. Whatever act he is engaged in, he does so devotedly and wholeheartedly. It is towards the result of the act, however, that he remains indifferent.

Whether he receives praise or blame, it matters not; he goes right on with his job. This spirit of action with total unconcern for the reward thereof is the hallmark of the truly great.

O Divine Mother Sai ! Whatsoever I think, speak or do, may it all be as worship unto Thee.

QUESTIONS:

(1) What do you understand by the term *karma*? Can sitting down idly be considered as *karma*? Give reasons.
(2) Explain the mechanism of *karma*?
(3) What is the Law of *Karma*?
(4) "Child is the father of man." Discuss
(5) Without the doctrine of rebirth, the Law of *Karma* can have no basis. Discuss.
(6) What are the differences between justice as dispensed by man and divine justice?
(7) Explain the analogy between 'deep-sleep' state and 'death'.
(8) Would you agree with the statement that the Law of *karma* is a defeatist doctrine? Give reasons.
(9) "We were the architects of our fate yesterday, today we are its slaves". Discuss.
(10) What possible reasons can there be for an 'innocent' child to be born blind? Why should it be denied a normal life?
(11) If there are many more lives to live, why not 'eat, drink and be merry' in this one?! Discuss.
(12) What are the distinguishing features of the Law of *Karma*?
(13) "Two actions bad and three actions good, you have the Law of *Karma* licked for good!" Do you agree? Explain with reasons.
(14) If the other person is willing to accept it, would you be able to off load some of your *kaarmic* debt on to him? Explain with reasons.
(15) What are the different types of *karma*? What is the connection between *karma* and fate?
(16) What is meant by "inaction in action, and action in inaction?"
(17) What is *akarma*? What action is binding and what is liberating?
(18) What is *nishkaama* (selfless) *karma*? Give examples.
(19) List the name of those historical personalities who can be regarded as *karma yogis*. Give reasons to support your answer.

> *"In the symbol, the particular represents the general, not as a dream, not as a shadow, but as a living and momentary revelation of the inscrutable."*
>
> *Goethe*

14. SYMBOLISM

Throughout the history of mankind, man has tried to grasp the abstract and the unmanifest through thought forms. God is spoken of as the Infinite; to comprehend the Infinity through our finite, limited resources therefore presents a problem. Being the product of time and space man, inevitably, thinks in terms of time and space and their concomitant, name and form. Yet, Infinity, by definition, transcends these limits. How then are we to relate to it? With the help of symbolism, of course. Comprehension of even the physical universe is made possible for us through symbolism. For example, it is through the symbolism of words and numbers that we are able to understand the physical sciences. Without their help, the present day awareness in the fields of science and technology would have been impossible.

What is a symbol? A symbol may be defined as a concrete form and name given to a subtle or intangible idea, feeling, principle, doctrine or truth, so that what is not ordinarily comprehended becomes easily intelligible to the human mind. Take the example of 'time'. What is time? How are we to cognize it? Even the definition that time is an interval between two events does not take us very far. We only feel the "passing" of time. This feeling is more realistically cognized by us through the symbol of a clock. However, the clock cannot measure time in its absolute sense since time is infinite; it can at best make the passage of time more intelligible to us.

In much the same way, deeper, profound spiritual truths can be made tangible through appropriate symbols. In fact, all religions have symbols, for example, the Cross in Christianity, the Star and the Crescent in Islam, the Flame in Zoroastrianism, etc. Symbols are not merely suggestive or indicative of Truth, but they are also powerful manifestations of Truth itself and therefore capable of leading us towards that Truth. However, the potency and the power of a symbol can come alive only through the purity and faith of the devotee; the deeper the faith, more meaningful the symbol. "Faith can move mountains" so the saying goes. The importance of faith is underlined by the story of the two friends – one an idolater and the other not. The idolater would go to the village temple everyday and perform ritualistic oblations believing God to be present in the idol. His friend the non-idolater, also undertook to go to the temple but only to hit the idol with his shoe, to prove his point that God did not exist in the stone idol. One day, however, there was a flood and the road leading to the temple was under water. The idolater, afraid of the flood waters and fearful for his own safety, convinced himself that God meant him to stay indoors until the flood waters subsided. So, he decided not to go to the temple. The non-idolater, on the other hand, in spite of all the odds against him, in upholding the sanctity of the promise he had made, took off his clothes, holding them head high in one hand, swam across to the temple and hit the idol with his shoe, as usual. Lo and behold, he got the vision of God! The moral of the story is not that the vision of God can be achieved by hitting the idol, but that faith without commitment does not mean much. The single-minded commitment of the non-idolater was ripe and the only thing missing was the correct direction. Seeing that he was worthy and ready in every other respect, God Himself appeared to him in order to teach him the principle of His omnipresence. On the other hand, his own lack of faith, devotion and steadfastness kept the idolater away from experiencing the Divine Grace. He, in reality, had no faith; his was only a faith of convenience.

"When there is no gust of wind, an iron ball and a dry leaf, both lie unmoved, and in similar manner, upon the ground," says Baba; "To conclude that they are therefore of the same nature would be wrong. Let but the wind blow a little fast, the leaf will rise and fly far, the iron ball is unaffected. Such is the nature of false and true devotees. When there is no pain or grief, both the false and the true are alike; when pain or discord presents itself, false devotion takes to flight. Devotion, that is confirmed in and through practice, alone can be the spring of lasting bliss."

Let us dwell on the inner significance of some selected symbols.

Lotus Feet of the Lord

Whatever prayer springs from the depths of one's heart, and whatever homage is offered with purest love, deepest faith and devotion are heard and unconditionally accepted by the almighty Lord; of that there can be no doubt. Why then are the Feet of God singled out for worship? Why are the Feet given such prominence when God can have hands as well to receive what the devotee has to offer with love? Well, there are three reasons:

1. Feet are symbolic of God's presence, it being a logical matter of faith that

God is where His Feet are. But He is also known as (*sahasra paadaakshi-shirorabahave*), one with thousand feet, a thousand eyes, a thousand hands, and so on, implying thereby His Omnipresence. "Where can I go leaving aside Thy Feet, Oh Lord, when every bit of space is permeated by Thee?" So, wherever the devotee deposes faith about God's presence, there He manifests Himself in response to that faith itself.

2. Touching the Feet symbolises and evokes in the devotee a sense of humility, surrender and the evanescence of the physical self. Through the act of prostration (*dandavat pranaam*), the devotee gets as close as is possible, physically, to effacing the ego.

3. The two Feet also represent the Creator (*Purusha*) and the Creation (*Prakriti*), the unseen and the seen principle. With the act of prostration as the forehead is lowered to touch the Feet, the devotee affirms "Wherever my Lord, my mind rests, let me realise the presence of both Thy Feet".

Touching the Feet of the Lord is to connect oneself with the current of His Grace and installing His Feet in one's heart is to let His Will prevail. The idea behind bowing one's head at the feet of *Bhagawan*, explains Baba, is that thereby sacred thoughts enter the devotee's mind. "This means that when one comes in contact with *Bhagawan's* feet, the sacred impulses from them flow to the devotee. When the devotee's head touches the Lord's feet, the Lord's divine energy flows towards him. This implies that you should keep away from impure objects."

Lotus is unaffected by the environment around it and so it symbolises purity and detachment; lotus, in *Sanskrit*, is *pankaja*, meaning "born out of mud". Although born out of mud, lotus remains unsullied by the dirt. So, lotus is an appellative used with the Feet of the Lord. But therein is hidden also a secret which is that only through purity and detachment which are symbolised by the lotus, can the Feet, ie, the presence of the Lord, be attained.

Prostration (*Pranaam*)

The act of bowing, bending or making reverential salutation or respectful obeisance before God or before the image, idol or picture or any other symbol of the Immanent–Transcendent Divine Principle, is called *namaskaar* or *namaste*. It is also called prostration, for, man has to give up his individuality and deny himself before he can win the joy of grace. The utterance of the word "*namah*" with the prostration means "*na mama*" –

says Baba; that is to say, "Not mine! I am not mine, but Thine!"

Prostration with eight links is called *sa-ashta-anga* (with-eight-parts) *namaskaar*; one has to touch the ground with the eight parts to indicate total surrender. The eight parts are: (1) the feet, (2) the knees, (3) the chest, (4) the forehead, (5) the palms, (6) the intelligence (*dhi*), (7) the word (one must repeat the word, *namah*, 'Not I but Thou'), (8) the sight (one must have one's eye directed upon the Master). That is to say, it is not a physical act involving some contortions or genuflections; it is an intellectual discipline, done with eyes open. The word, "*dhi*", that is used for the intelligence, indicates that the surrender is to be performed, after due discrimination and not in a fit of despair.

It is also called *danda-pranaama* or *dandavat-pranaama*, or simply, *dandavat* – that is to say, "stick-prostration", falling like a stick before the Master, signifying absolute surrender and denial of one's particularity.

Folded Palms

Baba has explained the significance of the 'folded palms, kept upright on the chest', with the prescribed attitude of *namaskaara*. (Incidentally, this avoids the contact with the other's body, and the embarrassing problem of how long and how vigorously to hold and shake the palm of another, which the ritual of shaking hands involves). When folded, the five fingers of the one hand representing the five senses of action (*karmendriyas*) and the five fingers of the other, representing the five senses of perception (*jnaanendriyas*) join together in a gesture of offering. In other words, all action and all the means of knowledge and awareness are thus offered at the Feet of the Master, before whom one bows, with folded palms. This is the meaning of the gesture, says Baba.

Baba has also given another illuminating interpretation of the 'hand-gesture', the folded palms placed on the chest, when one says, '*namah!*'

"Take the simple rite of *namaskaaram* (*namah-kaaram* is *namaskaaram*, the act of offering *namah*), the folded palms with which you greet reverentially, elders and others. What does it signify, that gesture?"

"The right palm is *Tatt* (The unseen Basic Universal Absolute, the *Paramaatma*, God), the left palm is *Twam* (the seen, the particular, the limited, the wave, the image, the *atma* in the *jiva*, the *jivaatma*, the individual). When the two palms are brought together, and kept in contact, the oneness of that and this, of *Tatt* and *Twam* (of all that is outside you and all that is inside you) is emphasised and demonstrated! The *namah-kaara* (*namaskaara*) is, indeed, the *mudra* (gesture, symbol) of *Aham Brahmaasmi* (I am *Brahman*), the *jivaatma* (individual) is *Paramaatma* (Universal).

Chin-Mudra or *Jnaana Mudra* (Gesture of Wisdom)

This involves the fingers. The little finger, the ring finger and the middle finger represent the three attributes (*gunas*) viz, *tamasic*, *rajasic* and *sattwic*, respectively. The middle finger, thus, signifies *sattwa*. The forefinger, ie, the index (indicator or pointer) finger is called the life-finger symbolising the individual (*jiva*) aspect of man. The thumb signifies God (*Brahman*), the source, the fountain-head of all life and power. While man can somehow manage without any of the other fingers, the thumb is indispensable. Without the thumb, the hand would be lost. That is why the thumb is identified with God (*Brahman*), but for whom the world is as good as lifeless and nothing would be possible.

The three attributes (*gunas*), by their interplay, create the phenomenal world (*praakriti*). The individual (*jiva*) is associated with the three attributes and this association alone results in binding the individual to the objective world (*samsaara*). Man, by liberating himself from the attributes (*gunas*) and associating himself with *Brahman* (God) in a spirit of subservience to Him, gets released and attains union and even mergence in God (*Brahman*). The joining of the forefinger with the thumb, with the other three fingers together but stretched apart indicates the desire for the mergence of the individual with the universal and the transcendence of the three attributes (*gunas*). This is called the *Chin-mudra* or *Jnaana-mudra*, the gesture of wisdom.

Joss Sticks

Look upon joss stick as the individual (*jiva*) and the covering on it as the five sheaths (*pancha koshas*), the impurities. Prior to lighting up, the stick is held in upright position. Look upon this stance as the ego of the individual, the *ahamkaaram* in the *jiva*, ie, the identification of the 'reality' with the stick and its covering. When the flame is applied to it, that is to say, when the light of knowledge and wisdom is kindled in the *jiva*, the impurities start to burn up and gradually the ego becomes smaller and smaller. And, finally, when this transformation is complete, ie, the ego is completely annihilated, the identity of the stick as the reality drops off and what remains is what in

The glorious God, whose bounty, mercy, grace,
And loving-kindness all the world embrace,
At every moment brings a world to nought,
And fashions such another in its place.

All gifts soever unto God are due,
Yet special gifts from special "names" ensue;
At every breath one "name" annihilates,
And one creates all outward things anew.

Philosophers devoid of reason find
This world a mere idea of the mind;
'Tis an idea - but they fail to see
The great Idealist who looms behind.

Both power and being are denied to us,
The lack of both is what is ordained for us;
But since 'tis He who lives within our forms,
Both power and action are ascribed to us.

Your "self" is non-existent, knowing One!
Deem not your actions by yourself are done;
Make no wry faces at this wholesome truth-
"Build the wall ere the fresco is begun".

Lav'aih of Jami
(Translation: E. H. Whinfield)

fact was the inherent reality all along, although masked for a while, ie, ash, which symbolises detachment, purity and evanescence of the body. In other words, burning of a joss stick symbolises the process of reducing our impurities, the desires and ego, to ashes. Also, since the process is purificatory, enlightening and uplifting, it naturally spreads fragrance and joy around. Whenever we light a joss stick, we should do so in a prayerful attitude, conscious of the inner significance and purpose of this symbolic act.

Aarati

Aarati is a *Sanskrit* word meaning "The Close". The *Aa-rati* is the prayer song sung at the close of each *bhajan (devotional singing)* session. It is of profound significance, for the camphor flame itself has been endowed by *Bhagawan* Baba with the value and validity of a grand prayer, the culmination of the hour-long yearning of all the devoted hearts – "While it is being waved, pray," Baba says, "O Lord! Make the allotted span of my life as pure, as fragrant and as transparent as camphor; let it consume itself in the fire, scattering light and the warmth of love to all around me and at the end of it all, let there be nothing left of me (as the camphor leaves no ash or residue) to render me liable to another sojourn amidst pleasure and pain".

Camphor is itself a fragrant substance, and one's essence is the fragrance of the spirit. When camphor burns, it gradually fades itself out in illumination, giving warmth and illumination to those around. So too, one should so live (burn oneself out, sacrifice oneself) as to be a source of comfort and inspiration to others with whom one comes in contact.

Aarati also means "*atma-rati*" or "union with the *atma* (soul) within and *Paramaatma* (Supersoul) around". This symbolism is vividly demonstrated by burning of camphor. When camphor and fire meet, where is the remainder of even soot; even so, my Lord, when I am united with Thee with all my impurities burnt away, both of us become one self-effulgent flame of Consciousness. Install light in your heart and be a light to others around you. This is the significance of *Aarati*.

Sarvadharma Aikya Stamba

The pillar (*stamba*) symbolising oneness of faiths is the symbol of the Sri Sathya Sai Organisations. It represents a confluence of all the religious streams. Baba says:

> "Let different faiths exist; let them flourish. Let the glory of God be sung in all the languages in a variety of tunes. Respect the differences between the faiths and recognise them as valid as long as they do not extinguish the flame of unity."

The *Sarvadharma* symbol consists of an open lotus on raised pedestal bordered by a circle to which is attached five petals and five leaves; the Crescent and the Star, the Cross, the Wheel, the Torch and the Aum, appear one in each petal, and the words, *"Sathya"*, *"Dharma"*, *"Shanti"*, *"Prema"*, and *"Ahimsa"*, appear one in each leaf.

Sri Sathya Sai Baba assures the world that the Sai era of harmony and unity has found roots in the hearts of millions and that each religion has something significant to contribute to the stream of human progress.

In the centre of the *Sarvadharma* symbol is the light in a lamp designed as a lotus resting upon nine tiers. Each tier indicates a step in man's pilgrimage towards union with God. The broad three-tiered base represents the three *gunas* (attributes): *sattwa*, *rajas* and *tamas*; the pure, the active and the dull, which have to be maintained in perfect balance and finally transcended to attain illumination. The two tiers just below the lotus represent the two kinds of hatred which man has to overcome. One type of hatred is caused by injury and the other one by frustration of one's desires. Thus when desire, anger and hatred have been uprooted from the mind, the spiritual aspirant attains contentment and equal mindedness towards all, thereby allowing the lotus of his heart to blossom with the effulgence of inner illumination.

The sacred symbols of the five world faiths (which subsume and represent others, too) teach that Truth has many facets and that every facet adds to its lustre and value.

1. The "Crescent and Star", symbol of the Muslims is an inspiration for steady faith and unswerving loyalty of Good and God. Be like the Star which never wavers from the Crescent but is fixed in steady faith.

2. The "Cross", symbol of Christianity, carries the message of the elimination of the "I". Cut the "I" feeling clean across and let your ego die on the Cross, to endow on you Eternity.

3. The "Wheel", *(Dharmachakra)*, symbol of the Buddhist faith is a reminder of the wheel to which we are bound and of the wheel of

righteousness that can release us. Remember the wheel of cause and effect, of deed and destiny and the wheel of *dharma* that rights them all.

4. The "Fire", symbol of the Parsis is an invitation to cast into fire the lower instincts and impulses. Offer your bitterness in the sacred fire and emerge Grand, Great and Godly.

5. The "Aum", symbol of Hinduism, that summarises within itself all the processes of Being and Becoming, is to be accepted as the ultimate formula of spiritual success. Listen to the primeval sound (*Pranava*) resounding in your heart, as well as in the heart of the universe.

All these religions point to one truth: "God is One; Truth is God." The Sai form bears the name *Sathya* which means Truth.

The five guiding principles inscribed on the lotus leaves of the *Sarvadharma* symbol are: *Sathya* (Truth), *Dharma* (Righteousness), *Shanti* (Peace), *Prema* (Love) and *Ahimsa* (Non-injury).

O Divine Mother Sai! Wherever my mind rests, let me realise the presence of Thy Lotus Feet.

QUESTIONS:

(1) What is a symbol?
(2) What is the purpose of symbolism?
(3) What is the significance of the lotus and why is it used as an appellative with the Feet of the Lord?
(4) What is symbolised by the Feet of the Lord?
(5) What does prostration symbolise and why?
(6) What is the inner meaning of folded palms salutation?
(7) What do the five fingers of hand represent and how do they symbolise wisdom?
(8) What does a joss stick represent and what is the inner significance of lighting it?
(9) Of what significance is the waving of a flame at the conclusion of a *bhajan* (devotional singing) session?
(10) What is the special significance of camphor?
(11) What is the emblem of the Sri Sathya Sai Organisation? Discuss in detail.

"The i that throbs in every heart,
exults in everybody and knows through every brain
is a spark of the Universal I which is God".

Sri Sathya Sai Baba

15. FROM 'i' TO 'I'

"I am no body, really", is a statement we often hear ourselves make in a bid to parade our modesty. However if truth be told, this statement is, more often than not, intended as a subtle ploy to fish for praise, or draw unto oneself attention and admiration. What should be a conscious and emphatic assertion of the fact that 'I' am, in reality, not the body, because of the veiled hypocrisy, inevitably comes across as a pathetic apology.

In *Sanskrit*, *'aham'* means I and *'aakaara'* means form. So *aham* (I) with an *aakaara* (corporal form) is *ahamkaara*, the ego, ie, the identification of 'I' with the body, or the body-consciousness. "When this tiny little ego assumes enormous importance, it causes untold bother!" That, Baba says, is the root of all travail of man.

Jeeva (the individual 'I'), it is said, is none other than *Shiva*, the pure Self. Just as the grain hidden inside the husk is called paddy and when dehusked, it is called rice, 'I' likewise, with a body, is called the *jeeva* (the individual), without the body and on its own, it is the Self. Through the supervention of mind, aided and abetted by the *'vaasanaas'* (residual impressions gathered in previous births), true identity of 'I' with the Self is forgotten yielding place to the false identity with the body. It is only when the intervention of the mind is removed and the false identity with the body drops off, that we will be able to glimpse 'I', the real Self, in its pristine glory.

Of what use is the knowledge of the universe, if of that of our own Self we remain ignorant? Sage Naarada, Baba says, was the master of all the sixty-four skills and yet had experienced no inner peace. He went to Sanat Kumara and asked him to explain the reason for his lack of peace in spite of having mastered all fields of human knowledge. The first thing Sanat Kumara asked Naarada was, "What are your qualifications?" Naarada replied, "I have learned and mastered every type of education; there is no field of human knowledge which is beyond my comprehension." "In that case", Sanat Kumara said, "You must have learned the knowledge of the Self, the *atmavidyaa*?" Naarada replied in the negative adding that that was the only exception. Upon learning this, Sanat Kumara pointed out to Naarada that only through the *atmavidyaa*, knowledge of the Self, could his peace of mind be vouchsafed, not otherwise. Only by knowing that which once known, everything else becomes known, can one be called educated. Otherwise, one will remain ignorant, however many fields of knowledge one may have mastered. The message is beautifully illustrated in the dialogue between Svetaketu and his father as described in the *Chandogya Upanishad*.

"When Svetaketu was twelve years old he was sent to a teacher with whom he studied until he was twenty-four. After learning all the *Vedas*, he returned home full of conceit in the belief that he was consummately well educated, and very censorious. His father, Sruni, said to him,' Svetaketu, my child, you who are so full of your learning and so censorious, have you asked for that knowledge by which we hear the unhearable, perceive what cannot be perceived and know what cannot be known?'
'What is that knowledge, sir?' asked Svetaketu.
His father replied, 'As by knowing one lump of clay all that is made of clay is known, the difference being only in name, but the truth being that all is clay - so, my child, is that knowledge, knowing which we know all.'
'But surely these venerable teachers of mine are ignorant of this knowledge; for if they possessed it they would have imparted it to me. Do you, sir, therefore, give me that knowledge.'
'So be it,' said the father... And he said, 'Bring me a fruit of the *nyagrodha* (banyan) tree.'
'Here is one, sir.'
'Break it.'
'It is broken, sir.'
'What do you see there?'
'Nothing at all.'
The father said, 'My son, that subtle essence which you do not perceive there - in that very essence stands the being of the huge *nyagrodha* tree. In that which is the subtle essence all that exists has itself. That is the True, that is the Self, and thou, Svetaketu, art That.'
'Pray, sir,' said the son, 'tell me more.'
'Be it so, my child,' the father replied; and he said, 'Place this salt in water, and come to me tomorrow morning.'
The son did as he was told.
Next morning the father said, 'Bring me the salt which you put in the water.'
The son looked for it, but could not find it; for the salt, of course, had dissolved.
The father said, 'Taste some of the water from the surface of the vessel. How is it?'
'Salty.'

'Taste some from the middle. How is it?'
'Salty.'
'Taste some from the bottom. How is it?'
'Salty.'
The father said, 'Throw the water away and then come back to me again.' The son did so; but the salt was not lost, for salt exists for ever. Then the father said, 'Here likewise in this body of yours, my son, you do not perceive the True; but there in fact it is. In that which is the subtle essence, all that exists has its self. That is the True, that is the Self, and thou, Svetaketu, art that.'"

Act of death brings home to us an invaluable truth: the existence of a force which is responsible for activating the body; a force that breathes life into what is otherwise, essentially, a corpse. The body is only an inert thing. According to Baba, it is nothing more than seven buckets of water, iron from four 2–inch nails, phosphorous of 1,100 matchsticks, carbon contained in four pencils and two pieces of soap. "When you put all these things together with a few other assorted substances, it becomes a body. So, the body just consists of this inert matter; but it is able to move about and exhibit life because there is an indweller , the activating life-force, inside." The moment life from the body goes, there is no longer "my", the sense of possession. After death, there is no one to proclaim the ownership of the body as would be the case before death. This can only be so because the owner, the resident in it, has bolted. Minus this life-force, the body on its own has no value whatsoever – not even a scrap value. Once the life-force has left the body, the body cannot be quickly enough consigned to flames or buried six feet underground. And yet so strong is our infatuation with the body that the very prospect of losing it is fearsome. "When does the fear seize us?" asks Ramana *Maharshi*. "Does it come when you do not see your body, say, in a dreamless sleep, or when you are under chloroform? It haunts you only when you are fully 'awake' and perceive the world, including your body. If you do not see these and remain your pure Self, as in dreamless sleep, no fear can touch you."

"If you trace this fear to the object, the loss of which gives rise to it, you will find that that object is not the body, but the mind which functions in it and through which the environment and the attractive world is known as sights, sounds, smells, etc. Many a man would be too glad to be rid of his diseased body and all the problems and inconvenience it creates for him if continued awareness were vouchsafed to him. It is the awareness, the consciousness, and not the body, he (really) fears to lose. Man loves existence because it is eternal awareness, which is his own Self. Why not then hold on to the pure awareness right now while in the body, and be free from all fear?" As Baba tells us that it is "as natural to die as it is to be born."

Writing about Baba's views on death, Professor Kasturi remarks: "Death is our birth-right, a gift every one can claim. It is a relief for the tired and a refuge for the persecuted, a lesson for the wayward, a jolt for the epicurean, a milestone for the pilgrim, a punishment for the poltroon and a paradise for the faithful." "Why do living beings die?" We ask. "For the reason they are born," He answers.

It is through the death of the body-mind complex that we find eternity. But the body-mind complex on its own is never alive, why fear death then? The great *Sufi* poet Jalal-Uddin Rumi sums it up beautifully as follows:

> "I died a mineral and became a plant.
> I died a plant and rose an animal.
> I died an animal and I was man.
> Why should I fear? When was I less by dying?
> Yet once more I shall die as man, to soar
> With the blessed angels; but even from angelhood
> I must pass on. All except God perishes.
> When I have sacrificed my angel soul,
> I shall become that which no mind ever conceived.
> O, let me not exist! For Non-Existence proclaims,
> 'To Him we shall return'."

When a person dies, we say: the life has gone out of that body. We do not say: life has died. In other words, knowingly or unknowingly, we assert that the life-force is not subject to death although the body itself is. The life-force by which the body becomes activated and appears to come alive, that consciousness present in the body as conscience is variously referred to as '*atma*', soul, Self, etc. *Brahman* (God) refers to the Universal Consciousness present in all beings. We can therefore conclude that the body-mind complex and the life-force (*atma*) represent the seen (manifest) and the unseen (unmanifest) principles respectively. The body-mind complex is the temporary abode of the *atma*. It is subject to birth, change and death and so belongs to the finite world of limitation, whereas the *atma*, is neither born nor dies and so belongs to the realm of eternity and infinity. Furthermore, as discussed in the next chapter, it is possible to 'kill' the mind without, in any way, endangering our fundamental well being. The world without, in spite of all its diversity and multiplicity is the finite world of time and space, whereas the world of spirit within is the infinite world of eternity. What is not born cannot die; what is time-bound cannot live for ever. What cometh, that goeth too; what cometh not, that goeth neither. Baba says that the finitude of the body and the infinitude of the soul have to be stoically accepted.

By stretching our imagination, we might be able to persuade ourselves to believe that the outside world is indeed limited; with regard to the possibility of the inner world being infinite, however, our understanding is made difficult because of two doubts:

- If the world within us is indeed infinite, how can it possibly be contained within a body which is finite? So, there would appear to be a contradiction in terms.

- Even if it was conceded that the inner world is infinite and eternal, if it is as close as being within us, why do we find it difficult to accept its existence and why is existence not patently manifest?

Both these doubts are raised by our mind. Mind, because of its sense-based perceptions and activity creates the hindrance. It deludes itself into believing that what it knows not is not worth knowing. It bases its judgement on the feed-back from the senses. But the senses, as tools of perception, lack versatility and depth. They have inherent limitations. For example, the eyes cannot hear, nor can they see beyond a certain distance; the ears cannot see, nor can they hear below a certain decibel, and so on. Clearly then, the mind and the senses have a defined, limited capability. With this handicap, how could the mind be expected to comprehend the Infinite and the Eternal?

The tendency of mind to size up or measure, as is its wont, constantly though not consciously, in terms of time and space that which in reality is beyond time and space, is the root cause of the problem. Mind, in reality, has no existence except as a collection of thoughts; with the cessation of thoughts, therefore, the mind also ceases to exist. When its own continued existence is not assured, how then can we expect it to have any concept of Eternity? Eternity does not imply an unending supply of time, nor does Infinity connote a sum total of finites or an unending continuum of space. These definitions are but poor attempts at pointing to that which, in fact, is beyond time and space. Besides, the world within is not meant to connote the spatial internality of our body but that unmanifest essence or reality of which the body is but a symbol, a manifest concretisation.

However clever a man may be, he will never know his own Self if his mind be turned outwards. To comprehend the inner world and the life-force (soul power), the mind and the senses as tools are useless. Instead, we need to cultivate the inner vision. As long as the mind is directed outwards into the objective world, developing inner vision is impossible. As long as thoughts persist, so long will the turning inward of the mind not be accomplished; as long as the mind is not turned inward, so long can the Self not be realised. Turning the mind inward is nothing more than the absence of all thought; how can the mind be fixed within if desires which keep us tethered to the outside world are not given up? When all thoughts are eliminated and all investigation ceases, one becomes aware of the Self. The sole requirement for the realisation of the Self, therefore, is the purity of mind; the only impurity being thoughts. In fact, every instant that is free from thoughts and musings in the 'wakeful' state offers us a glimpse of the Self. But, for want of acquaintance with it, sadly, such moments pass unnoticed! So, to keep the mind pure and inward looking is to render it thought-free. To achieve this, the sway of the senses has to slacken. The story of Ashtavakra and King Janaka further illustrates this point.

Ashtavakra lived in the reign of King Janaka. He was young in years, physically deformed but, spiritually, a realised soul. King Janaka once convened an assembly of learned scholars. When Ashtavakra was granted permission to enter the hall, all the assembled personages, with the exception of the king himself who maintained a dignified silence, burst out into an uncontrollable laughter at the sight of him. When the laughter subsided a little, it was Ashtavakra's turn to laugh even louder. This unexpected turn of events took the learned scholars by surprise. They felt that not only was he inexperienced, unlike them, and had no credentials to enter the learned assembly, but on top of that, he was also unsightly and deformed physically. These, they informed him, were reasons enough to justify their laughter, and proceeded to enquire the reasons for his impertinent outburst.

He told them that, for days together, he had waited outside the door patiently in the hope that he would be granted leave to enter the assembly of great scholars of the land; yet, when he was eventually granted permission to enter, he was shocked to find that the learned scholars he expected to see turned out to be no more than a bunch of cobblers parading as scholars! On hearing this, the 'scholars' felt slighted and thinking that he had overstepped himself, asked him to explain his outrageous remark. It appears that he addressed them thus:

"As I entered the hall, you looked at my body which is no more than a bag of leather, and seeing its defects and deformities came to the conclusion that you did. A cobbler who trades in leather, when his eyes fall on a foot will only remark at the styling or the defects of the material of the shoe but will not concern himself with the quality of the foot that wears it. Since the object of your observation and comment upon my entry into the hall, likewise, was this body, this leather casing and not the *atma* resident within it, the outer and not the inner, how then could I see you as anything other than the traders in leather? Do you still wish to challenge the reasons for my observation and reaction?" Upon hearing this, they were humbled and hung their heads in shame. However, whilst reprimanding them thus, Ashtavakra taught them two important lessons: firstly, the distinction between the real and the unreal, the *atma* and *unaatma*, and secondly, he demonstrated to them how the mind can mislead if it is allowed to dictate and is not kept under control.

To overcome the delusion of 'I am the body' brought about by mind, it is important to consider three points:

- If we look upon that which is unreal as real, the Reality will for ever remain obscure; that is to say, if we perceive the body as the Self, the real Self will never become apparent.

- As long as we perceive our reality as the body which is subject to birth and death, we cannot escape the succession of birth and death; only when we identify our reality with *atma* which knows no birth and death, will we also be free from that scourge.

- As long as we sleep the sleep of ignorance and the delusion of unreality as the Reality continues, no effort will be directed towards uncovering the Reality and so it will continue to remain beyond our reach.

It is important to recognise this, because only then is there a chance that we may apply our efforts towards the discovery of the Self single-mindedly.

However, how can a grain of sand measure the vastness of a desert? How does one 'define' that which is beyond definition? How does one explain that which defies explanation? How can a mere droplet of water, as long as it perceives itself as being distinct from the vast ocean and assumes a definition and limit, comprehend the size and fathom the depth of the ocean? The answer is that, as soon as the drop loses its own identity and distinction by merging with the ocean, that instant, it verily becomes the ocean, an integral part of its vastness. That moment onwards, all questions about the shape and size of the ocean become meaningless and redundant. In much the same way, when our inner vision opens and we lose all identity with the body-mind complex and experience and become aware of the Self, the *atma*, all doubts will dissolve.

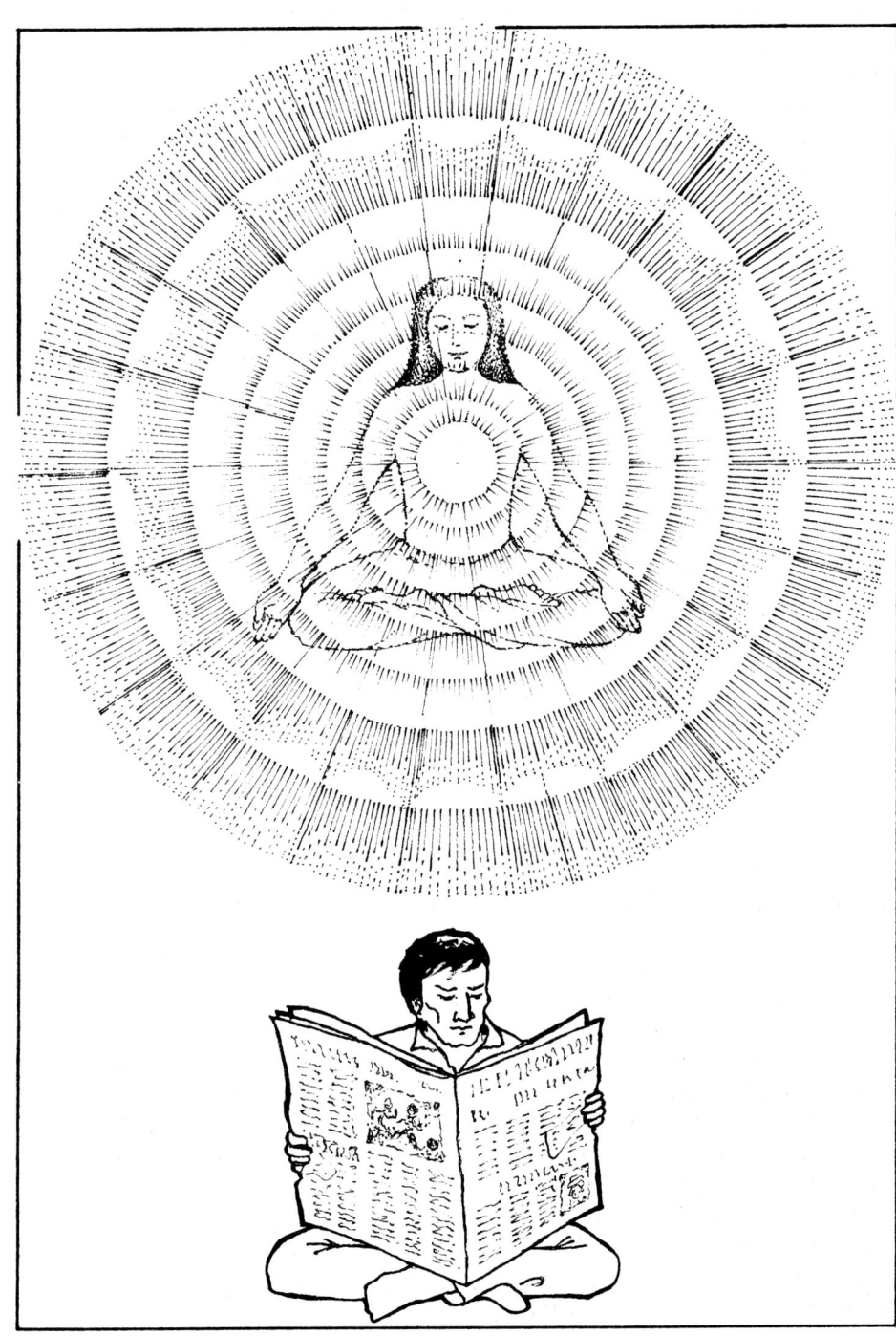

Atma is also known as 'Awareness'. It is this awareness that is responsible for the 'I' consciousness in all beings, which is called 'Aham'. When this Aham identifies itself with the body, it becomes Ahamkaara. This is the false 'I', and not the real 'I'. What hides the Atma always, is the mind. The clouds which are formed due to the Sun's heat hide the Sun itself. Likewise the mind which is the offspring of the Atma hides the Atma itself. As long as the mind is there, man cannot hope to understand anything about the Self, not to speak of realising and experiencing the bliss of the Self. That state in which one is established in the Self at all times and under all circumstances is called 'Saakshaatkaara' - Self-realisation.

The first sound that emanated from the Self is 'I'. The entire Creation began only after the emanation of this 'I' sound. If there is no 'I', there is no Creation. The terms 'I', Brahman, Atma or Self are all synonymous. The 'I' sans mind is the Atma or the Self in its pristine purity. The 'I' associated with the mind is the false self or Mithyaatma. There is only one Atma or Self and that is the 'I'...

It is important to recognise that as long as the mind is there, desires will not leave you. As long as you have desires, the false notion of 'I' and 'Mine' will not leave you. As long as the feeling of 'I' and 'Mine' is there, Ahamkaara - your wrong identification with the body - will not leave you. As long as Ahamkaara does not leave you, Ajnana - ignorance will not leave you. In effect, it means that there is no way other than the annihilation of the mind to attain Atma-Jnana - Knowledge of the Self, or Atma-darshan - Vision of the Self, or Atmaananda - Bliss of the Self, whatever you may choose to call it.

Sri Sathya Sai Baba

Mind's preoccupation with the body and its passionate concern for the personal ego reflect a sad spiritual illness. We fall from grace the moment our bodily weakness makes itself manifest. Hurled are we from high heaven the instant we taste of the fruits of 'I' and 'mine'. The paradise lost can, however, be regained by pouring the ego as libation into the crucible of life.

A person may play various roles in a drama, yet his true identity never leaves his mind. Likewise, when one is engaged in various empirical acts, there should always be the firm conviction "I am the Self", without allowing the false idea "I am the body", etc, to arise. "When, in this manner, the mind becomes quiescent in its own state," says Raman *Maharshi*, "Self-experience arises of its own accord. Thereafter, sensory pleasures and pains will not affect the mind. All phenomena will appear then, without any attachment, like a dream. When man has thus succeeded in dehypnotising himself from all the illusions of his own littleness and losing all sense of body consciousness, he will realise himself as the Self-sufficient totality, the *atma*." With that freedom won, he will have no reservation in joining *Swami* Vivekananda in the chorus:

> "Nor angel I, nor man brute,
> Nor body, mind, nor he nor she;
> The books do stop in wonder mute
> To tell my nature – I am He!
>
> Before the sun, the moon, the earth,
> Before the stars or comets free,
> Before e'en Time has had its birth
> I was, I am, and I will be!
>
> The beauteous earth, the glorious sun,
> The calm sweet moon, the spangled sky,
> Causation's laws do make them run,
> They live in bonds, in bonds they die.
>
> And mind its mantle, dreamy net
> Casts o'er them all and holds them fast,
> In warp and woof of thought are set
> Earth, hells or heavens, or worst or best.
>
> Know these are but the outer crust
> All space and time, all effect, cause,
> I am beyond all sense, all thought,
> The Witness of the Universe!

> Not two nor many, 'tis but One,
> And thus in me all ones I have
> I cannot hate, I cannot shun
> Myself from me – I can but love!
>
> From dreams awake, from bonds be free!
> Be not afraid. This mystery,
> My shadow, cannot frighten me!
> Know once for all that I am He....."

Baba says: "Each individual is born with the question, *koham* (who am I?) on his lips. And the answer is given by every breath – *So-ham* – He am I. The inhalation whispers *So* (He), and the exhalation, *ham* (I). But the question is brushed aside by the mind, impatient to dabble in the toy-land it pictures the world to be. The answer is denied admission into the understanding by the ego, which derives temporary pleasure thereby. Realize that your breath is answering the question correctly and live in the consciousness, that is God. Let your mind have no waves; let it be silent, level, calm – so that the *hamsa* (the celestial swan) that is the symbol of *So-ham* can sport thereon." Remember, " 'I' (Self) is not the physical self, nor is it the emotional self, nor the intellectual self, but the witness to all those changing aspects of what is commonly called as man. The Self is referred to as *jeeva* (the Life Factor), the *Atman* (Soul)."

The transition from the assertion that 'i' am the body to the realisation that 'I' am the *atma*, is the pilgrimage from "*Koham*?" ("Who am I?") to "*So-ham*" ("I am He"), from *shavam* (death) to *Shivam* (immortality). This progress of the pronoun, from 'i' to 'I', is indeed the pilgrimage from 'here' to 'Eternity'.

O Divine Mother Sai! May I be free from the bonds of death; may I never again forget my immortal nature.

QUESTIONS:

(1) What is ego?
(2) How does the identity of the Self with the body come about?
(3) What are the different aspects of human personality and how do they differ from each other?
(4) Kill the mind, you kill the body! Comment.
(5) How can the world within a finite, time-bound body be considered as infinite and eternal?
(6) Is Self-experience possible for the mind whose nature is constant

change?
(7) How can the delusion "I am the body" be overcome?
(8) "What the mind knows not is not worth knowing!" Examine this statement critically, illustrating your answer with appropriate examples.

I have come to light the lamp of love in your hearts, to see that it shines day by day with added lustre. I have not come to speak on behalf of any particular religion ... I have not come on any mission of publicity for any sect, creed or cause; nor have I come to collect followers for any doctrine. I have no plan to attract disciples or devotees into my fold or any fold. I have come to tell you of this Universal Unitary Faith, this Atmic (Divine) Principle, this Path of Love, this Duty of Love, this Obligation to Love ...

Believe that all hearts are motivated by the One and Only God; that all Faiths glorify the One and Only God; that all Names in all languages and all Forms that man can conceive denote the One and Only God; His Adoration is best done by means of LOVE. Cultivate that 'Eka-bhaava' (attitude of Oneness) between men of all creeds, all countries and all continents. That is the Message of Love I bring. That is the Message I wish you to take to heart.

– Sri Sathya Sai Baba

"To get at the core of God at his greatest,
one must first get into the core of himself at his least,
for no one can know God who has not first known himself"

Meister Eckhart

16. KNOWLEDGE OF THE SELF – 1

As discussed in the previous chapter, the starting point in the process towards the realisation of the Self is the enquiry, *'koham'* (who am I?). The greatest impediment in the path of this enquiry, however, is the mistaken identity of 'I' with everything other than its real Self. For example, in the 'wakeful' state, one identifies the 'I' with the gross body, whereas in the 'dream' state, it creates another body, the subtle body, to identify itself with, completely unmindful of the gross body it left behind in the bed. In 'deep-sleep', one enters into yet another state where one finds no attributes which would enable one to assert or deny one's existence. We thus pass through these states almost every 24-hour cycle and yet know not which, if any of these, conforms to our real nature. The question : 'Who am I?' therefore, continues to remain a persistent and unsolved riddle with us until it is investigated into.

Who or what this 'I',which appears to be hidden behind the mask of the body, in reality is, is the single most important quest of human endeavour. What appears to be hidden and what it is that is sought is none other than one's true identity, the real I. What makes the process of seeking more difficult is the fact that one cannot have the knowledge of the Self as Self, verily, is the knowledge itself. However, in the initial stages, the only way forward would appear to be to proceed from the standpoint of what we think is known towards that which appears to be the unknown.

There is often a vague notion that 'I' am the body itself (*dehoham*). But, *atma*, the real I is verily one and without parts, whereas the body consists of many parts; confounding these two as one, therefore, can only be seen as the height of ignorance. How very strange that a person should rest contented ignorantly with the idea that he is the body whilst knowing that the body is merely something that belongs to him and therefore apart from, and external to, him! *Bhagawan* Baba says : "During our life, we are always saying (things like) this is my body, this is my mind, this is my intelligence, these are my organs, etc. All the time you say so, have you at any time made an attempt to find out who you are before saying, this is mine or that is mine? Is it not that (only) after you have found out who you are, that you get the right to say that this body belongs to you? ....If I call this my towel, then I give rise to an opportunity by which I can throw the towel away and (yet) remain myself aloof and apart from the towel. So, if you say that this is your body, then you abrogate to yourself the power and the right to throw away the body and (yet) remain aloof and apart from the body. You are not the body. When you say that it is your mind, (you are asserting thereby that) you are not the mind ....." The act of death further lays bare the misconception by bringing into sharp focus three important facts:

(1) Body on its own is *jada* (insentient) having no awareness of its own.
(2) Presence of some other ingredient is therefore essential to activate the body. It may be appropriate to call this ingredient as the 'life-force' (*chaitanya*) since it is obvious that without it the body would be lifeless, a corpse.
(3) Body is the manifested and the life-force the un-manifested aspect of the human personality.

The body, because of its limitation in time and space, assumes a definition which allows it to be recognised readily by our mind through the senses, whereas the unmanifested nature of the life-force obviously makes such comprehension rather difficult. What is beyond doubt, however, is that the very unmanifested nature of the life-force must, at the very least, confirm that it can only belong to the realm which is beyond the limits and laws of time and space. This then forms the threshold of our quest. Further progress can be made only through a dedicated effort.

According to *Bhagawan* Baba, three-fourths of the effort should be in the nature of *vichaar* (earnest philosophical enquiry) and one-fourth as *sadhana* (disciplined spiritual exercise). The philosophical enquiry can be based either on the nihilistic (*Neti, Neti* – Not only this, Not only this) approach, excluding all that 'I' the real Self cannot be, or the process of assertion, ie, affirmation of what 'I' really is. The process of elimination is essentially the systematic removal of ignorance by using the powers of logic and discrimination. The process of assertion, however, can only be based on trust relying upon the testimony of the scriptures, great masters and the self-realised sages and, of course, one's own intuitive faith. For, in the words of Jalal-uddin Rumi :

> "When a mother cries to her suckling babe,
> 'Come, O son, I am thy mother!'
> Does the child answer, 'O mother, show (me) a proof
> That I shall find comfort in taking thy milk'?"

The bond of love and acceptance is natural and native and beyond question or doubt.

The two processes, ie, the rational and the intuitive, must not be looked upon as being mutually exclusive but as being complementary. In fact, by strengthening one, the other must become sharpened as well.

When, through the grace of God, man is able to separate from himself all that is not Himself, that is to say, peel off, step by step, and cast away all that is *un-atma* (non-Self) ie, body-mind related, and constantly bring back one's thoughts on to the life-force (*atma*), then 'I' shall stand revealed as the blissful "Self". This combined process of elimination and assertion is beautifully expounded in the following verses of "*Nirvaanashatkam*" (six stanzas on *Nirvaana* - Liberation) by the great spiritual master, Aadi Shankaracharya. For English rendering of these verses, see Appendix C.

(1) *Mano–buddyhankaara chittaani naaham*
Na cha shrotra–jihve na cha graana–netre
Na cha vyoma–bhoomir na tejo na vaayu
Chidaananda roopah Shivoham Shivoham.

Translation: "*Manas* (mind), *buddhi* (intellect), *ahamkaara* (ego) and *chitta* (memory) 'I' am not; nor am 'I' *shrotra* (ears), *jihvaa* (tongue), *graana* (nose) and *netre* (eyes). 'I' am not *vyoma* (sky), *bhoomi* (earth), *tejo* (fire) and *vaayu* (air) either. 'I' am Blissful Consciousness, *Shiva*, the Auspiciousness itself."

Manas is nothing but a bundle of thoughts; it does not have any specific form; it can be conceived as the process of thinking itself. There are four aspects of the mind; the lower or the impure mind, called the *manas*, the intuitive intellect and faculty of discrimination, called the *buddhi*, recollection of past experiences, called the *chitta* and the sense of personal self or ego, called the *ahamkaaram*. In other words, the mind wears four different caps; when the mind observes the impurities from the sense-organs, it can be described as the impure mind, but when the mind is turned away from the sense-organs and the sense impressions have been removed, it becomes pure. So, when the mind is associated with the sense-organs, it is *manas*, the impure mind; when it recalls past memories and deliberates, it is referred to as *chitta*. *Buddhi* examines the arguments for and against; *ahamkaaram* sways the decision for or against and, by attachment, slackens the hold of native intelligence.

Whether or not the mind is 'I', the real Self, can be easily resolved by

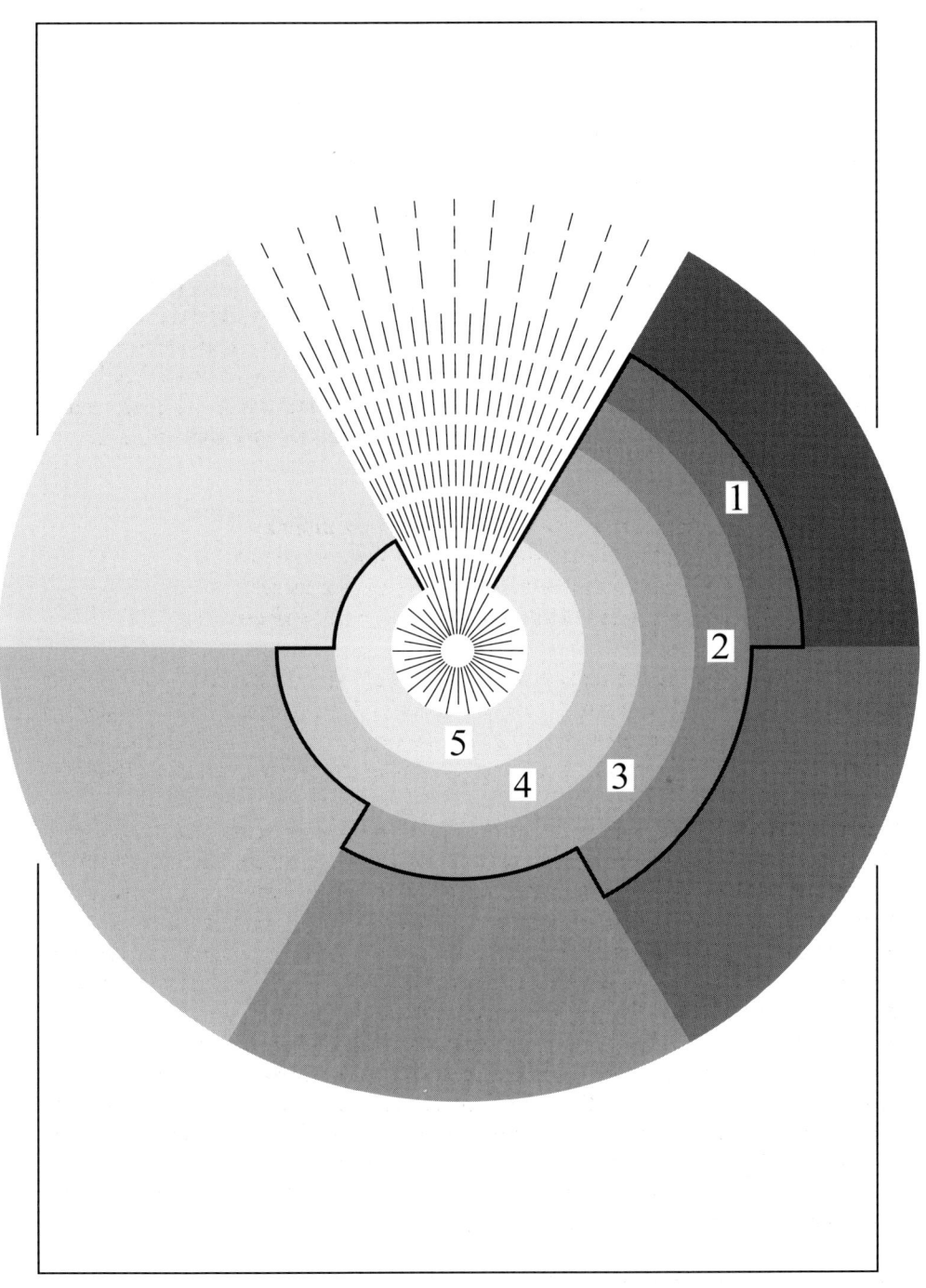

What is to be done, O Moslems? for I do not recognise myself.
I am neither Christian, nor Jew, nor Gabr, nor Moslem.
I am not of the East, nor of the West, nor of the land, nor of the sea;
I am not of Nature's mint, nor of the circling heavens.
I am not of earth, nor of water, nor of air, nor of fire;
I am not of the empyrean, nor of the dust, nor of existence, nor of entity.
I am not of India, nor of China, nor of Bulghar, nor of Saqsin;
I am not of the kingdom of Iraqain, nor of the country of Khorasan.
I am not of this world, nor of the next, nor of Paradise, nor of Hell;
I am not of Adam, nor of Eve, nor of Eden, and Rizwan.
My place is the Placeless, my trace is the traceless;
'Tis neither body nor soul, for I belong to the soul of the Beloved.
I have put duality away, I have seen that the two worlds are one;
One I seek, One I know, One I see, One I call.
He is the first, He is the last, He is the outward, He is the inward;
I know none other except "Ya Hu" and "Ya man Hu".
I am intoxicated with Love's cup, the two worlds have passed out of my ken;
I have no business save carouse and revelry.
If once in my life I spent a moment without Thee,
From that time and that hour I repent of my life.
If once in this world I win a moment with Thee,
I will trample on both worlds, I will dance in triumph for ever.
O Shamsi Tabriz, I am so drunken in this world,
That except of drunkenness and revelry I have no tale to tell.

From the Divan of Shams-e Tabriz (Translation: R. A. Nicholson)

> *Gabr: a Magian*
> *Iraqain: the two Iraqs, Iraqi Ajami (in Persia) and Iraqi Arabi (between Tigris and Euphrates)*
> *Rizwan: the angel who has the keys of Paradise.*
> *For I belong to the soul of the Beloved: when every trace of finite existence is swept away, the Infinite remains.*
> *"Ya Hu":" O He" (Jahve, Jehova), one of the most familiar darvish-cries.*
> *"Ya Man Hu": "O He who is".*
> *Carouse and revelry: spiritual rapture and ecstasy.*

comparing the experiences of the 'wakeful' (*jaagrat*) and the 'deep-sleep' (*sushupti*) states. During the 'wakeful' hours, mind is active. It ceases activity when it is too much fatigued. The complete cessation of the activity of mind, due to exhaustion, is known as sleep. In this state, it withdraws itself from both the physical as well as subtle objects and even the psychic activity ceases.

In the wakeful state, man is beset with all manner of problems. In spite of all the earthly possessions, with all the retinue of a kingdom and the power he can wield, he is agitated, vexed and worried. In the 'deep-sleep' state, on the other hand, in spite of the absence of an empire and power and even being unseen, unbefriended, unprotected and unrecognized, man's bliss is beyond compare. It is in fact everybody's experience that nothing in the 'wakeful' state can ever compare with the bliss and well-being experienced in the 'deep-sleep' state, This must conclusively point to the fact that the experience of bliss comes only from within ourselves and that it is most intense when we are free from all thoughts and perceptions which draw us out into the world without. In other words, the Be-ing alone being native to the Self is bliss and the mental activity being alien to it is simply the superimposition of ignorance and, therefore, the cause of misery. Attachment, desire, pleasure, pain, etc, are perceived when the mind is active, but are not perceived in the 'deep-sleep' (*sushupti*) state when the mind is not active. Therefore, these characteristics can only belong to the mind and not to the *atma*, the Self. The presence of problems in the 'wakeful' state and their absence in the 'deep-sleep' state can therefore be directly linked to the presence of mind in the former state and its absence in the latter. This then establishes two important principles in relation to mind:

(1)   Far from being our Reality, the mind can be the root cause of a lot of our problems.
(2)   It is possible to kill the mind without, in any way, endangering our fundamental well being.

The amazing revelation, however, is that the ratiocination that has led us to these conclusions and brought us close to the possibility of negating the mind has been helped by none other than the mind itself! This therefore, indubitably, points to the existence of a superior source, other than the mind, which must have within itself, the persuasive power to inspire the mind even to deny itself! Clearly then, the mind cannot be considered even as a contender for the title of 'I', the real Self; although it must be acknowledged that it is the mind itself, albeit in its purer form, that has to be instrumental in pointing us in the right direction. Every effort must therefore be made in using it towards that end.

The ears, the nose, the eyes, the tongue and the skin are known as the five senses of perception. These senses are the instruments, like any other instrument, through which certain specific tasks, ie, of hearing, smelling, seeing, tasting and feeling are carried out. Just as the power of perception itself cannot be attributed to a microscope even though it enables us to exercise that power through it, the various senses, likewise, cannot be credited with any awareness of their own even though the various acts, ie, of seeing, hearing, etc, are performed through them. Besides, it is the mind that uses the senses. Kill the mind and the senses will die of inanition. We must therefore infer that:

- The senses, as the instrument of perception, have defined, limited roles and therefore lack versatility.

- Perception and the instruments of perception are not synonymous.

This then leads us to conclude that 'I' am not the senses of perception.

Earth, Water, Fire, Air and Ether (Sky) are known as the *Pancha Mahabhutas*, the Five Primordial Elements. In the scientific parlance, they are recognised as Solid, Fluid, Energy, Movement and Space. The element Earth has five characteristics (impurities) of smell, taste, form, touch and sound. It is therefore the grossest (heaviest), has no freedom of movement and occupies the least amount of space. The element Water has only four characteristics, having lost the impurity of smell. It is consequently lighter than earth and has one degree of freedom of movement and so occupies more space then earth. The Fire element has only three characteristics, having lost smell and taste. It has therefore two degrees of freedom of movement; it can not only spread sideways, it also rises upwards. Since it is lighter than water, it occupies even more space than water. The element Air has only two characteristics that of touch and sound; having lost the other three, it has three degrees of freedom, sideways, upwards and downwards. It is lighter even than fire and therefore occupies even greater space than fire. The last element, Ether, is left with one impurity only, that of sound. It is the subtlest (lightest) of the five elements.

These five elements make up the entire *bhutaakaasha*, the gross physical universe, and therefore also the physical body. Just as all things found in the physical world are impermanent and subject to continuous change, human life, likewise undergoes change, namely, birth, growth, maturation, decline, decay and death. The atoms which form the human body, like atoms in any other form, change every moment, causing the body to undergo all these modifications. It is clear, therefore, that neither any one of the five elements on its own nor all of them put together constitute the real 'I' which is beyond modification and change. With regard to this 'I', the Cosmic Intelligence, *Brahadaranyaka Upanishad* (3–7–3) states: "It dwells in the earth, water, fire, air and space, (yet) they know It not, these elements being Its body". Besides, the five elements come alive only through the senses and the mind. Render the mind defunct, and the physical universe of the five elements will cease to be.

Beyond the mind, beyond reason and consciousness and beyond the I-sense, is the *atma*, the reality, the Cosmic I or God.

That awareness which is ever alive and vibrant, irrespective of whether the body consciousness exists, as in the so-called 'wakeful' state, or does not, as in the 'deep-sleep' state; whether the mind and the intellect are functioning or are defunct, that awareness is the Real I, the Self. That awareness, that 'I' never goes to sleep. How indeed could it be the awareness, the reality, the witness, if it even blinked for a fleeting second let alone went to sleep? That is why Baba says, "I never sleep." In our case, however, we have to settle for the impersonal statement: "'I' never sleeps", at least until such time as we truly realise our own reality as that 'I', when we can also proclaim: "I never sleep. 'I' am *Shiva*, the Blissful Awareness; 'I' am Auspiciousness itself".

(2) *Na cha praana sangyo na vai pancha vaayu*
Na vaa sapta dhaatu na vaa pancha koshah
Na vaak paani paadau na chopastha paayu
Chidaananda roopah Shivoham, Shivoham

Translation: "I am neither *praana* (life breath) nor the *pancha vaayu* (five vital airs). I am not the *sapta dhaatu* (seven substances), nor am I the *pancha koshah* (five sheaths). I am neither *vaak* (tongue), *paani* (hands) and *paadau* (feet), nor *upastha* (genitals), *paayu* (excretory organ). I am the Blissful Awareness, *Shiva*, the Auspiciousness itself".

Each subsequent element described above originated from the previous one. From Ether (*Aakaash*) was born Air (*Vaayu*); from Air, Fire (*Agni*); from Fire, Water (*Jalam*); and from Water, Earth (*Prthvi*). The cause of the first element Ether and therefore of all the five is *Brahman* (God), the unmodified, the fixed, the Basis. From *Brahman* originated Effort (*Yatna*) and Cosmos (*Mahat*) and from these were born the five elements. The human body is the result of the combination of all these five. However, in the composition of the body each element has again become five-fold.

The first, Ether (Sky) became Cognizer (*Jnaata*), mind (*manas*), intellect (*buddhi*), ego (*ahamkaaram*) and memory (*chitta*). They are recognised as the "inner senses".

The element Air (*Vaayu*) took the form of the five vital airs (*pancha praanas*) in the body. *Praana* (vital energy) appears in the form of breath. The five vital energies vitalize all bodily functioning; one of these is related to breathing, another to elimination, third to circulation, the fourth to digestion and the fifth to the upward flow which energizes the higher centres. *Praana* activates the head, *vyaana*, the right, *udaana*, the left, *samaana*, the central, and *apaana*, the lower parts of the body. The *praana* moves from the heart through the nerves of the face, the nose, etc, and reaches the head. From there, it motivates the various nerves flowing through the body under different names with distinct names and distinct functions. The *praana* that functions round the navel is, for example, called *samaana*.

The Element Fire (*Agni*) became the sensory organs; the ear, the skin, the eyes, the tongue and the nose. These are called the *jnaanendriyas*, the organs of knowledge.

The five (*jalapanchakas*) that the Element Water became are: sound (*shabda*), touch (*sparsha*), form (*rupa*), taste (*rasa*) and smell (*gandha*). These are known as the five subtleties (*pancha tanmaatraas*).

The Earth Element appears in the body in the form of the vocal organs, hands, legs, genitals, and the excretory organs. These are known as the *karmendriyas*, the organs of action. There are, in turn, five specific products attributable to the five elements that have united to form the gross body. The Earth element produces bone, skin, flesh, veins and hair; the Water element, blood, urine, saliva, phlegm and brain; the Fire element, hunger, thirst, sleep, sloth and comradeship; the element Air, activity, movement, speed, shame and fear and the element Ether produces lust, anger, greed, pride and envy. This group of gross qualities is the reason for the agony of man. That is why it is said that the physical body which is the product of the five-fold division of the Five Elements, is the medium for experiencing pleasure and pain as a consequence of past actions.

The seven substances referred to in the verse are: juice, blood, flesh, fat, bones, marrow and the seminal fluid. The human body constituted of the twenty-five elemental principles described above is also known as the gross body (*sthula deha*). The five senses of knowledge, the five subtleties, the five vital airs, the mind and the intellect – these seventeen categories combine to contribute the subtle body (*sukshma deha*). In the causal body (*kaarana deha*), the consciousness (*chittam*) is in association with the knower, the knowing principle (the *jnaata*). The 'wakeful' state is assigned to the gross body, the 'dream-state' to the subtle body and the 'deep-sleep' state to the causal body. The pure consciousness unmixed with any elemental principle, the Witness Eternal, the Self-Effulgent, is beyond all states of consciousness and is stateless. It is described as *a-kshara Purusha* (immortal Self). It is the resident in the body, the indweller (*dehi*) as distinct from the body (*deha*) itself. 'I' am therefore not the body that can be associated with either the five primordial elements or their derivatives; nor, indeed am 'I' the five sheaths.

The five sheaths can be thought of as various bodies interpenetrating each other in a successively more subtle way, each one finer than the previous one. These are called sheaths because they are like coverings on *atma*, the Self. The grossest sheath is the food sheath (*annamaya kosha*) which comprises the physical body; next is the vital sheath (*praanamaya kosha*) which relates to the life breath and physical energy; the one after that is the mind sheath (*manomaya kosha*) which is the subtle body relating to the lower mind or thought; then comes the intellectual sheath (*vignaanamaya kosha*) which is a still finer body associated with the higher mind and the intuition; the last sheath is the sheath of bliss (*aanandamaya kosha*), the subtlest of all the bodies, which is beyond all aspects of mind, where only the veil of ignorance remains to hide the *atma*, the Real I. By logical reasoning the pure *atma* should be separated from the five sheaths just as rice is separated from the husk by pounding it. When all the five sheaths are eliminated through discrimination and renunciation, what remains as the non-reducible substratum is the Self, the self-effulgent Witness, the changeless Reality, Absolute Knowledge and Everlasting Bliss.

The body is not evident before its birth nor after its death. It is seen only during the intervening period of time. The body has a beginning and an end, growth and decay. Such things are 'products', 'effects', and effects are conditioned. So the body too is a limited, conditioned thing. The wise man tells himself, "I exist always; I am not material; I have no cause and effect, I am separate from this gross body. So, I cannot be the food sheath. I am the knower of the food-sheath; I am the witness". When this knowledge is well established, he must realise that he is beyond the food-sheath. Besides, *praana* (life-breath) activates the body. Without *praana*, the body cannot survive. By contemplating that this sheath of life breath that activates the food-sheath is vital for the body, the notion that the body is the Self will disappear.

At night, when the individual is asleep, the *praanas* or vital airs are moving, but one does not know what is happening in or around one. One does not react in any way to any provocation during the sleep. One is inert and inactive like a log. Being the ever-conscious witness, one's nature cannot be this inertness. Discriminating thus, it is possible to transcend the vital sheath of life breath.

We have already seen that mind and intellect together with the senses are all the instruments of knowledge. They become activated by the life-force (*atma*) but are themselves devoid of intelligence. By reflecting upon this truth, the mind sheath and intellectual sheath can both be discarded as not representing the Self.

The last and the most subtle sheath gives the feeling of bliss. But this is so simply because of its immediate proximity to the Self within which is Bliss itself. So, even the sheath of bliss has to be transcended to reach the Self.

The five senses of action (*karmendriyas*), tongue, hands, feet, etc, being the component parts of the physical body, are also inert. Although action is performed through them, that is to say, they are the instruments of action, they have no awareness of their own. As such, they can also not qualify to represent our reality, the Self which is Blissful Awareness, *Shiva*.

O Divine Mother Sai! Vouchsafe unto me the necessary strength and make my effort fruitful. Through Thy Grace, leaving untruth, may I realise the Truth.

QUESTIONS:

(1) What is the purpose of Self-realisation and what is the chief impediment in this path?
(2) How can that which is known lead us to that which appears to be the unknown?
(3) What is the act of death and what lessons does it teach?
(4) What is the difference between the body and the soul?
(5) How can one proceed on the path of Self-enquiry?
(6) What is sleep? How does the experience of the 'deep-sleep' state differ from that of the 'wakeful' state?
(7) "Mind is the root cause of our problems." Discuss.
(8) What is mind and what forms can it take?
(9) "Mind can be used to kill the mind." Discuss.
(10) What are the five senses of perception, what role do they play and what is their relationship with the Self?
(11) What are the five Primordial Elements and their characteristics? What is their inter-relationship and their relationship with the body?

(12) What are the gross, the subtle and the causal bodies and why are they so named? What is their relationship with the various states of awareness.
(13) What are the five sheaths and what is it that they cover?
(14) What are the five senses of action and what role do they play?

God is all-pervading, but yet, we have some scientists who assert, "We have searched all outer space, we have looked for Him on the moon; no, He is nowhere to be found. He does not exist." They do not know what to seek and where, still, they have the impudence to assert that it is not found. Is God an occupant of an identifiable body or form; has He a habitation and a habiliment that is traditionally His? God is all this and more; He is in all this and beyond. He is the inner motivator of the very scientist who "denies" Him! Man himself is God; all matter, even in the moon, is suffused with the Divine Presence. To search for God with the instruments in the laboratory is like trying to cure pain in the stomach by pouring drops into the eye! There is a technique and a special instrument for that purpose which the past Masters in that science have developed and spoken about. Equip yourselves with a clear eye through detachment and love, sharpen your sense of discrimination so that it has no prejudice or predilection, then you can see God in you, around you, in all that you know and feel and are.

– Sri Sathya Sai Baba

> *"Self-enquiry is not the mind's inspection of its
> own contents; it is tracing the mind's first mode,
> the I-thought to its source which is the Self".*
>
> *Maharshi Raman*

17. KNOWLEDGE OF THE SELF – 2

Realization of the Self is not alien to us, nor is it something which is to be gained afresh. We are already the Self; in fact Self alone is. The Self is the all-pervading Reality, yet it is not perceived by those whose vision is beclouded by ignorance, just as the blind do not see the resplendent sun. It is the ignorance that makes us imagine that we are other than the Self. When this ignorance is removed through Self-enquiry, our eternal Self stands revealed in all its glory. The greatest obstruction to the removal of this ignorance, as discussed earlier, is the false identification of I, the Self, with the body. As long as the body-consciousness, the ego, exists, it is said, a body will continue to be available, since body is the carrier for the ego. When the body-sense drops off, body will no longer be needed. Remember, body cannot exist without the Self, whereas the Self can, and in fact always does, exist without the body.

That Self who is free from impurities, from old age and death, from grief, thirst and hunger, whose desire is true and whose desires come true - that Self, proclaims the *Chandogya Upanishad,* is to be sought after and enquired about, that Self is to be realised.

"The *Devas* (gods or angels) and the *Asuras* (demons or titans) both heard of this Truth. They thought: 'Let us seek after and realize this Self, so that we can obtain all the worlds and the fulfilment of all desires.'

Thereupon Indra (from the *Devas*) and Virochana (from the *Asuras*) approached Prajapati, the famous teacher. They lived with him as pupils for thirty-two years. Then Prajapati asked them: 'For what reason have you both lived here all this time?'

They replied: 'We have heard that one who realizes the self obtains all the worlds and all his desires. We have lived here because we want to be taught the Self.'

Prajapati said to them; 'The person who is seen in the eye - that is the Self.

That is immortal, that is fearless and that is *Brahman*.'

'Sir,' enquired the disciples, 'who is seen reflected in water or in a mirror?'

'He, the *Atman*,' was the reply. 'He indeed is seen in all these.' Then Prajapati added: 'Look at yourselves in the water, and whatever you do not understand, come and tell me.'

Indra and Virochana pored over their reflections in the water, and when they were asked what they had seen of the Self, they replied: 'Sir, we see the Self; we see even the hair and nails.'

Then Prajapati ordered them to put on their finest clothes and look again at their 'selves' in the water. This they did and when asked again what they had seen, they answered: 'We see the Self, exactly like ourselves, well adorned and in our finest clothes.'

Then said Prajapati: 'The Self is indeed seen in these. That self is immortal and fearless, and that is *Brahman*.' And the pupils went away, pleased at heart.

But looking at them, Prajapati lamented thus: 'Both of them departed without analysing or discriminating, and without comprehending the true Self. Whoever follows this false doctrine of the Self must perish.'

Satisfied that he had found the Self, Virochana returned to the *Asuras* and began to teach them that the bodily self alone is to be worshipped, that the body alone is to be served, and that he who worships the ego and serves the body gains both worlds, this and the next. And this in effect is the doctrine of the *Asuras*.

But Indra, on his way back to the *Devas*, realized the uselessness of his knowledge. 'As this Self,' he reflected, 'seems to be well adorned when the body is well adorned, well dressed when the body is well dressed, so too will it be blind if the body is blind, lame if the body is lame, deformed if the body is deformed. Nay more, this same Self will die when the body dies. I see no good in such knowledge.' So Indra returned to Prajapati for further instruction. Prajapati compelled him to live with him for another span of thirty-two years; after which he began to instruct him, step by step, as it were.

Prajapati said; 'He who moves about in dreams, enjoying and glorified - he is the Self. That is immortal and fearless, and that is *Brahman*.'

Pleased at heart, Indra again departed. But before he had rejoined the other angelic beings, he realized the uselessness of that knowledge also. 'True it is,' he thought within himself, 'that this new Self is not blind if the body is blind, not lame, nor hurt, if the body is lame or hurt. But even in dreams the Self is conscious of many sufferings. So I see no good in this teaching.'

Accordingly he went back to Prajapati for more instruction, and Prajapati made him live with him for thirty-two years more. At the end of that time Prajapati taught him thus: 'When a person is asleep, resting in perfect tranquillity, dreaming no dreams, then he realizes the Self. That is immortal and fearless, and that is *Brahman*.'

Satisfied, Indra went away. But even before he had reached home, he felt the uselessness of this knowledge also. 'When one is asleep,' he thought, 'one does not know oneself as "This is I." One is not in fact conscious of any existence. That state is almost annihilation. I see no good in this knowledge either.'

So Indra went back once again to be taught. Prajapati made him stay with him for five years more. At the end of that time Prajapati taught him the highest truth of the Self.

'This body,' he said, 'is mortal, forever in the clutch of death. But within it resides the Self, immortal, and without form. This Self, when associated in consciousness with the body, is subject to pleasure and pain; and so long as this association continues, no man can find freedom from pains and pleasures. But when the association comes to an end, there is an end also of pain and pleasure. Rising above physical consciousness, knowing the Self as distinct from the sense-organs and the mind, knowing Him in his true light, one rejoices and one is free."

There are *Devas* and *Asuras* (ie good and bad qualities) in all of us. We should cultivate the good qualities and weed out the bad. In this way, we will be able to peel off the layers of ignorance, and when its last vestige has been removed, Self shall stand revealed as Truth, Light and Beauty.

The third verse of *"Nirvaana-shatkam"* is:

(3) *Na may dwesha–raagau na may lobha–mohau*
Mado naiva may naiva maatsarya bhaavah
Na dharmo na chaartho na kaamo na mokhshah
Chidaananda roopah Shivoham, Shivoham

Translation: "I do not suffer from, nor am I subject to *dwesha* (hatred), *raaga* (desire), *lobha* (greed), *moha* (delusion), *mada* (pride, egoism) and *maatsarya* (malice). I have no need for *dharma* (righteousness, truth), *artha* (wealth), *kaama* (desire) or *mokhsha* (liberation). I am the Blissful Awareness *Shiva*, the Auspiciousness itself".

When the mind thinks of objects, attachment to the objects is forged; from attachment desire is born; from desire unfulfilled, arises anger. From anger comes delusion; from delusion the loss of memory; from the loss of memory the destruction of discrimination; from the destruction of discrimination, one perishes completely. For the one who is thus invaded by these disturbances and whose mind is therefore not tranquil and steady, there is no knowledge of the Self.

The mind becomes bound with attachment when it dwells upon an object or desire, it likes or dislikes. To break loose from such bondage, the mind should be trained not to dwell on any object nor to desire it or dislike it. It is the mind that binds and unbinds. But since we have already established that the mind is not the Self, that is to say that 'I' have no mind, the aberrations of the mind like hatred, desire, malice, etc, cannot have anything to do with 'Me' either.

Likewise the four *purushaarthas* (principal objectives) of human life, ie, righteousness, wealth, legitimate desire and liberation, are only the means of leading to the eventual realisation of the Self, and to that extent therefore are to be actively pursued. However, they do not constitute the Self itself. Baba says that wealth is to be earned through righteous means and put only to righteous use, and the desire has to be directed towards only the attainment of liberation, the goal. Through righteousness and liberation, the means and the goal, in this way, both wealth and desire are sanctified and given their correct place.

What is highlighted in this verse is the fact that, for the Self, the *atma*, there is nothing to be achieved, and so it has no limbs. *Atma* is inactive. Mind and the senses become activated by the very presence of the *atma*, but *atma* does not get anything done with them. Self or *atma* is merely the Witness.

(4) *Na punyam na paapam na soukhyam na duhkham*
Na mantro na teertham na Veda na yagnyah
Aham bhojanam naiva bhojyam na bhokhta
Chidaananda roopah Shivoham, Shivoham

Translation: "I am not subject to *punyam* (virtue) or *paapam* (sin), nor to *soukhyam* (pleasure) or *duhkham* (pain). I have no need for *mantra* (scared formula for liberation) or *teertham* (pilgrimage to a holy place), *Veda* (knowledge about God) or *yagna* (sacrifice). I am neither *bhojanam* (the process of eating), *bhojyam* (item of food, eatable) nor *bhokhta* (the eater of food). I am the Blissful Awareness *Shiva*, the Auspiciousness pure and simple".

The mind seeks *sukha* or happiness; it feels that happiness can be got in this world from fame, riches, power, property or from other individuals or relatives; further it builds up pictures of heaven where there is more intense happiness for a longer time; at last, it discovers that eternal undiminished happiness can be realised only by dwelling on the reality of one's own Self (*atma*) which is bliss itself.

Heaven and hell are the results of actions; they are objects made, and so they cannot be eternal; they are conditioned by birth, growth, decay and death. They do not exist from the very beginning; they were made; before that act, they were not. That which once was not and later will not be is as good as "not" even in the present.

Joy and grief, good and bad belong to the realm of the mind, not to 'I'. 'I' am not the doer nor the enjoyer of the fruits of the deeds. 'I' am ever-free. Joy and grief are, like right and wrong, to be transcended. Affection and hatred are of the nature of the internal instruments of man. They do not belong to the "resident" who lives with them, the Self or the *atma*, the essential reality of the individual.

Since 'I' am ever-free, what need can 'I' have for a sacred formula for liberation or a pilgrimage to a holy place. To the one who has known the Self, even all the *Vedas* are of as much use as is a pool of water in a place where there is an ocean. This does not, however, mean that the *Vedas* are useless. Only for the Self-realised are the *Vedas* of no use, because he is in possession of the infinite knowledge of the Self; to the neophyte, of course, they are the very life-breath.

The physical body is the gift of food. It is built-up on and sustained by food. It is ever in a flux; it was not before birth, nor will it be after death! It is perishable any moment. How can this gross physical frame of plasma and pus be the pure, the self-luminous, the ever witnessing atma, the Self? So, 'I' am neither the food, nor the eater of the food because both these are subject to change and decay. As 'I' am neither of these, 'I' cannot be the process of eating either, because its existence is dependent upon the other two only. 'I' am indeed the Blissful Awareness *Shiva*.

(5)   *Na may mrityu shanka na may jaati bheda*
       Pitaa naiva may naiva maata na janma
       Na bandhu na mitram gurur naiva shishyam
       Chidaananda roopah Shivoham, Shivoham

Translation: "Thought of *mrityu* (death) does not bother me, nor does the *bheda* (difference) of *jaati* (caste) concern Me. Father (*pitaa*) and mother (*maata*) I have not, nor indeed have I birth (*janma*). I have no *bandhu* (relations) nor *mitram* (friends). I am neither *guru* (teacher) nor *shishya* (taught). I am ever Blissful Awareness *Shiva*, the Auspiciousness itself".

The Self (*atma*) that resides in the body, unlike the body, is permanent and sacred. This sacred aspect of *atma* has neither birth nor death, nor attachment.

Creation or birth takes place only in the dimension of time and space; what is born or created must, in time, also die or be dissolved. That is the 'eternal' law. Consider the example of food. Wholesome, appetising food eaten with relish the night before turns into unwholesome, obnoxious refuse the morning after. This change from the wholesomeness to unwholesomeness is brought about by the passage of time. In fact, the change is projected by time. If we were able to reverse the clock and bring the passage of time to a halt, then the decomposition of the food could also be arrested. In other words, stop or remove the dimension of time, change will also cease. It is clear from this that death is synonymous with time. Outside the dimension of time, there can be no change, and therefore no death. For birth, and therefore also death, time is the basis. This is the reason why the word '*kaala*', in *Sanskrit*, stands for time as well as death. With the birth of the body is born the ego, the body identification; when death occurs, it is the death of this ego. Since 'I' am not the body, why should 'I' be attached to it or indeed feel concerned at its death?

Likewise, caste and creed apply only to the body and are commonly associated with its birth. The differences in the caste and creed merely reflect differences in the stations and circumstances of the birth of the body. Once again, having established that the real 'I' is not the body, the differences of caste and creed can be of no concern to it.

Father and mother are instrumental in the birth of the body. But for 'I', which is different from the body, since there is no birth (and no death), there can be, and is, no father or mother. Other relationships and friendships are also referred to in the context of the body only. Since the body is not permanent, these relationships cannot be permanent either. With the death of the body, the relationships also die. "Considering the number of births you have come through", Baba says, "You have had countless mothers and fathers, wives and husbands, sons and daughters, friends and enemies; but are they subsisting today? Do those relatives remember the relationships? You are no one to them; they are nobodies to you. But you and they both have the Lord in common as the unchanging relative; He subsists throughout all the births; He is eternal. He watches over you from birth to birth. What greater tragedy can there be than forgetting such a Lord!" And this Lord is none other than the Self, the *atma*.

The concept of the teacher and the taught commonly implies the existence of knowledge with one and its absence with the other and its communication from one to the other. But knowledge is not alien to one's Self. 'I' the Blissful Awareness is knowledge itself which is not acquired through a process of learning but which stands revealed in its pristine glory the instant the veil of ignorance masking it is removed. This is the reason why the word for teacher in *Sanskrit* is *guru*. *Guru* means remover of ignorance rather than the giver of knowledge. Clearly, the implication is that the Self is all knowledge; knowledge is already contained within and not acquired from without. By the process of knowing, other things can be known but not knowledge itself. The lamp will not crave for another lamp to see itself nor will it crave for its own light. It has light, it is light that is all. It sheds light on other objects; it does not shed light on its light.

The last verse is:

> (6) *Aham nirvikalpo niraakaara roopo*
> *Vibhurvyaapi sarvatra sarvendriyaanaam*
> *Sadaa may samattwam na mukhtir na bandhaha*
> *Chidaananda roopah Shivoham, Shivoham*

Translation: "*Aham* (I) am *nir* (without) *vikalpa* (doubt) and my *roopa* (form, shape) is *niraakaara* (formless). I am *vibhur* (supreme), *vyaapi* (immanent) *sarvatra* (everywhere) and in *sarva* (all) *indriyaas* (senses). May (I am) *sadaa* (always, ever) *samattwam* (in equipoise) and *na* (neither) bothered by *mukhti* (liberation) *na* (nor) *bandhaha* (bondage, attachment) because 'I' am the Blissful Awareness *Shiva*, the Auspiciousness itself".

The experiences such as "I came; I went; I did", etc, come naturally to everyone. From these experiences it would appear as if the consciousness, "I", is the subject of those various acts. But actions such as 'coming' and 'going', etc, belong only to the body. And so, when one says "I came, I went", it amounts to saying that the body is "I". But can the body be said to

REALISATION

So close! so close! my darling, close to me!
Above, below, behind, before You be.
Around me, without me, within me, O me.
How deeply, immensely and intensely You be.
My baby, lover, father, sister, brother.
My husband, wife, my friend or foe, my mother;
O sweet, my Self, my breath, my day, my night,
Gay garments, O love, Thou changest anon,
How charming are colours at day-break put on.
I am way-ward and careless, but leave me not please.
Say, All to All, whom else shall I tease?
All objects desired, ambition and glee,
Were wayside mind, true, goal only Thee.
O home, sweet home, by bedstead support, —
My shelter, my rest, my prayer, my fort.
In Thee do I bathe and in Thee do I swim,
In Thee live and move and of Thee full to brim,
My Lord and my liege, my meat and my drink,
O ocean of nectar in Thee let me sink.
Why clothe and conceal You in veils and in halls?
Nude, nude, I do strip You of masks and the walls.
I think You and drink You, I feel You, conceal You,
I talk You, I walk You, I am You, reveal You.
In rainstorms of tears as lightning You flash.
On Thee, roaring wave of my laughter doth dash.
O lightning and rainstorm! O sunshine of smiles!
I catch Thee, and hold Thee despite all Thy guiles.

Rama (Swami Ram Tirth)

be the consciousness 'I', since the body was not before it was born, is made up of the five elements, is non-existent in the deep-sleep state, and becomes a corpse when dead? Can this body which is inert like a log of wood be said to shine as 'I'? Therefore, the 'I' consciousness which at first arises in respect of the body is referred to variously as self-conceit, egoity, nescience, etc. All the thoughts that appear in the mind, says Raman *Maharshi*, have as their basis the cognition of the form, 'I am the body'; thus, it is the rise of the body-identification that is the cause and source of the rise of all other thoughts. Therefore if the self-conceit or egoity which is the root of the illusion is destroyed, all other thoughts will perish completely.

When the mind reaches out through the senses towards objects and envelopes them, it assumes the form of those objects and we acquire knowledge about them. This is called a *vritti* or function. The five senses and the mind are all, therefore, instruments of knowledge. Just as the sun illumines the world and makes it active in a thousand ways, so also does the body-mind complex become activated and illumined by the effulgence of the *atma*. Just as the electric current, in spite of it not being visible or concrete, energises the machines and makes them operational, the *atmic* effulgence is the invisible activating current that makes the various components of the body-mind complex function. It is the Ear of the ear, the Eye of the eye. The wonder is that the *atma* is inactive and without qualifications; it does not get anything done with the mind and the senses, yet they get activated by the very presence of the *atma*! Just as the rays of the Sun are not aware at all of the activity they invoke, the *atma*, likewise, is not responsible for the activity of the senses. This is why it is referred to as the Witness.

The *atma*, the Self, which is without attributes, actionless, eternal, without desires and thought, unsullied, changeless, formless, always free, ever pure, which is unaffected by the dualities, dichotomies and relativities of the world, which is not measurable and can never be contained by limitations though it may appear to be so, is like space pervading all things within and without. It has neither birth nor death, nor beginning nor end. Thus, using the powers of logical reasoning one should be able to eliminate all that is non-Self and with the powers of intuition march towards the realisation of the Self, towards the realisation that 'I' am the Blissful Awareness *Shiva*, the Auspiciousness itself.

When the mind, the intellect and the senses (the instruments of perception) rest, the body-consciousness drops off, and the pluralistic phenomenal world of perceptions ceases to exists. Then there is nothing seen and no seer; only the Self, the Awareness remains. *Vivekachoodaamani*, verses 124 to 135, help us to understand the real nature of the Self or the *atma* as:

"That which never goes to sleep and is aware of everything that happens in the wakeful, the dream and the deep-sleep states; that which is aware of the presence or absence of the mind and its functions."

"That which sees all but is not itself the object of seeing; that which illumines the *buddhi* (intellect) but is not itself the subject for illumination."

"That by whose very presence are the senses activated." That by which the entire universe is pervaded but which is not itself pervaded by anything ... ."

"The atma, the Self is neither born, nor does it die; neither does it grow, nor does it decay; being eternal, it is not subject to change. Even when the body is destroyed, it does not cease to exist, like the space in the jar which, being independent of the jar, continues to exist even when the jar is broken."

Remember, mere intellectual knowledge of the Self and its self-effulgent nature does not confer awareness of the Self. As long as the duality of the subject and the object persists, there can be no realisation. It is only when the knower and the known coalesce, that it becomes Self-knowledge for, in that state, there is no other object for knowing, there is only the Self.

Keep your thoughts and mind at home and centred in the real Self, says *Swami* Ram Tirth, and the sweetest melodies will spring from it naturally, spontaneously, without effort. "Your Godhood is not a thing to be accomplished; Realisation is not a thing to be achieved, you have not to do anything to gain God-vision; you have simply to undo what you have already done in the way of forming dark cocoons of desires around you. Fear not, you are free. Even your seeming bondage is imposed by your freedom. To you no harm can accrue unless you invite it; no sword can cut unless you think that it cuts. There is no need of loving your shackles and chains as ornaments. Shake off vain fancies, burn up all crookedness, and what power is there under the sun which will not be only too thankful to get the privilege of unlacing your shoes? Assert your Godhood; fling into utter oblivion the little self, as if it had never existed. When the little bubble bursts, it finds itself the whole ocean. You are the whole, the Infinite, All. Shine in your pristine glory. For you, O perfect One, there is no duty, no action, nothing to be done; all nature waits on you with bated breath. The world thanks her stars to have the good fortune of paying you homage."

"Trust, trust the Self Supreme,
The restlessness of the soul is due
To faith in things that seem,
The things that fleet as fog or dew.

The way to keep you fresh and new,
To every secret treasure clue,
Is to assert the real Self
And to deny deluding pelf.

There is no duty to be done
For you, O Everything, O One.
Why chafe and worry o'er the work,
Feel, feel the Truth, anxiety shirk.

Believe not when the people say,
'Oh, what a fine game you play.'
Believe not, never, in their praise,
No, ne'er can acts degrade or raise.

I never did a personal deed,
Impersonal Lord I am indeed.
In vain the raving critics fought;
The dupes of senses know me not.

I am for each and all, the home,
I am the Om! the Om! the Om!
O happy, happy, happy Ram!
Serene and peaceful, tranquil, calm.

My joy can nothing, nothing mar,
My course can nothing, nothing bar;
My livery wears gods, man and birds,
My bliss supreme transcendeth words.

Here, there and everywhere;
There, where no more a 'Where?'
Now, ever, anon and then,
Then, when's no more a 'When?'

This, that and which and what;
That, that's above a 'What?'

> First, last and mind and high,
> The One beyond a 'Why?'.
>
> One, five and hundred, All,
> Transcending number, one and all,
> The subject, object, knowledge, sight,
> E'en that description is not right.
>
> Was, is and e'er shall be,
> Confounder of the verb 'to be'
> The sweetest Self, the truest Me,
> No Me, no Thee, no He.
>
> The Infinite is that, the Infinite this;
> And on and on, unchanged is Infinite.
> Goes out the Infinite from the Infinite,
> And there remains unchanged the Infinite.
>
> The outward loss betrays the Infinite,
> The seeming gain displays the Infinite;
> The going, coming, subtracting, adding,
> Are seeming mode and truth the Infinite."

Howsoever daunting the path of Self-realization may appear to be, remember this: will sustained, sincere effort ever fail to draw unto itself the Grace of the Lord? How can the effort be in vain and the goal beyond reach when the God within be the Guide Himself? If the Mother of the Universe be pleased, will anything be witheld from the earnest seeker? Remember also that, in reality, the Self remains realised at all times; what is often missing is merely the true recognition of that fact!

O Divine Mother Sai! Lead me kindly by Thy hand all the way.

QUESTIONS:

(1) "Body cannot exist without the Self but the Self can without the body". Discuss.
(2) "It is the mind that binds and unbinds". Explain.
(3) What are the four Principal Objectives of the human life and what is their relationship with the Self?
(4) What is the difference between the *deha* and the *dehi*?
(5) Who suffers the dualities of joy and grief, good and bad, etc, and how can these be transcended?

(6) How can the *atma*, the Self, the real 'I' be infinite if it is contained within a finite, defined body? Discuss.
(7) Body is sustained by the food we eat, what sustains the *atma* and why?
(8) What are birth and death? What is their relationship with time.
(9) Explain by example the difference between the temporary and permanent relationships.
(10) Is it possible to 'acquire' the knowledge of the Self?! Explain.
(11) We know that body grows with food, why do we refer to it as being inert?
(12) What is the source of all thoughts and how can thoughtlessness be achieved?
(13) How do the mind and the senses perform intelligent functions when they are themselves devoid of intelligence?
(14) How can the powers of logical reasoning and intuition be used in the enquiry about the Self?

He is in you, and it is God that has prompted you to project Him into the outer world, as this idol or this image, to listen to your outpouring and give you peace. Without the inspiration, solace and joy that He confers from within, you will be raving mad, as one who has lost his moorings and is tossed about, rudderless on a stormy sea. Hold on to Him in the heart, hear Him whisper in the silent words of counsel and consolation. Hold converse with Him, guide your footsteps as He directs, and you reach the goal safe and soon. The picture before which you sit, the flowers which you place on it, the hymns you recite, the vows you impose on yourselves, the vigils you go through – these are the activities that cleanse, that remove obstacles in the way of your becoming aware of the God within.
– Sri Sathya Sai Baba

> *"My Lord is the Lord of the Universe;*
> *My Guru is the Guru of the Universe;*
> *My Self, verily, is the Self of the Universe".*

Visvasaratantra Puraana

18. THE MASTER WITHIN

Man is another name for a Self-contained body. When God created man, He made him Self-sufficient. Since what is born must also die, creation, likewise, could only be conceived in the dimension of time and space which is subject to change and which obeys the laws of relativity. So that man may not be helplessly lost but be able to pick for himself the right path in the unending dichotomy of dualities, the Creator bestowed upon him the power of discrimination between the real and the unreal, and the evanescent and the eternal. Out of His infinite love, He provided him with the necessary wherewithal for a safe and successful journey in the space-time odyssey.

But, of what use could this power of discrimination be if, in the first instance, man did not possess the knowledge of what is changing and what is changeless, what is time-bound and what is time-less? We can therefore safely conclude that when man was let loose in the space-time continuum, he embodied within himself the necessary knowledge and the power to set himself free from the cycle of birth and rebirth.

The question then arises: If man is the repository of the knowledge he requires, of what use is there for a *guru*? The answer to this question can, in part, be found in its meaning which has been given by Baba as follows :

> *"Gukaaro gunaateetam, Rukaaro roopavarjitah*
> *Gukaaro andhakaarascha, Rukaaro tannivaaranah."*

'*Gu*' stands for *gunaateeta* (one who transcends the three *gunas*) while '*Ru*' stands for *roopavarjitah* (one who is formless). Also,"*Gu*'means the darkness of ignorance and '*Ru*', remover. What can dispel the darkness? Only light can do it. Therefore *guru* is the one who removes or dispels the darkness of ignorance – ignorance of the assumption that 'I' am the body. When the seeker is steeped in body-consciousness, *guru* appears as man to remove "I-am-the-body" notion in him. So, *guru* is useful to teach man the truth about himself. In choosing the *guru*, however, it is important to remember that no one who is bound himself can break the chains of some one else; one who is free, alone can free others. Once the body illusion is broken, the seeker then realises the Master to be none other than his own Self.

Through our constant gaze at and persistent dwelling upon the objects of the material world, we have allowed ourselves to be hypnotised by the world of matter into believing that our reality is the material body and that what we cannot touch, taste, smell, see or hear, does not exist. Man lays a great deal of store by the exclusiveness of his mental and intellectual prowess and material attainment. If only we viewed life in the light of the infinite potential of our spirit, we would realise that even our so called scientific inventions, however fantastic they may appear to be are, in reality, no more than a fumbling progression from one minuscule discovery to another! The first step, therefore, is to break this spell by understanding that the body belongs to *mrityu lok*, the world of change and death and so cannot be the reality. This can be achieved with the help of the outside *guru*.

The outside *guru* does not necessarily have to be in the form of man. As long as one has the inclination, the thirst and the earnestness to seek the truth, as well as a sharp eye for learning, the whole universe and its bountiful manifestation can impart the best teaching. Dattatreya, the acknowledged universal *guru*, proclaimed the whole world as his *guru*. If you look at evil you feel you should desist from doing it. So, he said evil was his *guru*. If you see good, you would wish to do it, so he said that good also was his *guru*; both good and evil, he said, were his *gurus*. It seems that he asked a hunter which way he should go, but the latter ignored his question, as he was intent upon his aim to shoot a bird above. Dattatreya saluted him, saying, "you are my *guru*! Though killing the bird is bad, keeping your aim so steadfast in shooting the arrow as to ignore my query is good, thereby teaching me that I should keep my mind steadfast and fixed on *Ishwara* (God). You are, therefore, my *guru*". In the same way he looked upon everything as his *guru* till, in the end, he said that his physical body itself was a *guru*, as its consciousness does not exist during sleep and the body that does not exist should therefore not be confused with the soul, ie, the feeling that the body is the soul. Therefore, that too was a *guru* for him. While he looked upon the whole world as his *guru*, the whole world worshipped him as its *guru*.

Baba says: "Ignorance (*ajnaana*) has two powers: the veiling power (*aavarna shakti*) and the projecting power (*vikshepa shakti*). It veils the reality and projects upon it the unreal (*abhan-aavarna*)." When a wise person and an ignorant meet, though the wise teaches that the soul (*atma*) is One and non-dual, the ignorant will deny it and he cannot grasp the reality so easily. Even when he hears the truth, he has not got the faith and the steadfastness to imbibe it and he will dismiss it with a shrug of indifference. This is the veil of falsehood (*asat-aavarna*). Now about the veil of delusion, the (*abhan-aavarna*). Even when the person believes by his study of the scriptures (*shaastra*) and by the grace of providence that there is non-dual *atma*, he dismisses it as non-existent, carried away by mere cursory and superficial arguments. Though he has the Consciousness (*Chitta*) which is aware of that very thing which he denies, the delusion (*moha*) makes him declare that it is non-existent. This is the sinister role of the veil of delusion."

"With regard to the veiling power (*vikshepa shakti*), though you are formless, changeless and your nature is bliss (*aananda*), you are deluded into believing, feeling and acting as if you are the body, which has form, which changes and which is the seat of pain and grief. You refer to yourself as the doer and the enjoyer; you speak of I, you, they, this, that, etc, and allow yourself to be deluded into believing variety and multiplicity, when there is only One. This illusion of projecting many on the One is called *vikshepa shakti* or *adhyaropa* (superimposition)."

Ignorance gives rise to doubts and doubts can multiply. So, in order to avoid wasting time and energy in flitting from one doubt to another, whilst still fully entrenched in the outer world of ignorance, it is essential to complement the removal of ignorance by turning our gaze inwards through a conscious effort. This leads to, what *Maharshi* Raman calls, the concept of 'Push and Pull'; the *guru* without gives the 'Push' and the master within 'Pulls' inwards towards the centre. Remember that the *guru* outside, being an external addition, cannot be real. For he who 'comes' will also have to 'go'. "If he be a stranger whom you await", says the *Maharshi*, "he is bound to disappear also". "What use is there of such a transient being. In other words, his role is limited. The fact is that *guru* is none other than the goal an aspirant seeks, ie, the Self. So, in reality, the Goal, Master and the Self are one and the same".

Sages and seers of old used to pray to be born at a time when they could witness on the physical plane, first hand, the Lord and the Master Himself at work. That we are able to do so now, how uniquely fortunate must we be! The *guru* without (*Sai*) and the Master within (God) are one and the same. Those of us who are alive to the appearance of the Light of Truth and Love on the horizon right now and are able to sanctify our lives thereby will, for aeons to come, be the envy of all mankind. Whereas those who turn their backs upon the Truth staring them in the face and let the events pass them by will have missed the golden chance to redeem themselves and will have no one else but themselves to blame. For those who may wish to dispel their doubts on this, the clue to the nature of the Master Within and how to recognise him is given in the following verse from the *Visvasaratantra Puraana*:

"*Brahmaanandam parama-sukhadam kevalam jnaana-moortim,
Dwandvaateetam gagana–sadrsham Tatt–twam–assyaadi-lakshyam;
Aikam nityam vimalam–achalam sarva–dhee saakshi–bhootam;
Bhaavaateetam triguna–rahitam sad–gurum tam namaami.*"

Translation: "Embodiment of the divine bliss, the bestower of the greatest beatitude, the absolute, the personification of the highest wisdom, who is beyond the pairs of opposites (like pleasure, pain, good, bad, etc) and untouched by evil; like the sky; whom 'Thou art That' and similar scriptural passages have in view; the One without the second, the eternal, the pure, the immovable, the Witness of all mental activity, abiding ever beyond thoughts and attributes, to that True *guru*, I make my obeisance".

The above verse mentions fourteen aspects of the true guru. In His Divine Love, *Bhagawan* Baba has given us the inner meaning of these aspects as follows.

"The first aspect is *Brahmaananda* (transcendental bliss). The type of joy that man experiences when he is happy, healthy and contented, the type of joy that he derives out of wealth, property, pleasures and fortune, is called *manushyaananda* (human joy). Hundred times more than *manushyaananda* is *Indraananda*; hundred times more than *Indraananda* is *Devendraananda*; hundred times more than *Devendraananda* is *Brihaspati aananda*; hundred times more than *Brihaspati aananda* is *Prajapati aananda*; and hundred times more than *Prajapati aananda* is *Brahmaananda*. In other words, *Brahmaananda* (transcendental bliss) is ten billion (ie 10^{10}) times more than *manushyaananda* (human joy)! This is the true measure of *Brahmaananda* which is beyond all human imagination. It transcends the material, moral, religious and spiritual aspects of life. All other joys are inherent in this bliss. The true *guru* is one who experiences the supreme bliss of *Brahmaananda*. Who is he! None except God has the competence to experience such bliss.

The second aspect is *parama sukhadam* (highest happiness). This happiness is higher than all the happiness in the world. It is not worldly happiness, which has a beginning and an end, is ever-changing and comes and goes. But *parama sukhadam* neither comes nor goes. The happiness which changes is not true happiness. All the pleasures enjoyed by man in this world change with time and place. The highest joy has its source and spring in the *atma*, the spark of the cosmic splendour. A true *guru* is one who is ever aware of *atma* and enjoys and confers changeless supreme happiness.

The third aspect of the *guru* is *kevalam* (the ultimate). It means that which transcends the limitations of time and space. All the things in the world are bound by time and space. But the true guru is beyond time and space, and his consciousness is all pervasive. That is why He is called *kevalam*. He is none other than God.

The fourth aspect identifies the true *guru* as *jnaanamoorti* (embodiment of wisdom). What is true wisdom ? Is it material or worldly knowledge, or knowledge of science ? No, all this knowledge is related to materials in the world. But, true wisdom is the basis for all types of knowledge and is beyond them. It is infinite, unmanifest and remains ever as the One. The wisdom is the vision of Oneness. Real wisdom is the vision of one's own true nature. Knowing oneself is true wisdom. One who knows himself is the wise one. He is none other than God. God is the very embodiment of wisdom. He is the very form of truth and infinite. *Satyam, jnaanam, anantam Brahma* (Brahma is Truth, Wisdom and Infinite).

Dwandvaateetam, the fifth aspect refers to the One who is unaffected by the inevitable dualities of heat and cold, happiness and sorrow, gain and loss, or praise and blame. God alone has this power, no one else - He is the true *guru*.

The sixth aspect compares the true *guru* to *gagana* or sky. Where is sky? It is all pervading. But 'sky' is not the sky, it is merely a combination of clouds. Sky is what provides the space for them. This sky (space) exists everywhere. The nature of this *aakaash* (sky, space) is sound. Wherever there is sound, there is space. Even inhalation and exhalation are sounds. Therefore, where is the place without space? There is no such place at all. Space is present everywhere. One who is subtler, even more omnipresent than space is God Himself. Therefore such a God is the true *guru*.

There are four great pronouncements (supreme statements) culled from the four *Vedas*. These are :

- "*Pragnaanam Brahma*" - This is the essence of **Rig Veda**;
- "*Aham Brahmaasmi*" - This is the essence of **Yajur Veda**;
- "*Tatt Twam Assi*" - This is the essence of **Sama Veda**;
- "*Ayam Atma Brahma*' - This is the essence of **Atharvana Veda**.

All these four great declarations point to one Divinity. Though they state and explain differently, their goal is One Divinity.

Pragna, in the first pronouncement, is the constant integrated awareness

FOOTPRINTS IN THE SANDS OF TIME

I dreamt that I was walking along the beach with the Lord, and across the sky flashed scenes from my life. For most of the scenes which were reminiscent of the happier days of my life, I noticed two sets of footprints in the sand; one belonged to me and the other to the Lord. There were also many times along the path of my life when only one set of footprints could be seen in the sand. This, I also noticed, happened at the very hardest and saddest times of my life. This really bothered me and I questioned the Lord about it, "Lord, You promised me that once I decided to follow You, You would walk with me all the way. But I noticed that during the most troublesome times of my life, there has been only one set of footprints. I don't understand why, in times when I needed You most, You should have left me on my own." The Lord replied, "If only you knew how dearly I love you and would never, never leave you; during your times of trials and tribulations, when there was only one set of footprints to be seen, it was then My precious, precious child, that I carried you."

Anon

which is present in all the living and the non-living alike. Awareness is complete knowledge - knowledge of the principle that is immanent in the living and the non-living alike. Actually, *Pragna* and *Brahmam* are synonymous. *Brahmam* is immanent in the whole cosmos; it means pervasiveness.

Aham in the second pronouncement is taken to connote 'I'. But it has another meaning also. It is witness. He is witness to everything. He is the *atma*. *Aham* is the very form of *atma*. The Awareness or Consciousness which is present everywhere is installed as *atma* in man. *Atma*, Consciousness and *Brahma* are not different. Just as cloth, thread and cotton are in essence the same, so also the same principle takes upon the names of *Atma*, *Brahman* or *Aham* at different times and situations. Therefore, the second statement means that the witness *Atma* or 'I' in me is *Brahmam* Himself.

The third statement underlines the fact that the one without the *upadhi* (body) *'Tatt'* and the one with the body *'twam'*, ie, *Deva* (God) and *jeeva* (individual), are one and the same.

The fourth statement depicts the oneness of the three persons - the one you think you are (the body), the one others think you are (the mind) and the one you really are (the *atma*). You act with the body, think with the mind and you witness both as the *atman*....

The real *guru* is the very embodiment of the divine principle, which is the inner meaning of these four great pronouncements. He is the one who has experienced and enjoyed the essence of these declarations comprising the seventh aspect (*Tatt - twam - assyaadi - lakshyam*) and takes upon Himself to teach the same.

'Aikam' (one) is the eighth aspect. *Brahmam* (God) is the One without the second; all other things are merely diverse manifestations. A *guru* is one who has recognised that the many exist in the One. The *guru* is *aikam* (the One) and it is God Himself.

The ninth aspect is *'nityam'* - the eternal, untouched by time, the One who never changes under any circumstances... He has neither birth nor death, neither beginning nor end. He is God Himself : He is the *guru*.

'Vimalam' - faultless, without any impurity - is the tenth aspect. True *guru* is He who is pure, unsullied and sacred; he is not tainted by anything worldly; He has no desire or sense of want. He remains ever pure like fire. Such a *guru* is God.

Eleventh aspect of the true *guru* is '*achalam*' - steady and motionless. He need not move anywhere, because He is here, there and everywhere.

'*Sarvadhee saakshi bhootam,*' witness of everything, is the twelfth aspect. True *guru* is like the light shining which remains unaffected by any changes taking place on the stage. It remains as a mere witness. The *guru* is such an Eternal Witness, all pervasive, all activating intelligence.

Last but one aspect of the true *guru* is '*bhaavaateetam*', transcending mental comprehension and verbal explanation. None can explain His nature. He is beyond all emotions, feelings and thoughts.

The last aspect of the true *guru* is '*trigunarahitam*' - beyond the influence of the three qualities (*gunas*) - *sattwa*, *rajas* and *tamas*, the serene, the active and the dull modes. These are the characteristics of Nature. Wherever these qualities exist, happiness and sorrow follow - when these three are absent, there is neither happiness nor sorrow. When bound by these, you are human; when free from entanglements and limiting characterizations, you are divine. Who is beyond these qualities ? He is God; He is the true *guru*."

The true *guru* or the Master Within is of the form of *sat* (eternal existence), *chit* (total awareness) and *aananda* (absolute bliss) ie, the Self, the *Sai* within. No darkness or ignorance can coexist with it. It needs no oratory to proclaim Itself, nor to convince or to convert. It stands by Itself ever shining in its own effulgent glory! Mere contact with It is enough.

"No knowledge comes from outside"; says *Swami* Vivekananda, "it is all inside". "What we say a man 'knows' should, in strict psychological language, be what he 'discovers' or 'unveils'; what a man 'learns' is really what he 'discovers' by taking the cover off his own soul, which is a mine of infinite knowledge. We say Newton discovered gravitation. Was it sitting anywhere in a corner waiting for him? It was in his own mind; the time came and he found it out". "... the advance of knowledge is made by the advance of this process of uncovering. The man from whom this veil is being lifted is the more knowing man; the man upon whom it lies thick is ignorant; and the man for whom it has entirely gone is all-knowing, omniscient".

All knowledge does not just exist in the Self; Self is All knowledge. Eternal Existence and Absolute Bliss are also native to it. The fact that man is ever in search of knowledge, immortality and happiness rather than ignorance, death and unhappiness is proof positive of the communication from the Master Within. The Master Within speaks in the language of silence and it is through the medium of silence alone that it can be heard and reached. Silence is stillness of mind. Thoughts and desires cause agitation, agitation means movement and movement is accompanied by sound. Supervention of mind, therefore, is responsible not only for putting up an obstruction to the communication from the Master, but through its contact with the outside phenomenal world, it also distorts the Truth into the shape of desires, preferences and prejudices.

For communication between different persons, ie, when duality exists, language of the spoken word is required; when there is no duality, ie, for communion with the Self, there can be no need for verbal communication, it is the language of silence that is necessary. In fact silence is interrupted by speaking, for words obstruct this mute language. Baba says: "The illumination of soul is silence (*mounam*)! How can there be silence without the *atma* being illuminated? Silence is ever with you. What you have to do is only to remove all things that disturb it!" Silence, the ever speaking perennial flow of language, it is said, is unceasing eloquence and more emphatic than all the scriptures put together. It is the best language; when words cease, silence prevails. "What is better", *Maharshi* Raman asks, "preaching loudly and without effect or to sit silently sending inner force?" "Again, how does speech arise? There is abstract knowledge, whence arises the ego, which in turn gives rise to thoughts and thoughts to the spoken word. So, the word is the great-grandchild of the original source. If the word can produce a great impact, judge for yourself, how much more powerful must be the preaching through silence! ...."

The following verse from Shankara's '*Dhakshinamurti Stotram*' further underlines the power of silence.

> *Chittram vata-taruh moolay vriddha shishyaa gurur–yuvaa,*
> *Guru–astu mounam vyaakhyaanam shishyaastu chhinna samshayah.*

Translation: "How strange a sight! Youthful Master and elderly disciples seated under a banyan tree; the Master's communication is silence and yet the disciples have all their doubts dispelled!"

Silence also charges our spiritual batteries. Einstein has been the greatest scientist of this century; who was his teacher? Who are the teachers of the sages and the seers? Greatest sages uncover the most subtle and sublime, supreme spiritual truths but only in moments of deep silent reflection. Greatest scientists make marvellous discoveries but only in moments of inspired silence. This is because through silence alone can the Master Within, ie, the Self, be contacted, and since the Self is total Awareness itself, no knowledge can exist outside it. To be awake to the eternal Self, however, presents a problem. According to *Maharshi* Raman, because our conscious experience is now limited to the duration of the extroversion (contact with the outside world) of the mind, we call the present moment the 'wakeful' state, whereas all the while, our mind has been asleep to (not in contact with) the Self, and therefore we are now really fast asleep. Furthermore, the mind would also have us believe that we have no awareness during the 'deep-sleep' state although we exist in that state. But of what value is the testimony of the mind about our existence or experience during 'deep-sleep' if during that state it was absent. "Remember," says *Maharshi* Raman," existence and awareness are not two different things but one and the same. However, if for any reason you feel constrained to admit the fact that you existed in 'deep-sleep', be sure you were also aware of that existence. What you were really unaware of in sleep is your bodily existence. You are confounding this bodily awareness with the true Awareness of the Self which is eternal ...." "The Self is beyond the three states, because it can subsist without them and in spite of them". "...The mind and its three states are unreal and that you are the eternal, infinite Consciousness of pure Being, the Self".

To conclude: The Master Within is, by its very presence, pouring out instruction constantly and continuously through the language of silence. The difficulty lies in not being able to hear that voice. But rather than disproving the existence of the Master (Sai, God) Within, it simply proves that we are either not listening to Him or that we have grown used to and are therefore more readily able to recognise, by the sheer force of habit, other sounds (of outer world) to which we keep our ears pitched. Consequently, we find ourselves out of tune and out of frequency with the inner voice. However, on rare occasions, when we find ourselves feeding a hungry beggar, helping a blind man cross a busy road, attending on a sick and ailing old person and wiping the tears of orphaned children, shedding tears at others' pain and feeling happy at others' joy, and all this spontaneously, without premeditation or being motivated by reward or recognition, we then know that we are in tune with the inner voice coming from the Master Within. Ask not a man in pain the name of his religion, look not for the colour of his skin, seek not to know the size of his purse, crave not for reward or recognition; respond instead, in humility, with eyes full of kindness and heart full of love, with prayers on the lips and hands ready to serve, and be thankful for the chance given. When we experience love, for its own sake, welling up in our hearts saturating our every thought, word and deed, without any trace of intervention or calculation on the part of the mind, it is in those inspired moments of grace that we not only walk in the company of God but we truly affirm our godhood.

Bhagawan Baba has given us the following four directive for sanctifying our lives and purifying our mind, so that we can contact God, the Master within:

Tyaja durjana samsargam: Give up the company of the wicked;
Bhaja saadhu samaagamam: Welcome the chance to be among the good;
Kuru punyam ahoraatram: Do good deeds day and night;
Smara nityam - anityataam:Remember what is lasting and what not.

"Man is consumed by time; God is the master of time. So, take refuge in God. Let God be your guru, your path, your Lord. Adore Him, obey His commands, offer Him your grateful homage, hold Him fast in your memory. This is the easiest way to realise Him as your own reality. This is the one and only way."

O Divine Mother Sai! Remove the veil of ignorance that envelops me in darkness and let the Light of Truth, Goodness and Beauty reign supreme.

QUESTIONS:

(1) How is man equipped for the pilgrimage of life?
(2) Who or what is a *guru*? What is the need for a *guru*?
(3) Why is the phenomenal world referred to as the *mrityu lok*, the world of death?
(4) What are the characteristics of a disciple and a *guru*?
(5) Discuss the concept of "Push and Pull".
(6) What is the difference between the *guru* without and the MasterWithin?
(7) How will you recognise the Master Within?
(8) In what language does the Master Within communicate and why?
(9) List some of the greatest 'inventions' of man!
(10) What do you mean by extroversion of mind? What is introversion?
(11) "The realised 'sleep' when the world is 'awake' and when the world is 'asleep' they are awake". Discuss.
(12) We are able to affirm our existence in 'deep-sleep' state only through circumstantial evidence and not by direct experience, why?

"Bear all and do nothing;
Hear all and say nothing
Give all and take nothing;
Serve all and be nothing."

Sri Sathya Sai Baba

19. PRINCIPLE OF SURRENDER

There are two aspects to the human personality: a phenomenal ego and the Eternal Self. Ego (*ahamkaara*) is born of mind and manifests itself in terms of the attachment to the body; that is why it is often referred to as the knot between the Self and the body (*jada-chaitanya-granthi*), whereas the Eternal Self, the Essential Man is the life-force, the spark of divinity within. The purpose of life on earth is the realisation of the Self. Annihilation of the ego and the dissolution of the mind are variously referred to as liberation (*mokhsha*), realisation of the Self, union with God or simply surrender.

In common parlance, surrender means relinquishing one's possessions and control. It connotes loss of freedom, bondage and servitude. That is why the term "surrender" generally meets with a certain amount of suspicion and reticence. In the spiritual sense, however, surrender means overcoming the delusion of the mind, sublimating the ego and restoring the native sovereignty of the Self; it signifies freedom and supremacy. The former amounts to an unwelcome imposition from the outside and represents defeat, whereas the latter amounts to an assertion of the native aspiration and signals victory.

It is often claimed that man has the freedom of thought and action including the freedom to err. God has also granted man the power of discrimination between good and bad, right and wrong, eternal and evanescent, etc. It is in exercise of this freedom of choice, it is argued, that man is seen to perform acts which can be construed as good, bad or indifferent. Whether, and to what extent, this claim is true will be discussed later; for the present, however, let us assume that man has the freedom of thought and action as claimed, and see where such a claim leads to.

If we take a panoramic view of world affairs today, it is not difficult to realise that, in the pursuit of his own selfish ends and with total disregard for the needs of others, man is racing towards the brink of disaster. He has forgotten how to tap the fountain-head of absolute knowledge and infinite bliss within himself and is therefore unable to discover his true strength.

Man's fall from grace is essentially the consequence of the misuse of his 'free' will. Far from being chained by the shackles imposed by some mythical, merciless monster, man is bound by the fetters of his own misguided indulgence. It is an accepted fact that man has an insatiable thirst for and is therefore ever in search of the secrets of long life, total knowledge and unending happiness, these being the natural attributes of the Self. Since, *sat*, *chit* and *aananda* are native to us, it therefore stands to reason that no one would, knowingly, lead oneself to despair and disaster. It would also appear then that mistaken is the belief of man if he thinks that *sat*, *chit* and *aananda* can either be acquired from without or secured through power and pelf. In spite of his 'freedom' of thought and the power of discrimination, which if used judiciously could enable man to realise his native divinity, there appears to be a kind of distortion of vision and miscalculation which are responsible for the plight of man today. Given that he is relentlessly pursuing an insane course towards disaster and appears to be unable or unwilling to alter it, is there no hope for his redemption? Is God not likely to intervene in the affairs of man, His own creation?

Well, God created the whole universe; He also created man and gave him 'freedom'. That He is all powerful, He can make or unmake, do or undo anything if He so wills, is beyond doubt. The question is not whether He can intervene, for nothing in this universe is impossible for Him nor beyond His reach, but, whether He will do so. For, if He stepped into the affairs of man, would His help, even though well meaning and benign, not be perceived by the jaundiced vision of man as being unsolicited and therefore as an act of interference? Besides, is He likely to break or transgress His own rule or take back the gift He has willingly made to man? If He is, what then, it could be argued, would be the point in bestowing the gift in the first place and could it, in that case, be called freedom?

So, if man finds himself helpless in bringing order into his life and God will not make an unsolicited intervention, is all hope lost? Thankfully not! Divine intervention is possible but only if, out of his own free will, man earnestly invites the Lord to take over his affairs. In verse 66 of the eighteenth canto of the *Bhagavad Geeta*, Lord Krishna assures Arjuna, the representative man, thus:

"*Sarvadharmaan parityajya maamekam sharanam vraja;*
Aham twaa sarvapaapebhyo mokhshayishyaami maa shuchah."

Translation: "Abandoning all allegiances and attachments, take refuge in Me alone; I will liberate thee from all sins, grieve not."

Only if man surrenders his will totally in favour of the Divine Will, will the Lord intervene. As long as the slightest feeling in man that he may be able to devise a way by which to put his affairs in order, persists, God will not step in but will allow him to sort things out for himself through his own experience; after all, the mess man finds himself in, is of his own making. Not even when, out of sheer desperation, may man lament: "I give up, O Lord! I know not where my duty lies; I am confused," will He intervene, because doing so could easily be misconstrued as an act of exploitation of the helplessness of man. However, if the cry is earnest and the anguish heartfelt, God will take the first step which is to remove the confusion and point out to the errant man where his duty lies. It is only after all the doubts have been dissolved and the helplessness has gone, when man has regained his composure and strength, and is able to surrender completely in the knowledge that all is the Will of God, that He will take over, and not before. But God "taking over" surely cannot mean that, having uttered the magic words, "I surrender", man can sit back and do nothing. If it is the affairs of man that have to be put right then, whether he likes it or not, man has to be the principal and active participant; he cannot delegate action to someone else or abdicate his duty. Surrender does not imply giving up of action but only renouncing the fruit thereof. If God be the doer, how can man lay claim to the fruit? If a scholar writes the magnum opus, how can the pen expect to get the credit for it? However efficient and proficient one may consider oneself to be, in reality one is merely an instrument in the hands of the Lord. To think otherwise is sheer folly.

However, for the Lord's instructions to be understood and carried out implicitly, man has to be fully receptive and without any reservations; for the Lord's Will to prevail, there has to be total absence of any intervention from the mind of man. Unfortunately, man finds himself subjugated by the mind to such an extent that he is unable to summon his powers of discrimination. In that state, when man is unable to sublimate the waywardness of his mind and take the right decision, he is prone to falling a prey to the **A**ttachment, **I**llusion, **D**elusion **S**yndrome, ie, contracting the **'AIDS'** disease.

In Chapter 15, it was established that the body, on its own, is no better than a corpse. It comes alive and functions only due to the presence of the life - force (*praana*) in it. Without the life-force the body is worthless. However, it is the attachment of mind with body that is responsible for the mistaken identity of I, the real Self, with the body. Once 'I' is identified as the body, then the possessive tendency, 'mine', does not lag far behind. In fact, 'I' leads to 'mine'. So, attachment with the body causes the malaise of 'I' and 'mine' and is responsible for our distorted vision. The statements like: 'This is my body', 'That is my house', 'He is my friend', etc, are attributable to the mind alone. We must remember that these have no relevance to the life-force (*atma*), because the life-force needs no body, no home, etc; it is Self-sufficient. Whereas the body and the senses need a location habitation, and they cannot exist without the life-force, the life-force itself does not depend on the body for its existence; it always exists.

The attachment to the body also causes the 'illusion' of seeing the 'unreal' as the real: perceiving the manifested universe as the reality with great gusto and, sadly, ignoring the underlying reality with extreme neglect. And all because the former can be perceived through the senses and so the mind asserts its existence whereas the total inadequacy of such tools to comprehend the latter conveniently leads the mind to proclaim its non-existence! What an operator this mind!

The attachment and the illusion further lead to the 'delusion' of doership. Man assumes doership, although he may tend to be selective about it at times. Whenever our planned activity meets with success, our mind is quick to stamp its doership on it but only because of the success achieved. It conveniently chooses to ignore the ninety-nine other activities which were similarly planned and executed but which failed to achieve success. As discussed in Chapter 13, this should surely bring home to us the fact that there is a deeper, more profound intelligence than our individual mind at work, that things happen not in response to our command but at some One else's behest, and that we are merely the instruments.

Evolving from the animal, Baba says, man developed the mind and in due course was able to discover whatever was necessary for his comforts. "He discovered many things but could not discover the cause of birth and death. Death is certain for one who is born, but one does not know whether a dead person is born again. What is the secret of this phenomenon? The ancient sages sought to unravel the mystery of birth, death and rebirth. They found that this secret is beyond the power of man; they realised that this was due to Divine Will and not the result of human effort. If one wants to live, can he live as long as he wants? A man may consider himself healthy and strong and think that he will live for at least ten more years. But he may die the same night in a car accident. Is health the cause of longevity? No. What then is the means of preventing death? Not our health; not our own abilities and devices; nor all our various possessions. The root cause of death is Divine Will."

"Innumerable things are happening in the world without any effort on man's part. Is man doing anything for the functioning of his heart, or for his continuous respiration? Is he in any way responsible for the circulation of blood in his body? These are not dependent on human effort. They are the result of Divine Will....Do not concern yourself as to when death will happen, where and how. No one can alter what is destined by the Will of the Divine."

Over five millennia ago, on the *Kurukshetra* battlefield, Arjuna the great hero, uncharacteristically, displayed faint-heartedness in the face of the enemy. The reason for his loss of nerve was that he too fell victim to the AIDS disease. As long as he perceived himself as a body-mind complex, he remained infatuated with worldly attachments, got confused by the illusory world and inevitably suffered from the delusion of doership. Amongst those arrayed opposite him ready to do battle were those whom he called his kinsmen, teachers, friends, etc, and for whom he had nurtured attachments in his heart. This befogged his vision. He took the manifested diversity, which was apparent to his mind and senses, to be the reality and so the underlying Reality, the One-ness, the unseen *atmic* principle, eluded him. Having allowed himself to be caught in this illusion thus, the prospect of taking up arms against his 'near and dear ones' and the consequences of incurring the sin of killing them unnerved him.

Man gets confused when he becomes egocentric. "*Aham karomi iti bhaavaha, Ahamkaara*" - "The feeling that I am the doer is the ego (in man)". We carry the load of problems in our little minds and on our slender shoulders not knowing how to disburden ourselves. An hour of work, if only offered at the Lotus Feet of the Lord, would become an hour of worship. With that attitude how simple would the whole life become! Unfortunately, we go out of our way to complicate it. When man starts to think in terms of 'I' and 'mine', there is so much to get confused about. Such was Arjuna's predicament too. Although he knew that when wickedness is on the ascendence, the evil must be eradicated and where battle is necessary, it must be fought, yet Arjuna was overcome by doubt and emotion. He became confused, unable to decide wherein his duty lay - whether to follow the dharma (duty) of *ahimsa* (non-violence), run away from the battle and save himself from the sin of slaying those who deserved his reverence, love and obedience, or to follow his *kshatriya dharma* (ordained duty as a warrior) to uphold justice and fair play and put down the wicked, but incur, as he thought, the sin of slaying them. In that state of confusion, Arjuna argued: "How can the aftermath of war ever be peace and happiness? Of what merit would the glory of winning such a war through the bloodshed of the near and dear ones be? I would much rather beg for my sustenance than kill; gaining the crown and kingdom is not worth the price it will exact in blood and tears".

It is not out of choice that man comes to birth, nor does he depart of his own accord. If he did, he would not come crying, nor be dragged away unhappy or unwilling. Forced is he to come and perforce does he depart. Placed between these two dictates and subject to the constraints thereof, wherefore then, O man of intelligence, can you lay claim to freedom of will? Besides, if one chooses to be a willing slave to the illusory delights of matter and is therefore unable to shake off one's attachment to the 'finite', aspiring for the freedom of the 'infinite' then is a meaningless pastime. It is our mind that produces within us the illusion that we possess a separate identity of our own over which we have total control. Because of this, it is also deluded into believing that it has the freedom of will. However, since everything around and including us in nature is intrinsically linked, one to another, by the Doctrine of Causation, the concept of freedom or free will can have no existence other than as a figment of our imagination. When even the most essential functions of our body such as breathing, heart beat, etc, are beyond our control, what free will can there possibly be for man? The fact is that there is no such thing as freedom or free will - there is only Divine Will.

However, those who see fit to question this often protest that, on the human plane, ascribing doership for everything that happens around us to God would be highly dangerous. Doing so, they argue, would subscribe to anarchy by conferring upon the criminally inclined the freedom to commit crimes with impunity and the licence to get away with them simply by attributing their own aberrations to the Will of God. But for those who truly believe that not even a blade of grass moves without Divine Will and in consonance therewith consider themselves only as His instruments and completely surrender to Him, they will find that God will not be outdone in courtesy; He will play sweet music through them and their godliness will shine forth confirming their true faith. For those of the criminal bent of mind who may not be this way inclined, however, who might feel tempted to exploit the argument but only to escape responsibility, their own cleverness can be turned around upon them by ascribing the appropriate retribution likely to be meted out to them also to the will of God, thus giving them a taste of their own medicine! One cannot ride far on the horse of pretence; to expect that merely assuming a posture of devotion as a facade to hide the collusion between mind and matter, will make the 'spirit' reveal its treasures, is to live in a fool's paradise. In the realm of the 'spirit', cleverness does not pay but humility and surrender are most valued and rewarded.

PKK

Seeing the plight of Arjuna, Lord Krishna admonished him thus: "Who is the slayer and who the slain? Mistaken is your belief if you think that you are either of these. When ego is deluded, it appropriates to itself, wrongly, the doership. Such is the nature of ignorance that you are suffering from."

"Why do you shed tears like a coward? Is it because Bhishma, Drona and the rest are about to be killed? No; you weep because they are 'your men'. It is egoism (attachment) that makes you weep. People weep not for the dead, but because they think the dead are 'theirs'. Have you not killed until now many who were 'not yours'? You never shed any tears for them. Today you weep since you are under the delusion that these whom you see before you are somehow 'yours' in a special way. When you sleep (ie, your mind is defunct), you are unaffected by this feeling of "I" and "mine", so you are unaware (and unconcerned) what happens to your body or the bodies of 'your men' or to your possessions, items which you carefully remember while 'awake' (ie, when your mind is active). The fundamental ignorance, my dear fool, is the identification of yourself with something that is not you, viz, the body."

"You did not bestow life on those you call your kinsmen, nor indeed upon anyone else; how then could you possibly claim the responsibility for slaying them? You have no power to kill nor have they the power to die by their own efforts. Living and dying are both directed by My Will. I bear the burden of the Earth; I create the burden; I relieve it. Consider also these questions: Why is it that the very body with a name and form that might be the object of one's deep attachment one moment, becomes the object of total revulsion the moment that something within it which makes it look as if full of life, departs? How can such objects be worthy of one's attachment? Reflecting on these questions will make you realise that the bodies that carry the names of your kinsmen, just as all other bodies, are already dead. In fact, they were never alive. That which makes these corpses come alive is the *atma*, the true self, the essential man; that essence cannot be touched by death; it is ever alive; it is immortal. Therefore your grief at the prospect of seeing your kinsmen doff their bodies like the old clothes, and your cowardice in not performing your ordained duty, are unbecoming a hero like you. They are unfounded since they are the result of your ignorance born out of your ego the body-consciousness. Recognising this truth, stand up and do your duty; that is the only way to attain supreme peace."

"You say that you would rather beg; but begging demands a different kind of mettle, a different kind of temperament, a different *dharma*. Forsaking your own *dharma* (duty) and following alien *dharma* cannot confer on you peace." If a cobbler and a judge were to swap places for a day, both would end up doing a bad job and being thoroughly unhappy; each to his own *dharma*.

Turning now to the question of freedom and free will: what is freedom? In common parlance, one's ability to think, speak and act as one pleases, without any let or hindrance, is seen to represent one's freedom. But as long as the mind holds the sway and our thought, word, and deed are open to outer and inner influences, no one can claim to enjoy true freedom.

When we think, it is about something; when we speak, it is to convey our thoughts to someone; and when we act, it is towards some end. To that extent therefore, our thought, word and deed cannot stand alone, they must inevitably be linked to and be influenced by that something, someone or some purpose. Moreover, mind as we know it, is a mixture of the three *gunas* (attributes) - *sattwa* (harmony), *rajas* (activity) and *tamas* (inertia). One or the other of these, says *Bhagawan* Baba, may become dominant at any given time in a given person and accordingly influence his thought, word or deed at that time. For example, one may claim that by giving away money in charity, one is exercising one's freedom. In reality, however, it is the influence of the *sattwa guna*, and not freedom, that moves him this way. As long as the mind is active and it operates under the sway of the *gunas* (attributes), there can be no freedom of will in the real sense. Freedom can be experienced only after the *gunas* are transcended - not before! In other words, it is impossible for anyone who is part of the creation to have absolute freedom. What you find in this world, Baba says, is a hierarchy of controls, the one at a higher level controlling the one at the lower level. This results in the lack of freedom for all except for the one at the top of the hierarchy. However, that freedom too is only relative and not absolute.

People believe that it is because of man's will, determination, spiritual practice, effort, etc, that he is able to achieve success. That belief, Baba says, is due to the aberration of the ego (*ahamkaara*) and a reflection of the false sense of doership. Existence is one (*ekam sat*); when there is no second, how can the question of freedom, or indeed bondage, arise? The concepts of freedom and bondage are the concoctions of our mind. Man can experience real freedom only when the mind is laid to rest. "True freedom consists in recognising and realising the divine principle, knowing which one becomes the knower of everything. One who knows the Self, knows all. Today's man tries to know everything about the world but nothing about the Self ... Engage yourself in activity, but always keep in view your true nature as the Self or *atma*. If you do so, you will surely enjoy real freedom. There are no two kinds of freedom - individual and spiritual. Spirituality alone is Freedom; Freedom alone is Spirituality. True freedom consists in the spontaneous expression of what comes from the heart; it can come only when one is free from the influences of the mind."

Giving up the body-consciousness by constantly reminding ourselves of our essential nature, the immortal Self, renunciation of the feeling of possessiveness by recognising that the essence in each one of us is a part of that totality which is the One without the second, and eschewing the feeling of doership by performing actions as divine instruments without identifying ourselves with the actions or the rewards thereof, will inevitably lead to the acceptance of whatever comes our way as the grace of the Lord. Such prayerfulness sublimates the ego, removes the veil of ignorance and brings about surrender.

The words: "Thy will be done" can meaningfully form on one's lips only after being educated into humility and when the veil of ignorance is lifted and not at the peak of one's deluding ego. It took 18 chapters and 659 verses of ego-blasting for Arjuna's ignorance to be removed and for his surrender. Eventually, when the light of wisdom dawned, he had no hesitation in proclaiming:

> *"Nashto moha smritir-labdhaa twat-prasaadaat-mayaachyuta;*
> *Sthitosmi gata-sandeha, karishye vachanam tava."*

Bhagavad Geeta : 18, 73

Translation: "Destroyed is my delusion, as I have regained my memory (ie, Truth) through Thy Grace, O Achyuta (Krishna)! I stand firm, free of all doubts, ready to do Thy bidding."

What does surrender mean? Baba says: "People talk glibly about surrender. Some persons complain that they have completely surrendered themselves to *Swami*, but that there is no end to their problems, hardships, suffering and sorrow. This is no surrender at all. True surrender never takes into cognizance the presence or absence of sorrow, suffering, misery and the like." "It is only when we accept and believe that the divine is present in everything that we can understand the meaning of surrendering in thought, word and deed. Becoming one with God is true surrender (*sharanagati*). So long as there is distinction in the mind of the individual between God and 'I', there is no surrender. To think that one who gives orders is God and one who executes these is man, there is no surrender. There is bliss and happiness in unity and not in duality. So the feeling of unity with God is the real meaning of the word surrender."

Baba says, "For you, birth is an anxious moment; childhood is fraught with anxiety; living is a series of anxious moments; livelihood is earned through a chain of anxious events; old age and death cause dire anxiety; even joy brings about the anxiety that you might lose it soon; all activity is saturated with anxiety. But barter all this anxiety for only one anxiety - how to win the grace of Sai - and you will be free from the big brood of worry and unrest." Let us not lose hold of or let go the Lotus Feet of the Saviour and all will be well.

As long as one harbours expectations, nurtures preferences and prejudices and is moved by one's likes and dislikes, merely repeating the words "I surrender", however many times, is meaningless and a waste of time. Surrender requires giving up of individual thinking, calculation and will, totally and completely, in favour of the Divine Will so that It can operate through one, unhindered and as It sees fit, with total unconcern on one's part as to the type of experience it might bring. When the individual identity 'I' is lost, its concomitant 'mine' will vanish too, because it cannot survive on its own. When the attachment of 'I' and 'mine' are gone, gone too will be the grand illusion and the delusion of doership. In that state, one will neither be elated by praise or profit nor depressed by blame or loss, because in that state of equal-mindedness (*sama-dhi*), nothing will be perceived as anything other than the Will of the Lord. When one's mind turns its gaze away from the objective world thus and becomes centred on, and loses itself in, the *atma*, the Lord within, that dissolution of the thinking mind and its thought process is the highest form of surrender.

O Divine Mother Sai! Grant that I may have no other will than Thine.

QUESTIONS:

(1) What is ego?
(2) What is the difference between servitude and surrender?
(3) How can Divine intervention in the affairs of man come about?
(4) Compare the predicament of Arjuna with the modern day man.
(5) What causes ignorance in man?
(6) What are freedom and free will?
(7) How much freedom does man enjoy? Give reasons.
(8) What is true surrender? How can it be achieved?
(9) What should we expect of God when we 'surrender'?!

"In the root, divine Wisdom is all - Brahman;
in the stem, she is all - Illusion;
in the flower, she is all - World;
and in the fruit, all - Liberation."

Tantra Tattwa

20. ROAD TO DESTINY

A noble family once dwelt in a beautiful mansion. The parents, *Atma Ram* and *Jyotirmayi* were enlightened souls. They were blessed with two sons. The elder son *Bodh Ram* led a sheltered life and grew up to be intelligent and wise. He was wedded to *Chetna*, who had dedicated her life to the service and welfare of her husband. Her voice hardly ever rose above a whisper. The younger son was named *Manasa Ram*. As a toddler, *Manasa* enjoyed the full freedom of the house. Soon, however, he learnt to walk and in his natural curiosity to explore the unknown, he started to venture out of doors and make contact with the neighbours. The neighbours began to fill him up with the tales of excitement, adventure and fortune awaiting him in the green pastures of the valley yonder. Whenever *Manasa* peeped out of the windows he would be fascinated by the bright lights that could be seen and the accompanying guffaws of merriment that could be heard in the far distance. The desire of enjoying the experience gradually took hold of him. And one morning, without consulting his family and knowing that they would not approve of his so doing, *Manasa* left his home in search of fame and fortune.

While thus embarked, young *Manasa* began building a mental picture of the acquisitions which would satisfy him as constituting the fortune he set out in search of. Pleasure, comfort, wealth, power, etc, were added to the never ending list. Soon, however, he came to the cross-roads and the question whether to take the road to the left or to the right faced the young man. He promptly climbed a nearby tree in order to scan the horizon and the information gleaned thereby, he argued, would enable him to make the right decision. He cast his glance 'as far as his eyes could see' and having established, or so he thought, that the left hand road led to the orchard of trees laden with an assortment of appetising fruits, he decided to take that road to satiate his hunger. But, however close he appeared to get to this garden (of Eden), the farther the fruit laden trees seemed to recede! Yet, turning back homewards was firmly ruled out because the mango grove on the horizon appeared to him tantalizingly nearer than the wholesome food of the home he left behind.

On and on *Manasa* went without any pause or care; the roads multiplied and criss-crossed into a maze. Suddenly he came across a carriage by the roadside which had got bogged down in slush. *Manasa* lent the strength of his shoulders and helped put the carriage back on the firm ground. In recognition thereof he was invited to cover the rest of his journey inside the comfort of the carriage. This he readily accepted.

Inside the carriage, young *Manasa* found himself face to face with a beautiful damsel, *Mayavati* by name and a danceuse (*nartaki*) by profession. She appeared to be in some distress and poured out on to the young man her tale of woe. It transpired that the owner of the carriage was a powerful and ruthless Marquis at whose behest the carriage was sent to fetch *Mayavati* against her wishes, to serve a life of servitude in his castle. Crack after crack of the whip on the horses and the impending confrontation with the Marquis were enough to send shivers down *Manasa's* spine. Yet, bewitched and beguiled by her looks, *Manasa* took it upon himself to save her from the clutches of the Marquis and marry her himself.

At the journey's end, on the fateful day, the Marquis and *Manasa* met. The Marquis warned him of the fate other men met at his hands for displaying impertinence similar to his and for getting involved, but to no avail. In the ensuing duel, *Manasa* was fatally wounded. As he lay dying, he could not help wondering: had he not left his home, had he not taken the road to the left, had he not helped the carriage, had he not fallen for the damsel in distress, had he not offered to marry her, had he not challenged the Marquis, his fate might have been different!

A closer look at the story will reveal an all too familiar a plot. The young *Manasa Ram* is none other than *manas*, the mind. The elder brother *Bodh Ram* is *buddhi*, the intellect and his wife *Chetna* is the power of intuition. The parents together represent the *atma-jyoti*, the Self-Effulgence.

As the light of effulgence shines in full splendour upon the intellect, the power of intuition sharpens and it is the whispered promptings of the intuition that endow intellect with the power of discrimination. When the mind is guided by and looks towards the intellect, it also receives reflection of the light and the stranglehold of the native instinct slackens yielding place to the sway of intuition which guides it towards the kinship with the *atma*. With the mind thus sublimated, the mansion becomes *devalaya*, the Abode of God, where *atma-jyoti* is ever effulgent and where peace and harmony reign supreme.

The windows through which the mind looks out are the five *jnaanendriyas* (the senses of perception: sight, sound, smell, touch and taste). When the mind reaches out into the objective world, it does so in the mistaken belief of gathering unto itself the treasure trove of happiness it believes lies hidden in the world outside. As it parts company with the intellect and turns away from the very source of light, a veil of darkness and ignorance descends and keeps it company. The peace and tranquillity experienced hitherto fade out into a dim memory of the past. The identity with the *atma* is lost in the delusion of the I (ego) consciousness. When the the principle of non-duality (*adwaita*) is lost sight of, one inevitably finds one-self at the crossroads of duality (*dwaita*).

The two roads referred to are the *shreyas* (superior, righteous) and the *preyas* (pleasure-seeking) paths. In the absence of the wise counsel of the intellect and putting total reliance on the biased feedback from the imperfect senses, the tempting fruits of desire, greed, anger, attachment, ego and lust that the laden tree of the sensory world hold out for us, soon lure us on to the *preyas* path, the path of comfort. In spite of tasting one fruit after another, craving for more grows. All this is like the magician's art. (*Indrajaalam idham sarvam*). The further and farther the mind strays into the objective world, the more difficult and daunting the trek back to the *atmic* reality becomes. The criss-crossing of roads into a maze symbolises the unending multiplication of desires.

The carriage is the body *dehalaya*, the carrier for ego (*ahamkaaram*). It gets bogged down in the quagmire of the sensory world. Whilst mind has the power to put the body on an even keel, yet, bereft of the powers of discrimination, it jumps into the life of comfort with the *nartaki* (danceuse). *Nartaki*, the damsel, is *maya*, delusion personified. She is well versed in the art of creating illusions. By shedding tantalizing tears of emotion and attachment, and through her wiles, she deludes the mind into believing the body (*dehalaya*) to be the Abode of God (*devalaya*). It creates desires which put on cloak of mercy marshalling all efforts towards their fulfilment. The mind, which once was pellucid and pure, gets drunk and lost in the lap of *maya* and in its drunken stupor, it loses all track of time. With the ensuing chaos, compounded by the desertion of the lieutenants (senses) on account of their failing health, vision becomes befogged, the speech slurred and finally, senility sets in. Mercifully, soon the curtain is about to fall; the time is up. The appointment with the Marquis, the Lord of time (*Kaala*), which was fixed at the very birth, has to be kept and in His compassion at its plight and misery, He puts an end to the torment of the mind.

In the seven-stage-slide to oblivion, the tragedy begins with the sense pulls, mind's rushing forth towards the sense objects. Even whilst engaged in action, the mind constantly, though not quite consciously, contemplates over the expected fruits of action. This leads to attachment. This action-with-attachment together with the active connivance of the doer's ego sets up currents of reaction in the Cosmic Energy. Attachment and ego let loose desires and passions such as falsehood, hatred, anger, etc, which open the gateway to beastly existence. These passions are the highway robbers who snatch away all peace and tranquillity. With the subsequent delusion of doership comes the loss of memory of the Truth. From the loss of memory stems the ruin of discrimination between the real and the unreal. With the loss of discrimination, self-destruction is, inevitably, assured.

The tragedy, however, does not end there. The lingering and overwhelming desire of finding out what could have been awaiting one if only one had taken some other route on the journey, sows the seed and forms the cause for the next life cycle. So, the whole pathetic cycle starts all over again. What has to be realised is the fact that on the journey of life, we will always come to crossroads at every twist and turn; there will always be a bogged down carriage; we will always meet a damsel in distress and there will inevitably be the Marquis (the Lord of Time) at the journey's end. Besides, both the paths, *shreyas* (virtuous) as well as *preyas* (pleasurable), are binding. To save ourselves from the sorry plight, therefore, we must follow the route that transcends both these paths; we must refuse to be shackled by chains even those made of gold. Since our destiny is divinity, the road leading to it cannot be one of duality. As eloquently stated in the Third Patriarch of Zen:

> "The Perfect Way knows no difficulties,
> Except that it refuses to make preferences.
> Only when freed from hate and love
> Does it reveal itself fully and without disguise.
>
> A tenth of an inch's difference,
> And heaven and earth are set apart.
> If you wish to see it before your own eyes,
> Have no fixed thoughts either for or against it.
>
> To set up what you like against what you dislike-
> This is the disease of mind.
> When the deep meaning of the Way is not understood,
> Peace of mind is disturbed to no purpose ...
>
> Pursue not the outer entanglements,
> Dwell not in the inner void;

Be serene in the oneness of things,
And dualism vanishes of itself.

When you strive to gain quiescence by stopping motion,
The quiescence so gained is ever in motion.
So long as you tarry in such dualism,
How can you realize oneness?

And when oneness is not thoroughly grasped,
Loss is sustained in two ways;
The denying of external reality is the assertion of it,
And the assertion of Emptiness (the Absolute) is the denying of it ...

Transformations going on in the empty world that confronts us
Appear to be real because of Ignorance.
Do not strive to seek after the True,
Only cease to cherish opinions.

The two exist because of the One;
But hold not even to this One.
When a mind is not disturbed,
The ten thousand things offer no offence...

If an eye never falls asleep,
All dreams will cease of themselves;
If the Mind retains its absoluteness,
The ten thousand things are of one substance.

When the deep mystery of one Suchness is fathomed,
All of a sudden we forget the external entanglements;
When the ten thousand things are viewed in their Oneness,
We return to the origin and remain where we have always been...

One in all,
All in One -
If only this is realized,
No more worry about not being perfect!

When (Cosmic) Mind and each believing mind are not divided,
And undivided are each believing mind and (Cosmic) Mind,
This is where words fail,
For it is not of the past, present or future."

"*Anapeksha*", Baba says, "goes beyond both the paths (the pleasurable as well as the virtuous paths)..." "*Anapeksha* means freedom from any kind of '*apeksha*' (desire or expectation). The objects desired may be sensual pleasures and comforts, and things of the world or, those that relate to non-sensual, non-physical and ultramundane. Almost all desires fall into one or the other of these two categories. How, then, is it possible to be rid of both kinds of desires? It is when a man gives up the feeling, in the performance of all actions, that 'I am the doer' (the sense of ego), 'I am the experiencer' (the sense of fulfilment of desire), that the true '*anapeksha*' emerges. This means that conceit of doership and the sense of enjoyment of desired things should be wholly renounced ... It is only when all actions are done as an offering to God that they become 'desireless' actions and '*anapeksha*' prevails ..."

Offering actions to God means performing all actions with the conviction that the Indwelling Lord is the real doer. In order to make steady progress on this path, we must bear with us the torch of intellect *(buddhi)* reflecting the light of *atmic* splendour and illumining the path in front. With our sights firmly fixed on the milestones of *sathya* (truth), *dharma* (right conduct), *shanti* (peace), *prema* (Love) and *ahimsa* (non-violence), we shall assuredly proceed on the path of redemption and liberation. With the antidote of *kirtana* (singing the glory of God), even the wiles of *nartaki* will cease to distract and disrupt and instead ensure godspeed towards self-realisation. Such a life will transform the journey into a holy pilgrimage. All agitation and wander-lust will cease and the deliverance from the cycle of birth and rebirth will come. We shall be spared the confrontation with the Marquis. Instead who shall be waiting at the journey's end, with His benign gaze and unbounded love, reassuring us with His *abhaya hasta* (benediction of fearlessness) "Why fear when I am here?" – who else but our own sweet SAI. And we shall hear Him say: "Welcome home my dear child; I missed you so". With bended knees, palms folded, head bowed down at the Lotus Feet and with grateful tears of homage, we shall render the account thus:

"O, My Lord! I fixed my sights and ran after what I mistakenly thought was the treasure trove of happiness; I pitched my ears to catch what I mistakenly thought was the whisper of Thy sweet name; I kept my feelings attuned to what I mistakenly thought was Thy presence. In ignorance, I confused the evanescent pleasures for the eternal bliss; I mistook the noise of laughter for the sweet vibrations of Aum; I mistakenly plighted my troth to the body instead of the *atma*. It was 'i' blazing its ego-trail that brought in its wake trouble and turmoil. But through Thy compassion, my Lord, the light has now dawned, the veil of ignorance has been rent asunder, the shackles undone and the spell broken. The twenty-five have joined their

"All beings are actors on this world stage. They exit when the curtain is wrung down or their part is over. On that stage, one may play the part of a thief; another may be cast as a king; a third may be a clown; and another, a beggar. For all these characters in the play, there is One who gives the cue. He will not come out on the stage in full view of all. If He did that, the play would lose its appeal. Therefore, standing behind the screen at the back of the stage, He prompts each actor, irrespective of his role. The Prompter provides the cue for the dialogue, speech, or song, just when the help is most needed."

"In the same way, the Lord is behind the screen on the stage of the world, giving the cue to all the actors for their various parts. Each actor must be conscious of His Presence behind the screen of illusion. He must be eager to catch the faintest suggestion the Director might give, keeping the corner of his eye always on Him and having the ear pitched to catch His voice. If the player forgets the plot and the story, neglecting to watch the Presence behind the screen, the audience will laugh and he will have spoiled the show. For these reasons, every actor who has to play the role of Man on the world stage must first learn his lines well; then, remembering the Lord behind the screen, await His direction."

Sri Sathya Sai Baba

parents five, the five have merged with the three and, through Thy grace alone, the three have found, and lost their identity in, the One".

In the human body, each of the five primordial elements (earth, water, fire, air, ether) become five-fold, making the count twenty-five. The five elements themselves are the products of the three *gunas* (attributes, qualities): inertia (*tamas*), activity (*rajas*) and harmony (*sattwa*). *Maya* (grand illusion) is directly associated with these three *gunas*.

As long as these three *gunas* take up residence in our heart, beclouding our understanding, we remain in bondage. Among these *gunas*, *rajas* and *tamas* are responsible for all the sorrows, grief, troubles and problems that we experience. Fear, rage, laziness, drowsiness or sleep are the characteristics by which we can recognise *tamo guna*. When *rajo guna* holds sway, our true human nature is forgotten; *rajo guna* brings out the animal and the demonic nature in us. Whenever there is intense anguish at the feeling of separation from God, at that time all *gunas* merge and become one.

Baba says: "The whole universe surges towards God, which longing is expressed in the process of evolution. Why does the universe evolve? Because it is restless until it reaches that state. So, we are driven to that state of perfection, and this urge is the urge for cosmic evolution. God realisation, therefore, is the Goal of life." How can that realisation come about? In the following, Bayazid, the *Sufi* saint, gives us a clue:

> "For twelve years, I was the smith of my soul. I put it in the furnace of austerity and burned it in the fire of combat; I laid it on the anvil of reproach and smote it with the hammer of blame until I made of my soul a mirror. Five years I was the mirror of my self and was ever polishing that mirror with diverse acts of worship and piety. Then for a year I gazed in contemplation. On my waist I saw a girdle of pride and vanity and self-conceit, and reliance on devotion and approbation of my works. I laboured for five years more until the girdle became worn out and I professed Islam anew. I looked and saw that all created things (for whatever comes out of the mould of creation must also suffer dissolution) were dead. I pronounced four *akbirs* over them and returned from the funeral of them all, and without intrusion of creatures, through God's help alone, I attained unto God."

To the neophyte, the road to destiny, ie, realisation of the native divinity, may appear to be synonymous with privation and austerity and it may conjure up a path fraught with hardship and suffering of all kinds. As a result, one may find oneself reluctant even to take the first step even whilst acknowledging the inevitability of having to come to terms with one's own reality, the Self. However, such apprehensions are born out of one's ignorance of the richness and the strength of the native spirit. In the words of Silver Birch, the renowned guide of the spirit world, "There is no trouble in your world of matter which is greater than the power you have within you for overcoming it, because the troubles are of the earth material, and you are part of the Great Spirit, Divine. There is no problem that comes to anyone which he is incapable of solving. There is no difficulty that you cannot conquer, if you would but allow the latent Divinity to rise to the surface."

'S'(Supersoul) without 'I'(Individual Soul) and 'I' sans 'S' are both incomplete. It is only when the 'A' (Awareness) unites 'I' with 'S', and 'I' finds its rightful place in S ♣ A ♣ I that the true destiny will be realised.

O Divine Mother Sai! Inspire me with courage and steel me with fortitude that I may realise my destiny.

QUESTIONS:

(1) Identify the different characters in the story and discuss their relationships.
(2) What is the mansion and what do its doors and windows represent?
(3) How does the behaviour of *Manasa Ram* differ from that of *Bodh Ram*?
(4) What are the contact points between mind and the objective world?
(5) How far can the feed back through the senses be relied upon and why?
(6) What do the cross-roads represent?
(7) What does the tree with the assorted fruits represent? How do these fruits differ from the wholesome food in the mansion?
(8) " The closer we get to the tree, the farther it recedes!" Discuss
(9) Discuss the mechanism of the seven-stage slide to oblivion.
(10) What is the connection between time and death?
(11) What are the One, the three and the five?
(12) What is the destiny of man?
(13) What is *anapeksha*? How can one offer action to God?

> *"The Infinite is that, the Infinite this;*
> *And on and on, unchanged is Infinite;*
> *Goes out the Infinite from the Infinite;*
> *And there remains unchanged the Infinite."*
>
> Upanishad

21. THE SPIRIT OF NUMBERS

Mathematics, it is said, is the science of total intellectual order. Basis of mathematics is the numbers and the basis of numbers is the universe. The secrecy with which the primordial numeral One conceals within its bosom the mysteries of the universe and the sheer precision with which it, through its proliferation, makes nothingness come alive and reveal to us some of its secrets is simply breathtaking. However, the secrets stand revealed only when approached in a spirit of prayerfulness and humility.

Remember, it is beyond the ken of man to 'invent', for he cannot tap what already exists not in the cosmos. The so-called inventions are merely attempts by man to comprehend but a fraction of the majesty and excellence of the Supreme. And through divine compassion, when man is so inspired, the ego is made to flee by the enormity of its own ignorance and the head bows down in grateful homage.

Before Creation started there was nothing other than the One. With the dawn of Creation, duality and multiplicity appeared. "I am One; I want to become many." (*Ekoham bahusyaam*). And so to comprehend the glory of His Creation, God gave man the knowledge of numbers. A deeper understanding of numbers and their science gives us not only an insight into the underlying unity in the manifested diversity but also reveals to us the beauty, harmony and order in nature. If we develop an insight into the very basis of numbers and also realise their deeper spiritual truths, the science of numbers can open the doors to a new spiritual experience.

Zero (*Shunya*)

> *"The giving to airy nothing, not merely a location habitation*
> *and a name, a picture, a symbol, but helpful power is the*
> *characteristic of the Hindu race whence it sprang."*
>
> Halsted

Shunya in *Sanskrit* means void, nothingness. Nothingness, a zero may be, but a nothingness that cannot be ignored. Baba says: "In what you call everything, there is nothing; what you call nothing has everything. Everything is nothing and nothing is everything."

The entire manifested universe is in reality nothing and in that nothingness is concealed everything. Everything that we are able to see, hear, taste, smell and feel is subject to change, decay and death. All such manifestations therefore which are not eternal, cannot be referred to as truth-absolute, but may be seen for what they really are – nothing! The realisation of this nothingness, this truth is, in essence, everything. Prof. Timothy Ferris emphasises this point further by quoting the physicist Heinz R. Pagels, (The Cosmic Code), "Nothingness contains all being. All of physics – everything we hope to know – is waiting in the vacuum to be discovered."

Zero conjures up at once not only the infinitesimal but also the infinite. A circle has no beginning and no end. As a symbol of zero, circle therefore also represents space-time continuum or eternity. The zero symbol itself, however, was a source of great difficulty for a lot of people around the world. They found it hard to understand how it was that a symbol which stands for 'nothing' could, when put next to a numeral, suddenly multiply its value ten-fold.

Imagine, if the basic numerals numbered from 1 to 9 only and zero did not exist, 2×9 would not have made 18, nor 3×9, 27; $9 + 1$ would not have made 10 but would have had to remain as 9 and 1, and so on. Counting beyond 9 itself would become extremely difficult, tedious and cumbersome, and calculations involving large distances, such as from the earth to other planets, would have been well nigh impossible and remained beyond the reach of man. As a simple example to illustrate this, the answer to 5×5 could, at best, be written as $9 + 9 + 7$ which, instead of simplifying the requirement, actually complicates it.

It is, therefore, obvious that without the concept of zero, man could not have had the freedom to enable him to take a quantum leap into space and touch the stars. The mathematical calculations which have made it possible for man to achieve the incredible progress in the fields of science and technology and revolutionise the very life on our planet, owe their very existence to the concept of zero. Man, therefore, stands forever beholden to those rare moments of Divine Inspiration and Grace when "nothingness" assumed a shape, a symbol, out of which in course of time arose, among other things, even the ability to catapult man on to the moon.

One (1)

Baba says: "All experiences in daily life are variations in form of the basic reality which reveal how the changes in the primary energy bring about the emergence and the disappearance of material substances. The experience is One only with no difference. Different combinations of atoms result in objects of different kinds like copper, gold or oxygen, which have varying utility and value. But the primary energy which manifests itself in different kinds of atoms and objects is One and the same. The *Vedas* indicated this truth when they declared: 'The One willed to become the many' (*Ekoham bahusyaam*). 'The reality is One, the wise call it by many names' (*Ekam sat, viprah bahudaa vadanti*). 'The universe is permeated by God' (*Ishaa vaasyam idam sarvam*). If the universe is itself the manifestation of the One primary energy, everything in it is also an expression of that energy". "Blessed are those who keep God as their goal and strive accordingly", says *Sri* Ramakrishna *Paramhamsa*. "Zeros have no value, but they gain in value when linked to the number One. God is number One and all the worldly things are zeros. Independent of God, they are mere ciphers, but when associated with Him, they gain importance."

Unlike other numbers, One (1) contains within itself nothing other than itself; it also manifests itself in the multiplicity of other numbers. That is to say, all other numbers are simply expressions of One basic number. Illustrated mathematically, all numbers are simply the proliferation of the primary number, 1; 1+1 become 2, 2+1 become 3, and so on. Without the One (1), all other numbers have no basis at all. It should be clear from this that there is One primordial power which is the basis of all that is.

So, in numerology, (1) represents God who is one without the second. One is not only the basis, it permeates and exists in all the other numbers, in the same way as God permeates the whole universe. Even in the Pythagorean view of creation, 1 was the basic unit from which all others were created – it therefore was symbolic of divinity, of reason and of all that was eternal and unchanging. One also signifies unity, singularity, uniqueness and supremacy.

Two (2)

Two stands for the apparent duality in the universe – This (manifested universe) and That (God). It represents: *Purusha* (God) and *Praakriti* (Nature); indivisible consciousness, spirit and primordial matter; birth and death; positive and negative; day and night; heat and cold; pain and pleasure; right and wrong; inhalation and exhalation. Two also represents: action and reaction; cause and effect; real and unreal; microcosm and macrocosm; time and space, etc.

The relative manifestation of darkness and light, pain and pleasure, etc, although appear to be different are, in reality, not distinct but contained in each other. Falsehood is nothing but truth distorted. In the absence of light, a room may become dark, but when the light is switched on, where does the darkness go? Does it slip out of the door or escape through the window? No! The answer is simply that one is inherent in the other. Light and darkness, when thus looked upon as the presence or absence of the same thing, emphasise the underlying unity in spite of the apparent duality.

Mind is the root cause of the duality. In the 'deep sleep' state, when the mind is rendered defunct, there is no duality. It is only when the mind is active that the matter and energy, Creation and the Creator, are seen as two. Remove the influence of the mind and the illusion of the two, or the parallax, is removed.

Three (3)

The world is based on three entities: Fire, the Sun and the Moon. The combination of these three attracts and sustains all beings in the world. Thus, the number 3 figures prominently in the life of man and his relationship with his Creator. Three stands for: The trinity *Brahma* (Creator), *Vishnu* (Preserver) and *Maheshwara* (Destroyer); The Father, the Son and the Holy Spirit; the triple process of Creation (*Srishti*), Preservation (*Sthiti*) and Dissolution (*Laya*).

There is only One God who has the absolute power. The trinity merely symbolises that the process and the powers of Creation, Preservation and Dissolution, rest with God.

Nature (*praakriti*) has three qualities or attributes (*gunas*) which are therefore in man also. These are: *sattwa, rajas* and *tamas*. *Sattwa* is the quality of light and harmony. *Rajas* is the quality of activity. *Tamas* is the quality of inertia. In the beginning, these three qualities are in equilibrium. When this precosmic equilibrium is disturbed by the association of Spirit (*Purusha*) with matter (*Praakriti*), cosmic evolution is set in motion, resulting in the Universe. Though independent of matter and inactive, the Spirit is regarded as the prime mover, the First Cause of the Cosmic process.

Man is made up of three constituents - the body, the mind and the *atma*. Body is needed for performing actions. But, if actions are performed on impulse without discrimination, man will be seen to behave like an animal. Moreover, if the mind, without relying on the eternal and ever pure *atma*, follows the demands of the body and the senses, the actions that follow will be demonic. However, when one is installed in the *atmic* principle, transcending the body and the mind, one attains the divine.

The nature of *atma* is three-fold: *sat* (eternal existence), *chit* (absolute knowledge) and *aananda* (total bliss). Three is also associated with the three paths of God realisation: *jnaana maarga* (path of knowledge and wisdom), *karma maarga* (path of selfless service) and *bhakhti maarga* (path of devotion and surrender).

Man's relationship with God, has been explained through the three philosophies of dualism (*dwaita*), qualified monism (*vishishtadwaita*) and monism (*adwaita*) as propounded by the three great masters, Madhava, Ramanuja and Shankara, respectively. The dualistic philosophy represents the first step on the ladder and looks upon the individual as being distinct from the Universal. This also explains what Christ meant by saying: "I am the Messenger of God", implying a distinction between the two entities – Messenger and God. If we look upon the *atma* (soul) or individual as the reflection of the Universal (Supersoul), ie, the concept that the reflection has an existence only because of what is reflected, that is qualified monism. This was referred to by Christ as being the "Son of God" – the son being the reflection of the father. However, with further progress when the reality dawns, we realise that there exists nothing other than *Brahman* (God). This philosophy of monism was asserted by Christ by declaring: "I and my Father are One". The three kings, likewise, on seeing Jesus at birth, in turn, declared that he would be a 'lover of God', 'loved by God' and 'one with God'. These are also seen as the three stages in the spiritual evolution of man. The best synthesis of these three views or stages is found in Hanuman's prayer to *Sri* Rama:

> *"Deha budhya tu daaso ham, jeeva budhya*
> *twadamshakhaha, atmabudhya twamewaham,*
> *iti may dridha matihi."*

Translation: "O my Lord ! I stand apart from Thee as Thy servant when I feel I am the body (**Daasoham**). I become a part of Thy Self when I feel that I am a *jeeva* (individual soul) detached from the body (**Soham**). And when I feel I am the pure *atma* or consciousness within, I realise, my Lord, that I am Thyself (**Om**)."

The whole of monistic philosophy is summed up in the three principles contained in the following couplet by *Sri Aadi* Shankaraachaarya:

Brahma satyam, jagan mithyaa,
Jeevo Brahmaiva naa paraa.

Translation: "(1) *Brahman* (God) alone is real; (2) Apart from God, the world (of matter) is illusory; (3) the *atma*, ie, the individual soul (*Jeeva*) is, in essence, not apart from *Brahman* ; *Jeeva*, in reality, is *Brahman* (God) Itself".

Human personality comprises the gross body (*sthula deha*), subtle body (*sookshama deha*) and the causal body (*kaarana deha*) which are, in turn, related to the three states of awareness: the 'wakeful' (*jaagrat*), the 'dream' (*swapna*) and the 'deep-sleep' (*sushupti*) states. In the 'wakeful' state, the world of matter comes alive through the experience of our sense perceptions. The mind reaches out and makes contact with the objects of the world through the senses. In the 'dream' state, the gross body and the senses are at rest whereas the subtle body is active. The experiences in the 'dream' state are, in many respects similar to those in the 'wakeful' state. Just as experiences in the 'wakeful' state appear to be real, the experiences in the 'dream' state, during the duration of the dream, likewise, appear to be very much real. However, just as the unreality of the 'dream' becomes apparent upon coming out of the 'dream' state, so also, it is said, will the reality of the so-called 'wakeful' state become apparent when waking up from the 'wakeful' state into the *atmic* state. In the 'deep-sleep' state, the activities of both the gross as well as the subtle bodies cease completely. Since there is no activity of the mind and no thoughts and desires to agitate us, it is naturally a state of bliss. However, the absence of mind in this state is not a result of conscious design but rather the helplessness of the mind. Such bliss is therefore born out of ignorance. This is patently obvious since it is the feeling of satisfaction beyond compare, the feeling of rejuvenation and quiet peace that one finds oneself in after the event that leads one to conclude that one had the experience of bliss. For this reason, it is referred to as the pseudo-bliss. So, the state of 'no mind' during the 'deep-sleep' state is a state of ignorance whereas the state of 'no mind' while fully awake is Awareness itself, although both the states, because of the absence of the mind, are blissful.

The reference to the so-called 'wakeful', the 'dream' and the 'deep-sleep' states as the three states of Awareness is actually not correct. Awareness simply is; it has no states or parts; there is no duality or multiplicity. These 'states' are, in reality, the three states of experience of the mind. Remember, it is our thoughts and the thinking process that constitute the mind. When our thought process, ie, the mind, is active, it is referred to as the wakeful state; when our unfulfilled desires seek expression through our thoughts in a dream, it is referred to as the 'dream' state; when the thoughts and the thinking process are absent, it is referred to as the 'deep-sleep' state. So, it is clear that, in the three states, it is the mind that is either awake, dreaming or in deep sleep. For the mind to describe the experience of the 'deep-sleep' state is impossible because of its very absence in that state. How can it describe something which it has not experienced or been a witness to? Although the instruments for gathering the information, ie, the senses, are present even in the 'deep-sleep' state, yet no information is gathered because the mind is absent. So, it can be safely said that in the 'deep-sleep' state, the mind is dead. It is patently clear then that, far from being our reality, the mind is an imposter, a pretender, which is redundant and which can be dispensed with altogether without endangering our fundamental well-being in any way. The Awareness which is ever present whether the mind is active, as in the 'wakeful' state, dreaming, as in the 'dream' state or totally absent as in the 'deep-sleep' state, and even beyond, is our reality, the true blissful Self.

Being born in the dimension of time and space, man is bound by the past, present and the future and by the three types of *karmas* (actions): *praarabdha*, *sanchita* and *aagaami*. Three also refers to the three sources of sound: *saamaanya* (ordinary), *varna* (vernacular) and *mooka* (silence).

The three syllables: "*Bha*", "*Ra*" and "*Ta*" represent the *bhaava* (feeling), *raaga* (melody) and *taala* (rhythm) which are the essentials for proper singing. Even the name *Bharat* (for India) signifies the combination of these three elements *(Bha-Ra-Ta)*.

Number three reminds us of the three principles: *Daiva preeti* (love of God), *paapa bheeti* (fear of sin) and *sangha neeti* (morality or ethics in society). Baba also exhorts us: "Never to forget God, never to believe the world as reality and never to be afraid of death."

Four (4)

Four refers to the four *Vedas* – *Rig* (10,578 verses), *Yajur* (1,975 verses), *Saam* (1,064 verses) and the *Atharvana* (5,847 verses).

There are 4 *purushaarthas* (principal objectives of human life): *dharma* (righteous living), *artha* (wealth), *kaama* (legitimate desire) and *mokhsha* (liberation). Earn *artha* (wealth) through *dharma* and for *dharma*; develop *kaama* (desire) for *mokhsha* (liberation).

Four also symbolises the *Vedic* injunctions: *matru devo bhava* (honour your mother as God), *pitru devo bhava* (honour your father as God), *aachaarya devo bhava* (honour your spiritual preceptor as God) and *atithi devo bhava* (honour your guest as God). By guest is not meant a person who comes by prior invitation but anyone, known or unknown, who calls unexpectedly.

In the spiritual path, we have to clearly understand the interrelationship of four aspects: (1) the soul, (2) the intelligence, (3) the mind, and (4) the sense organs. For the sense organs, the mind is the master; for the mind, the intelligence is the master; and for the intelligence, the soul is the master.

For the yearning to understand the nature of *Brahman* (*Brahma Jignyaasa*), four qualifications are necessary. These are:

- Discrimination between the transitory and eternal. In other words, the discovery that the *atma* (soul) alone is beyond time, and that all objects perceivable by the senses of sight, sound, etc, are only transitory. *Atma* alone is *Nitya Sathya* (Timeless Truth).

- Renunciation of the desire to enjoy here and hereafter, the fruits of one's actions. This is also known as *vairagya* (non-attachment). Renunciation does not involve giving up of hearth and home, of wife and children and taking refuge in forests. It involves only the awareness of the transitoriness of the world and as a consequence of this awareness, discarding the feelings of 'I' and 'mine'.

- The group of six virtues - this is described under number (6).

- Longing for *mokhsha* (liberation). This longing cannot arise from either riches, scholarship, wealth or progeny, rites and rituals, or charity, for liberation can come only from the conquest of *ajnaana* (ignorance).

According to Pythogorean view, 4, the first square number represents justice – perhaps it is from this that we get the expression: "square deal"!

Five (5)

Five represents the five sheaths covering the life-force, *atma*, and the five Human Values of the truth (*sathya*), right conduct (*dharma*), peace (*shanti*), love (*prema*) and non-violence (*ahimsa*) which constitute the pillars of life.

There are five kinds of suffering (*kleshas*) which stand in the way of one's spiritual progress. These are: Ignorance (of the *atmic* principle); Immaturity (mental infirmity); Unsteadiness (due to vagaries of senses and the mind); Attachment (to one's possessions); Hatred (due to failure to fulfil desires).

True aspirants on the spiritual path are required to steer clear of the five transgressions beginning with the letter 'A' (*Akaara Panchaka Arishtas*), viz, *Alakshyam* (Negligence), *Avinayam* (Disobedience), *Ahamkaaram* (Ego), *Asooya* (Jealousy) and *Asabhyata* (Lack of Social Etiquette).

Number 5 reminds us not only of the five primordial elements but also of the five-fold process (*panchikaran*), ie, their quintuplication. According to it, each of the elements must be divided into two equal parts. One of these two parts is further split up into four equal parts forming 1/8th part each. One gross element is then formed by compounding the half part of the element itself with the eighth part of each of the other four elements put together. Thus in ether, for instance, there will be five constituent parts; half of it will be ether and the other half will consist of the four parts contributed by all the other four elements. The gross elements thus compounded make up the objects of the universe.

Number 5 also reminds us of the WATCH-word which we must never lose sight of; we must always WATCH our:

Word (W), Action (A), Thought (T), Character (C), and Heart (H).

Six (6)

Number 6 reminds us of the six foes of man, the enemy within, and our constant endeavour to conquer these enemies. The six foes are: desire (*kaama*), anger (*krodha*), greed (*lobha*), attachment (*moha*), pride (*mada*) and malice (*maatsarya*).

Number 6 also reminds us of the six good qualities like: truth, righteousness, peace, love, non-violence and sense of fullness (*poornattva*).

The human body is associated with six stages of transformation, namely: (1) birth, (2) growth, (3) change, (4) decline, (5) death, and (6) disintegration. *Atma* alone, the resident in the changing body, is the unchanging Truth.

The six virtues known as *sadhana sampath* (treasure of spiritual struggle) and referred to under Number (4) are explained by Baba thus:

- *Sama*: Mind-control (through control and abandonment of desires). Mind is capable of causing bondage as well as conferring liberation. It is easily polluted. It relishes in hiding the real nature of things and casting on them the forms and values which it desires. So, the activities of mind have to be regulated. Mind is a bundle of thoughts, a complex of wants and wishes. As soon as a thought, a desire or wish raises its head from the mind, *Buddhi* (Intellect) must probe into its value and validity - is it good or bad, will it help or hinder, where will it lead or end. If the mind does not submit to this probe, it will lend itself on the path of ruin; if it does and obeys the Intelligence, it can move along the right path.

- *Dama*: Keeping body and senses under control, ie, restraint of external function. This can be achieved by *sadhana* (disciplined spiritual exercise), avoiding spending precious time in useless pursuits and being ever vigilant.

- *Uparati*: State of mind which is above and beyond dualities. One has to escape from blame etc, which agitate and affect the mind, and attain balance and stability. This can be achieved by carefully avoiding entanglements with bondage to differences or distinctions of class, caste, age, gender, etc, and firmly establishing in the *atmic* Reality alone. Do not look upon the world with the worldly eye but with the eye of *atma*. (Turning away from sense objects is the height of *Uparati*).

- *Titiksha*: Attitude of forbearance which refuses to be affected or pained when afflicted with sorrow and loss, and ingratitude and wickedness of others. In fact, one is happy and calm, for one knows that these are the results of one's own actions now recoiling on him. One does not retaliate nor does he wish ill of them. One bears all blows patiently and gladly. Paying evil for evil can never lighten the burden of *karma* (action); it will only become heavier. So, return good for injury.

- *Shraddha*: Unwavering faith in the sacred scriptures and the moral codes they contain, as well as in the *atma* and the *guru* (preceptor). *Gurus* are worth worshipping. They show us the path of fulfilment. The scriptures are designed to ensure peace and prosperity of the world and the spiritual perfection of mankind. They show the way to the realisation of these aims.

- *Samaadhaana*: The conviction that what the scriptures make known and what the *Guru* attempts to uncover within us are both one and the same. One's intellect must rest upon and draw inspiration from the *atma* at all times and under all circumstances. One must place implicit faith in the dictum that all living beings are facets or fractions of *Ishwara* (God).

Seven (7)

Number 7 is associated with the seven notes (*Saptaswaras*) in music, ie, *Sa, Re, Ga, Ma, Pa, Da, Ni*. The Sun's rays are made up of seven colours. There are seven oceans in the world. The supreme sages (*Saptarishis*) are seven in number. It is significant that certain religious observances are spread over seven days of the weak. The unique significance of number 7, however, is that, numerologically, *Pranava*, the Sound of creation, ie, AUM amounts to a total of this number. 'A' equals O, 'U' equals 2 and 'M' equals 5, so that the numerological vibration present in AUM is 7. Same numerological vibration is also present in the name RAMA, since 'R' also equals 2.

Eight (8)

Nothing in this manifested universe of name and form is eternal; everything is subject to change, decay and death. Everything that we can see, touch, taste, smell and hear is ever changing. If number 8 is multiplied by numbers 1 to 8, in turn, and the digits of each answer added, we obtain numbers changing from 8 to 1:

ie, $8 \times 1 = 8$, $8 \times 2 = 16$ and $1 + 6 = 7$, $8 \times 3 = 24$

and $2 + 4 = 6$, $8 \times 4 = 32$ and $3 + 2 = 5$, and so on.

So, the number 8 keeps constantly changing, and decreasing, from 8 to 7 to 6 to 5 and so on. This decrease in value, this inconstance, this unsteadiness is typical of the Grand Illusion (*Maya*) that the manifested universe presents. It is therefore aptly symbolised by the number 8.

Number 8 reminds us of the eight letters with the use of which the great seers fostered the *Vedas*. These are : "A, Ka, Cha, Ta, Tha, Pa, Ya and Sa." All the *Vedic mantras* (formulae) with their musical rendering were remembered by reflecting on these eight letters.

Number 8 is also associated with the eight *siddhis* (yogic powers). These are:

(1) *Aneema*, the capacity to assume a very small form, however big one's actual form.
(2) *Lagheema*, the power to become as light as cotton fluff.
(3) *Maheema*, the ability to assume a very big size.
(4) *Praapti*, the power to bring near oneself any object from whatever quarter and to enjoy it. By acquiring this power, it is said, that one can even touch the moon or the sun by one's fingers.
(5) *Praakaamyam*, the power to enter fire or immerse in acid as harmlessly as bathing in water.
(6) *Vasitvam*, mastery over the five elements and to control them at will.
(7) *Easitvam*, the power of creating (and destroying) the five elements.
(8) *Kaamaavasaayitvam*, the capacity to acquire anything desired.

Number 8 reminds us about the eight attributes of Aum (*Pranava*). Aum is :

(1) *Shabda Brahma* (Word of God). Sound is the essence of creation. Aum is the very breath of God.
(2) *Charaacharam*. It is both movable and immovable. It contains all that we see in the Universe, eg, sun, planets, stars, oceans, land, minerals, other life forms.
(3) *Jyotir Mayam*. It is of the form of self-effulgent light.
(4) *Vaanga Mayam*. All that comes under the purview of the spoken word is included in it. All sacred mystic formulae (*mantras*) are its expression.
(5) *Nityaananda Mayam*. It is eternal bliss.
(6) *Paraat Para*. It is beyond all ultimates.
(7) *Maayaa Mayam*. It is mysterious.
(8) *Shree Mayam*. It is the embodiment of truth, goodness and beauty.

Nine (9)

Number 9 is the *Para-Brahma sankhya*, ie, the number representing the Supreme Lord; it symbolises Truth, indicating the immutability of *Brahman* (God) and the *niraakaara* (formless) aspect. It always remains 9 however many times we may multiply it. Multiply it by any number and add up the digits of the result, they will, unlike that of number 8, always add up to 9 only. Even 8 itself which is ever changing, if it crosses its path with 9, the immutable symbol of Truth, it also becomes 9, the Truth!

Number 9 also symbolises detachment. The sum of all the digits of any number (of any length) containing one or more 9's remains unaffected

An Ode to Zero

Zero on its own
May seem forlorn,
But placed right-ly,
See it come alive sprightly.
Zero to the left of a number if placed,
May seem inept and a sheer waste;
But when it stands on the side that is Right,
Behold its magic and awesome might!
The seeming nothingness of old,
Then packs a punch ten-fold.
Should a number dare cross its path,
Nothing it becomes by tasting its wrath.
Zero below the line, no longer a pity,
But a concept sublime that reveals Infinity.
A void to confound?
No! A Reality so profound!

PKK

whether the 9's are counted or ignored. For instance, in the number 3479, if all the digits are added, ie, 3+4+7+9=23 and 2+3=5, we get 5 as the answer. If, however, the digit 9 were to be ignored and only the remaining digits added, ie, 3+4+7=14 and 1+4=5, we still get the same answer, illustrating the detachment of number 9.

It is also significant that by adding 1 to 8, it becomes 9; that is to say, with the Grace of God (1), even in this phenomenal changing world (8), one can attain the Truth (9). Again by adding 1 to 9, it becomes 10, ie, One and nothing (else)! In other words, it is through God's Grace again that one can further progress beyond the Truth (9) to the awareness of the One without the second (since all else is nothing).

Number 9 also reminds us that the *Vedas* developed under nine heads: *(1) Shruti; (2) Anuswara; (3) Trayee; (4) Aamnaayam; (5) Samaamnaayam; (6) Chhandas; (7) Swaadhyaayam; (8) Gama; and (9) Aagama.*

Baba has explained these thus:

"*Shruti*": refers to the process of learning the *Vedas* from a preceptor by practising the precise manner of chanting the *mantras* (formulae) and thereby acquiring proficiency in the recitation of the *Vedas*. The sounds have to be reproduced exactly as taught by the preceptor by listening to him with intense earnestness. The *Vedic mantras* are thus learnt entirely by listening.

"*Anuswara*': refers to the practice of repeating the mantras learnt from the preceptor, contemplating on them and preserving them in their purity by constant recitation.

"*Trayee*": refers to the Triad. Originally only three *Vedas* - *Rg, Yajur* and *Sama Veda* - were considered "*apourusheya*", without a human origin (that is, emanating from the Divine). The *Atharvana Veda* comprises hymns taken from the *Yajur Veda*. Because of their Divine origin, the first three *Vedas* were called "*Trayee*" (the Triad).

"*Aamnaaya*": refers to constant contemplation of the root syllable "*na*". Acquiring the knowledge of the *Vedas* by this practice has been described as "*Aamnaaya*" and "*Samaamnaaya*".

"*Chhandas*": One of its meanings is that it is knowledge which should be guarded in secret and propagated with care. The *Vedas* are also described as *Chhandas*. The entire *Sama Veda* consists of *Chhandas*.

"*Swaadhyaayam*": refers to the process by which the *Vedas* have come down from generation to generation, through father to son, in geneological succession. Acquisition of *Vedic* knowledge was not through books. It was transmitted from preceptor to disciple over the years. It is because this knowledge was handed down directly from preceptor to pupil that it has been described as "*Swaadhyaaya*".

"*Gama*" and "*Aagama*": are the names given to the inhaling and exhaling of the Lord's breath which was the origin of the *Vedas*. All in all, the *Vedas* represent the emanations from the breath of the Lord.

Infinity – Infinity = Infinity

This Truth is illustrated in the *Upanishadic* prayer:

> "*Aum poornamadah poornamidam poornaat poornamudachyate,*
> *Poornasya poornamaadaaya poornamevaavashishyate.*
> *Aum shanti shanti shantihi.*"

Translation: That (*Brahman*, God) is Whole; This (Creation) is also Whole. From That Whole (ie, *Brahman* only), This Whole (Creation) has come out. But even though This Whole has come out of That Whole, yet That Whole remains Whole only. In other words *Brahman* remains unaffected, undiminished and retains Its Fullness and Completeness. Let there be no discord anywhere; let Peace only prevail.

From the above it follows that *atma* (soul) cannot be a part of but must be *Brahman* (God) Itself. Infinity cannot have parts; it cannot be divided, it always remains infinite. If it were possible to divide Infinity, each part would limit the other and both would thus be finite. However, aggregation of finites can only make a bigger finite but never an Infinite. So, Infinity can only be One, undivided. The conclusion must therefore be that This Whole (Universe) is only a reflection of That Whole (*Brahman*).

Looked at in another way, Infinity or Fullness is the attribute, the nature of Supreme; it is found in part or portion, half or whole in full measure. Quantity is not the criterion, quality is. In the visible, manifested world that has emanated from the Divine, this quality is found equally full, just as the sweetness in a sweet, in the lump of jaggery that the sweet is made from, and in the kilo of jaggery that the lump comes from, is of equal fullness. So the sweetness undergoes no diminution or change.

Three minus One is One

Consider a man standing in front of a mirror. If the person looks into the mirror, his own form is projected on to it as his image. Thus, three things can be observed: man, mirror and mirage or image. In reality, the image is like a mirage; it has no substance, no existence. It is the mirror which causes the confusion. Remove one object, ie, the mirror, out of the three, and only the Self remains.

In much the same way, the universe is like a mirror and the apparent diversity and multiplicity that is seen in it is nothing but the reflection or image of *Brahman* (God); it is the Grand Illusion (*Maya*)! If we look 'through' the mirror rather than 'at' it, which is the same thing as removing the mirror, *Maya* (Illusion) will be removed, what remains then is God alone, ie, One without the second. This Truth can be stated mathematically as:
$$3 - 1 = 1.$$

Which is greater 1 or 9?!

Nine (9), as we have already seen, is an immutable number; that is the reason why it symbolises Truth. But One (1), on the other hand, represents One without the second, ie, *Brahman* (God) who has no equal. Nine (9) is made up of nine ones; without One (1), nine (9) could not be. In other words, 9 has emerged out of 1. As the Truth (9) has emerged out of *Brahman* (1), *Brahman* (1) must be more than just the Truth (9) itself. Therefore, Baba says that 1 is greater than 9!

One and One make Eleven!

This is a mathematical expression of the proverb: "Unity is strength." It suggests that the strength of a united whole is many times more than the sum of the strengths of its individual components.

When the scattered rays of Sun pass through a magnifying glass and converge at a point, the unified ray gains such intensity and power as to set the object on which it falls, alight. In much the same way, if our wayward thoughts, which are scattered outwards in different directions in pursuit of sense 'enjoyment' in the objective world, are gathered and directed inwards towards the very core of our being, the resultant illumination will burn all dross and dispel all ignorance and enable us to have the vision of our Real Self, the *atma*.

Why 108 beads in a Rosary?

When 12 is multiplied 9 times, the product is 108. 12 is the number of the luminaries (*aadityaas*), that reveal the objective world and who are the formful (*saakaara*) manifestations of the formless *Brahman* (God). Number 12 also represents the 12 *raashis* (planets) or points through which the sun moves, each *raashi* representing one month.

Number 9 indicates the immutability of *Brahman* (God) and represents the formless (*niraakaar*) aspect. *Brahman* (9) with its 12 manifestations (*aadityaas*) ie, 9 × 12, makes 108. Thus, 108 indicates the totality of Godhead, the formless (*niraakaar*) and the formful (*saakaara*) aspects together.

Expansion of π (Pi)

The devotees of mathematics throughout the world must be beholden to the *Vedas* for revealing the key to what many historians and translators had dismissed as meaningless jargon. There, as commented upon by Desmond Doig, contained in certain *Sutras* (aphorisms), are the processes of mathematics, psychology, ethics and metaphysics.

"During the reign of King Kamsa" read a *Sutra*, "rebellions, arsons, famines and insanitary conditions prevailed." Decoded, this little piece of libellous history gives decimal answer to the fraction 1/17; sixteen processes of simple mathematics reduced to one.

In his book on *"Vedic* Mathematics", *Swami Sri* Krishna Tirthaji Maharaja says: "It is a matter of historical interest to note that, in their mathematical writings, the ancient *Sanskrit* writers did not use figures in their numeral notations but preferred to use the letters of *Sanskrit* (*Devanaagri*) alphabet to represent the various numbers! And this they did, not in order to conceal knowledge but in order to facilitate the recording of their arguments ...., to help the pupil to memorise the material studied and assimilated, they made it a general rule .... to write .... text-books in *sutras* or in verse .... for lightening the burden ..."

One such instance recorded in the book is the two line verse which is so worded as to bear three different meanings – all of them quite appropriate. The first is reported to be a hymn to Lord *Sri* Krishna; the second is similarly a hymn in praise of Lord *Sri* Shankara; and the third is a valuation of π/10 to 32 places of decimals! (with, allegedly, a "Self-contained master-key" for extending the evaluation to any number of decimal places!). Considering the fact that the expansion of π does not generate a cyclic number, the concept of a master-key enabling the evaluation to be extended to any number of decimal places is absolutely mind-blowing. However, no direct clue as to the form of the master-key is apparent from the two line verse.

The verse is reproduced hereunder with the corresponding numerical values for the consonants in the *Sanskrit* alphabet in accordance with the known alphabetical key.

"G o P i BHA a   G-YA   MA DH u V-RA a T − SHR-N G i SH o DA DH i   SA N-DH i GA
 3   1   4   1   5 9   2   6   5 3 5   8 9 7   9   3

 KHA LA   J ee V i TA   KHA a TA a VA   GA LA HA a LA a RA   SA n-DHA RA"
  2   3   8 4 6   2   6   4   3 3 8   3   2   7   9   2

π/10 = .3 1 4 1 5 9 2 6 5 3 5 8 9 7 9 3 2 3 8 4 6 2 6 4 3 3 8 3 2 7 9 2 ...

The alphabetical key is given in Appendix D.

Age of Creation

The knowledge about the age of Creation has been revealed in the "*Atharvana Veda*" (80–1–20). It is explained thus:

> "The length of time in years over which Creation will exist can be obtained by adding 7 places of zeros after 4 3 2, ie, 4 320 000 000 years."

This has been further elaborated in verses 18, 19 and 20 of the "*Surya Siddhanta*". According to it, the Creation has been divided into 14 parts, each part representing a *Manu-Mantra* (chronology of Life). Each *Manu-Mantra* is further divided into 71 *Chaturyugis* or 4-Age time cycles (*Mahayugs*). 1000 such cycles (*Sahasra Mahayug*), known as '*Kalpa*', over which life is sustained represent 1 day in the life of the Creator (ie, 1 *Brahma* Day). His night, known as '*Pralaya*', is also of even duration.

Creation remains in existence during the *Brahma* Day and it is dissolved during the *Brahma* Night. During this dissolution, only the life disappears by merging within the Creator Himself but the earth, the sun and the planets continue to exist.

Every day of *Brahma* sees 14 *Manus* lording over the Universe. So each *Manu* is the master for more than 70 *Mahayugs*.

<u>Yugs (Ages)</u>		<u>Man Years</u>	
Sat Yug or Krita Yug	:	1 728 000	(Kali Yug x 4)
Treta Yug	:	1 296 000	(Kali Yug x 3)
Dwapara Yug	:	864 000	(Kali Yug x 2)
Kali Yug	:	432 000	
Total of 1 Cycle, or Chaturyugi or Mahayug	:	4 320 000	(Kali Yug x 10)
71 Chaturyugis, or 1 Manu-Mantra	:	306 720 000	
14 Manu-Mantras or 994 Mahayugs	:	4 294 080 000	
Sandhya or Contact Period between Manu-Mantras (Equivalent to 6 Mahayugs)	:	25 920 000	
Grand Total of 1 'Kalpa', or 1000 (Sahasra) Mahayugs	:	4 320 000 000	

So, **1 Brahma Day (Kalpa)** = **4 320 000 000 years**
1 Brahma Night (Pralaya) = **4 320 000 000 years**

According to *Puraanas*, this figure is also arrived at in the following way:–

8 Yamas	:	1 Day
30 Days	:	1 Month
12 Months	:	1 Man Year
1 Man Year	:	1 God Day
360 God Days	:	1 God Year
or 360 Man Years	:	1 God Year

NB: "God Day" referred to here is not the same as *Brahma* Day, ie, Creator's 1 day or *Kalpa*.

Age		God Years		
Kali Yug	:	1 000		
Contact (*Sandhya*) Period	:	+ 200	=	1 200
Dwapara Yug	:	2 000		
Contact (*Sandhya*) Period	:	+ 400	=	2 400
Treta Yug	:	3 000		
Contact (*Sandhya*) Period	:	+ 600	=	3 600
Sat Yug	:	4 000		
Contact (*Sandhya*) Period	:	+ 800	=	4 800
TOTAL	:	**12 000**		**God Years**

12 000 God Years	:	1 *Mahayug*
1 000 *Mahayugs*	:	1 *Brahma* Day
So, 1 **Brahma Day** or ***Kalpa***	:	1 000 x 12 000 x 360
	:	**4 320 000 000 man years**

The 4-Age cycle of Time is also related to the solar and lunar eclipses. It is claimed that *Treta Yug* started after 2 000 solar and 2 000 lunar eclipses occurred in the *Sat Yug*. Likewise, after further 22 000 solar and 22 000 lunar eclipses in the *Treta Yug*, *Dwapara Yug* started. After another 20 000 solar and 20 000 lunar eclipses, the present *Kali Yug* started. The *Kali* Age will come to a conclusion after the sun and the moon have been eclipsed for 96 000 times each.

Age of Present *Kalpa*

Of the 14 *Manu-Mantras* of the present *Kalpa*, 6 have since passed. These are:

(1) *Swaayambhu*,   (2) *Swaarochish*,   (3) *Aautami (Aadatam)*,
(4) *Taamas*,   (5) *Raivat*,   (6) *Chaakshush*.

The name of the present *Manu-Mantra* is *"Vaivasvat"* (*Dev-Sut*). The names of the remaining 7 are:

(8) *Saavarnih (Saadarnih)*,   (9) *Daksh Saavarnih*,
(10) *Brahma Saavarnih*,   (11) *Dharma Saavarnih*,
(12) *Rudr Saavarnih (Rudr Putr)*, (13) *Dev Saavarnih (Rochashch)*,
(14) *Indr Saavarnih (Bhowtak)*.

		Years
6 *Manu-Mantras* have passed ie, 6 × 306 720 000	=	1 840 320 000
7th *Mano-Mantra* of which 27 *Chaturyugis* have since passed, ie, 27 × 4 320 000	=	116 640 000
28th *Chaturyugi* of which 3 *Yugs* have since passed ie, 1 728 000 + 1 296 000 + 86 400	=	3 888 000
Total at the end of *Dwapara Yug*	=	1 960 848 000
Kali Yug, the 4th *Yug* is current, having started on	:	20th of February, 3102 BC.
Time elapsed since the start of *Kali Yug* to 23rd November 1995 ie, (3102 + 1994) years, 9 months, and 1 day	=	**5096 years, 9 months, 1 day.**
Therefore **Age of Present *Kalpa*** as on 23rd November 1995	=	**1 960 853 096 years, 9 months, 1 day.**

Life Span of *Brahma* (Creator)

360 *Brahma* Days and Nights make one *Brahma* Year. 100 Such years represent the Age of *Brahma*. At the end of His Age, there will be the Final Dissolution (*Maha-pralaya*) of the Universe and *Ishwara* too, Baba says, will be non-existent; the Primordial Elements will also revert to their causal

be non-existent; the Primordial Elements will also revert to their causal state. In other words, the grossest of the five elements, namely, earth will be drowned in water, water will be drawn in by fire, fire will be absorbed by air and air will vanish into space, and so on until all merge back and revert to their causal state.

So, **Life Span of** *Brahma* **(Creator)**
ie, 4 320 000 000 × 2 × 360 × 100   =   **311 040 000 000 000 years**

(311 Thousand and 40 Billion years !!!)

Age of Creation

50 Years of *Brahma* (Creator) have already passed,
ie, 4 320 000 000 × 2 × 360 × 50   =   155 520 000 000 000 years
ie, 155 520 Billion years

The Creation is currently in the *Shveta-Vaaraaha-Kalpa,* which is the very first (*Brahma*) Day of the first (*Brahma*) Month of the 51st (*Brahma*) Year.

Recalling from page 214, the Age of present *Brahma* Day (*Shveta-Vaaraaha-Kalpa*) as on 23 November 1995 is   :   1 960 853 096 years, 9 months, 1 day.

So, **Age of Creation** as on 23 November 1995 is   :   (155 520 000 000 + 1 960 853 096) years, 9 months, 1 day

= **155 521 960 853 096 years, 9 months, 1 day**

O Divine Mother Sai ! Bless me that I may never lose myself in the many but ever remain centred on the One.

QUESTIONS:

(1) Discuss the concept of zero.
(2) What number symbolises God and why?

(3) What is the connection between mind and the number 2?
(4) What is the significance of number 2?
(5) What is the connection between the senses, the mind, the intellect and the soul?
(6) What is the WATCH-word?
(7) What are the characteristics of the Primordial Elements?
(8) How can we overcome the inner foes?
(9) What is the connection between the phenomenal world, the Truth and God?
(10) What are the 8 *Yogic Siddhis* (Powers) and the attributes of AUM?
(11) What are the two main characteristics of number 9?
(12) What is Infinity? When Infinity is taken away from Infinity, how can the residue be Infinity?
(13) How can three minus one equal one?
(14) Which is greater 1 or 9, and why?
(15) What do one and one make?
(16) What is the significance of 108?
(17) What is a *Chaturyugi* (4-Age time cycle)?
(18) What is a *kalpa*? How long is its duration?
(19) What happens during *Brahma* Night?
(20) What happens at Final Dissolution (*Maha-Pralaya*)?

> *Make your heart soft, then success is quick in sadhana (spiritual practice). Talk softly, talk sweetly, talk only of God – that is the process of softening the subsoil. Develop compassion, sympathy; engage in service, understand the agony of poverty and disease, distress and despair; share both tears and cheers with others. That is the way to soften the heart and help sadhana to succeed.*
> *– Sri Sathya Sai Baba*

APPENDIX A

A SUGGESTED FORMAT FOR A TYPICAL STUDY CIRCLE

The circle may be formed with the picture of Sai at the head to serve as a constant reminder of His omnipresence and therefore of the discipline and behaviour expected of every participant. Just as an assortment of flowers on their own does not constitute a garland until they are joined together by a common thread, so also a study circle can be complete only when there is a feeling of kinship and brotherhood and a shared love of and faith in Sai amongst all the participants. "Man's life is a garland," says Baba, "with birth at one end and death at the other". "Between the two ends are strung together flowers of all kinds, troubles, worries, joys sorrows and dreams. Few men are aware of the string that runs through all the flowers. Without the string there can be no garland. Only the person who recognises the string can become a real man. This string is called "*Sutra*" or "*Brahma-Sutra*" (The Divine String). The Divine *Atma* Principle is the string which is found in all human beings and which is the source of all potencies in them.

In a study circle, active participation by all is most desirable. Topic or the theme chosen for a study session should be announced at least one session in advance so as to give the participants a reasonable notice to do their home work on the subject preparatory to the study circle session and to enable them to contribute meaningfully to the discussions. Ideally, all participants should take it upon themselves to do the presentations of the topics in turn; otherwise the responsibility should be rotated amongst those who are best able to shoulder it.

Presentation may take the form of putting across the presenter's understanding of the topic, his doubts and difficulties, or a series of logically structured questions aimed at the various aspects of the topic and its relevance in the day-to-day life. Whatever method the presenter feels comfortable with, that choice should be left to him.

A suggested format for a typical study circle is given below:–

Venue and Time :	Fixed
Size of the group :	7–15 members
Duration of session :	1hr 10mins to 1hr 30mins
Frequency :	Once a week

- Begin session with 3 AUMs
- Silent Prayer for Divine Guidance
- Main Presentation : 30 – 40 mins
- Discussion : 30 – 40 mins
- Summing up : 5 mins
- Conclude session with 3 AUMs
- Universal Prayer before dispersal

The person nominated to do the summing up may also be called upon to be the moderator for the session.

Suffering and misery are the inescapable acts of the Cosmic Drama. God does not decree these calamities, but man invites them by way of retribution for his own evil deeds. This is corrective punishment which induces mankind to give up the wrong path and return to the right path so that he may experience the Godlike state of Sat-Chit-Aananda (Being-Awareness-Bliss) ... All this is part of the grand synthesis in which the negatives serve to glorify the positives. Thus death glorifies immortality, ignorance glorifies wisdom, misery glorifies bliss, and night glorifies dawn.

You are reaping in the present what you had sown in the past. And what you are sowing in the present, you will reap in the future. Thus, both the past and the future are contained in the present only.

— *Sri Sathya Sai Baba*

APPENDIX B

YOGA, KUNDALINI AND THE CHAKRAS

Yoga means union; union of the individual self (*jivatma*) with the Universal Self (*Paramatma*), the human with the divine. This union, the blossoming of the human consciousness into divine consciousness, is the consummation and fruition of an intense discipline or a set of disciplines (*sadhanas*) involving body, mind and spirit. In common parlance, this *sadhana*, the physical, mental and the spiritual practices that lead to the final consummation is referred to as *yoga*.

The *yoga* that pertains to the control and disciplining of the body is known as *Hatha Yoga*. Its constituents are : *Praanayama* (breath control), *Aasanaas* (balanced body postures), *Shatkarma* (exercises for the six purifications of the body) and the awakening of the *Kundalini* (the serpent energy latent at the base of the spine). *Hatha Yoga* aims at a total mastery over body, breath and the nerves and, through it, Self-realisation. **Such exercises, especially the awakening of the *Kundalini* however, should be undertaken only under the instruction and the expert supervision of a well experienced master.**

- 1. *Praanayama* : See Chapter 8.

- 2. *Aasanaas* : For the practitioners of *Hatha Yoga*, 84 postures to make all parts of the body supple preventing muscular deterioration, have been prescribed. Some well known ones of these are :

  - *Padmaasana*   (Lotus posture)
  - *Sarvaangaasana*   (All - parts exercise posture)
  - *Mayuraasana*   (Peacock posture)
  - *Matsyaasana*   (Fish posture)
  - *Dhanuraasana*   (Bow posture)
  - *Paschimothanaasana*   (Posterior stretching posture)
  - *Chakraasana*   (Circle posture)
  - *Bakaasana*   (Crane posture)
  - *Shirshaasana*   (Head - stand posture)

For further details, the reader is referred to the book 'Sai Baba and Sai Yoga'.

- 3. *Shatkarmas* : These exercises are undertaken to cleanse the impurities of the body and are known as : *Neti, Dhoti, Basti, Nyoli, Bhasrika* and *Trataka*.

- 4. **Kundalini Awakening (*Laya Yoga*):** *Kundalini* is considered by *Hatha Yogis* to be a vital energy of awesome power situated, in its dormant state, at the base of the spinal cord. Within the physical spinal cord, it is said, is a central canal known in *Sanskrit*, as *Sushumna Naadi* with two other canals - *Ida* on the left and *Pingala* on the right - entwined around the spine. *Ida*, also known as the *Chandra* (Moon) *Naadi* is connected with the left nostril and *Pingala*, also known as the *Surya* (Sun) *Naadi*, with the right. *Kundalini* Power is said to lie at the base in three and a half coils like a sleeping serpent. As the *Kundalini* is awakened, it is said to flow in the three canals. In the *yogis*, the main flow is said to be through the *Sushumna Naadi* (canal).

    Sushumna Naadi, however, is not the physical spinal cord. Just as the spinal cord is the centre of the nerves in the physical body, *Sushumna Naadi* which is situated in the spinal cord, is the ethereal cord of the subtle body. In the *Sushumna*, right from the base where the *Kundalini* energy lies latent up to the space between the eyebrows, are situated six spiritual centres, known as *Chakras* (Wheels). When awakened, *Kundalini* moves upwards through these centres.

    Meditation, according to *Hatha Yoga*, is always on the *Sushumna*, with the object of arousing the sleeping *Kundalini* and causing it to rise, gradually, up the *Sushumna* canal activating each higher centre in turn. However, as it is subtle and since the subtle body can be reached only through the physical body, the concentration has, in effect, to be on the centres of the spinal cord. Meditation on the spinal centres automatically affects the subtler centres of the *Sushumna*.

    By concentration and other methods, the heat in the body becomes very powerful. *Kundalini*, feeling this heat and being disturbed by it, is aroused from her sleep in much the same way as a serpent struck by a stick hisses and straightens itself up. It then enters the *Sushumna*. The ascent of the *Kundalini* from one spiritual centre to the next is very graded. As it enters it, the centre becomes illumined and enlivened, and as the *Kundalini* leaves each centre in her upward movement, the illuminated and enlivened centre becomes latent for the illumination and the enlivenment of the subsequent higher centre. It is because of this that *Kundalini Yoga* is also called the *Laya Yoga*; Laya means latency or disappearance. It disappears in the lower centre to

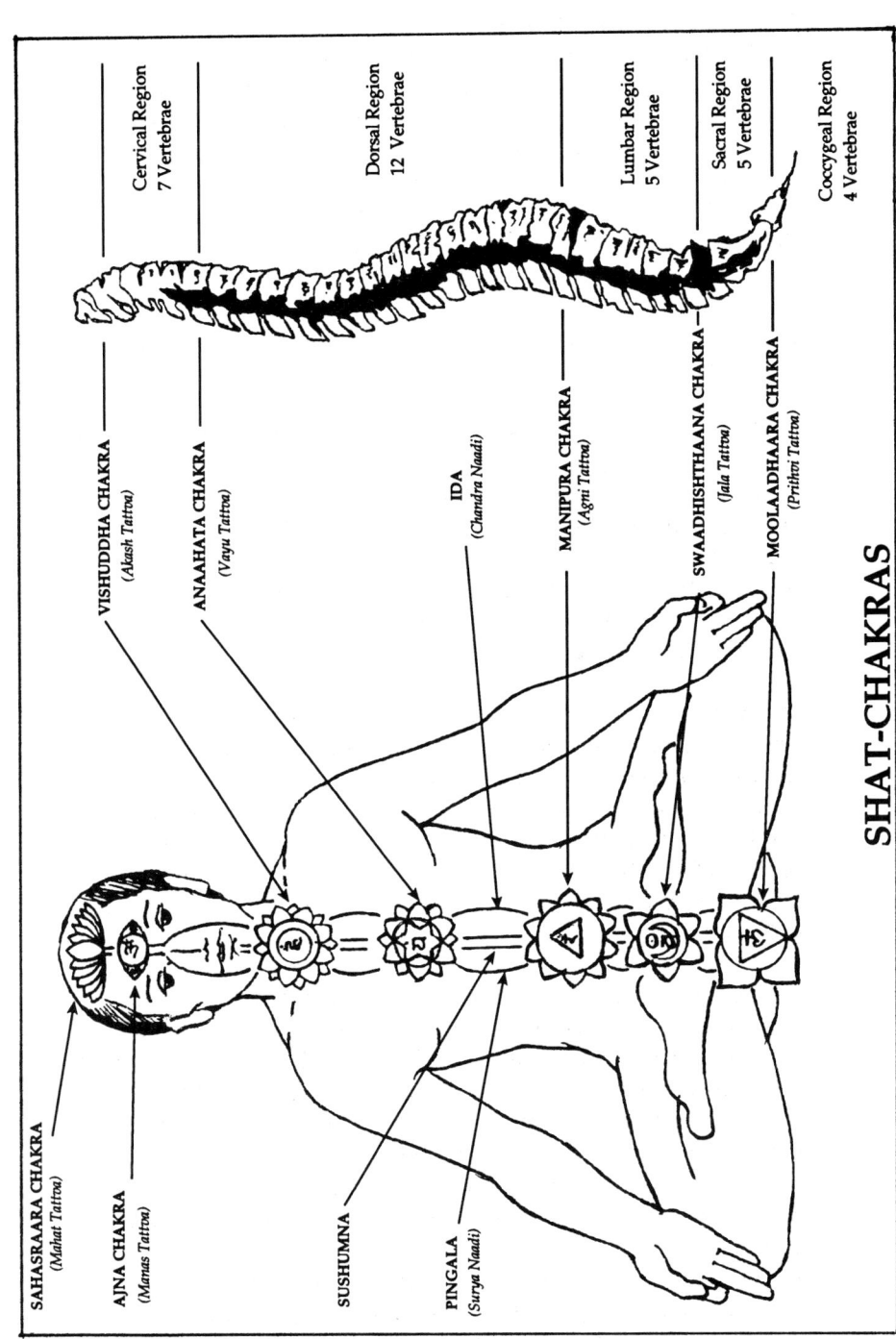

"It is a mistaken notion to believe that things happen as a result of human effort and planning, and human intelligence and care. No one can succeed in any venture without Divine Grace. It is God's plan that is being worked out through Man, but Man prides himself that it is he who is working for it. Man will realise his mission on earth when he knows himself as Divine and reveres others as Divine. Man must worship God in man. God appears before him as a blind beggar, an idiot, a leper, a child, a decrepit old man, a criminal or a mad man. You must see behind even these physical veils the Divine Sai and worship Him through service. All names are His and all forms are His, including yours. You appear as separate individual bodies because the eye that sees them, seeks only the outer bodies. When you clarify your vision and look at them through the Atmic eye, (that is the eye which penetrates behind the physical with its attributes and appurtenances) then you will see others as Waves on the Ocean of the Absolute, as the thousand heads, the thousand eyes and the thousand feet of the Purusha sung in the Rigveda. The vision of the Virat (the Cosmic Form) is given to those who surrender their ego and take refuge in the Lord. God is omnipresent. He is the inner motivator of every particle in the Universe. To declare that He is amenable only to your style of worship and that He will answer only to the Name you have learnt to use, is to insult His Omniscience and His Glory. See Him, serve Him and revere Him, in all. Pray, "Let the whole world prosper and let all mankind be happy.'"

Sri Sathya Sai Baba

illumine the next higher one.

When the ascent through the six spiritual centres is complete, in its final state the *Kundalini* reaches the topmost, the seventh location called the *Sahasraara Chakra* (Thousand petalled centre) where the Hindus always used to wear tuft of hair on their heads even while otherwise clean shaven. At this point, it is said, there takes place the union of *Shakti* (*Kundalini* Power) with her Lord *Shiva* in the *Puranic* terminology, or *Atma* (the individual soul) with *Paramatma* (the Supersoul) in the *Vedantic* terminology. This is said to be the stage of spiritual bliss, unalloyed with physical and sensual pleasures. This is the transcendental experience of a *Hatha Yogi* whereby he realises in his own person the individual and separate existence of the soul from the body.

Each spiritual centre (*Chakra*) is associated with a certain location of the body, a primal element, a lotus flower with a certain number of petals, a geometrical shape with a special significance, a letter of the *Sanskrit* alphabet representing a particular sound, etc. Each *Chakra* enshrines both the strength for spiritual evolution as well as the potential for degeneration and appalling dangers; that is why *Hatha Yoga Pradipika* warns us that : "It gives liberation to *Yogis* and bondage to fools." Specific techniques are therefore required for a successful and beneficial passage of this awesome *Kundalini Shakti* (Power) up the *Sushumna* through the various *Chakras*. These *Chakras* are :

- 1. *Moolaadhaara Chakra* (**Pelvic Wheel**) : It is situated in the *Sushumna* at the base of the spine, in the coccyx or pelvic region. This is the root where the *Kundalini* as a spiritual force lies dormant sleeping in three and a half coils as a serpent.

- 2. *Swaadhishthaana Chakra* (**Generative Wheel**) : It is located in the area of the generative organs, two inches above the Pelvic Wheel and represents the creative potential in man.

- 3. *Manipura Chakra* (**Navel Wheel**) : It is located in the abdominal area, at the navel over the solar plexus of the spinal cord. It is called *Manipura* meaning the 'city of the jewel'.

- 4. *Anaahata Chakra* (**Heart Wheel**) : *Anaahata* means ever new. This *Chakra* is located at the intersection of the spinal canal with the line joining the nipples of the chest. As this location is that of the spiritual (not the biological) heart, it is referred to as the Heart Wheel. The lotus of the heart (*Hridayakamala*) has eight petals. These eight petals symbolise the eight worlds, the eight directions, the eight guardians of the world, the eight spirits (*bhutas*) and the eight parts of the earth. Because Krishna is the Lord of these eight petals, He was described as the husband of eight queens.

- 5. *Vishuddha Chakra* (**Laryngeal Wheel**) : It is located in the *Sushumna* on a level with the throat.

- 6. *Ajna Chakra* (**Frontal Wheel**) : It is located in the front (hence Frontal) between the eyebrows.

- 7. *Sahasraara Chakra* (**Thousand petalled Wheel**) : It is located at the crown of the head and is said to be represented by thousand petalled lotus. Each of these petals has 16 *kalas*. The Lord is described as the embodiment of the 16 *kalas*. As Lord of the *Sahasraara* (thousand-petalled lotus), He presides over the 16 000 *kalas* which are present in this lotus. The *Kundalini Shakti* (Power) which starts at the base of the spinal column (*Moolaadhaara*), rises and merges with the 16 000 thousand entities in the *Sahasraara*. This is the esoteric significance and the meaning of the role of the Divine within the body. Oblivious to this inner meaning, people indulge in misinterpretations and perverse expositions.

It is interesting to note that the *Gopikas* during the sojourn of Krishna *Avataar* on earth as well as Meera the great devotee of Lord Krishna during the recent past, exhorted their minds to travel to the place where *Ganga* and *Yamuna* meet. *Ganga* and *Yamuna* are symbolic of the two *naadis*, *Ida* and *Pingala*, through which one takes in and gives out breath. The place where they meet is the centre of the forehead. However, it is said to be the confluence of not only *Ida* and *Pingala* but also the *Sushumna* (*Triveni sangham* -- confluence of three rivers). This spot is sacred, pure and calm and the self should be located in this place.

APPENDIX C

NIRVAANA SHATKAM
(Six stanzas on Liberation)

(AN ENGLISH RENDERING)

1. Mind and Intellect I am not,
   No Ego, nor Recollection ever sought;
   Neither the Senses of Perception Five[1],
   Nor the Primordial Elements Five[2],
   Blissful Awareness Shiva am I!
   Blissful Awareness Shiva am I!

2. With the Life-Force and the Vital Airs Five[3],
   With the Substances Seven[4] and the Sheaths Five[5],
   With every Action of the Senses Five[6],
   No claim of any dealings have I;
   Blissful Awareness Shiva am I!
   Blissful Awareness Shiva am I!

3. Loathing and Liking I have none,
   No Greed nor Deluding Infatuation;
   Of Ego and Pride, no sense any more,
   Nor of the Principal Objectives Four[7];
   Blissful Awareness Shiva am I!
   Blissful Awareness Shiva am I!

4. No Virtue, no Vice, no Pleasure, no Pain,
   No yen for the Vedas, all Sacrifice - in vain;
   No Mystic Formula, no Pilgrimage either,
   No Eater, no Food, the Act of Eating neither;
   Blissful Awareness Shiva am I!
   Blissful Awareness Shiva am I!

5. No Death to fear, no Caste to beware,
   No Father, no Mother, no Birth either;
   No Friend nor Kinship,
   No Teacher - Taught relationship;
   Blissful Awareness Shiva am I!
   Blissful Awareness Shiva am I!

6. No Form, no Fancy, for the All-Pervading Supremacy,
   Ever Existing, yet Senses Transcending;
   Ever serene, calm and Equipoised,
   Free of Fetters and Freedom Realised;
   Blissful Awareness Shiva am I!
   Blissful Awareness Shiva am I!

1. Senses of Perception	Touch, Taste, Sound, Sight & Smell
2. Primordial Elements	Earth, Water, Fire, Air & Ether (or, Space)
3. Vital Airs Five	*Praana, Vyaana, Udaana, Samaana* & Apaana
4. Substances Seven	Juice, Blood, Flesh, Fat, Bones, Marrow & Seminal Fluid
5. Sheaths Five	*Anna Maya* (food related), *Praana Maya* (life-breath related), *Mano Maya* (mind related), *Vignaana Maya* (discrimination related) & *Aananda Maya* (bliss related)
6. Senses of Action	Tongue, Hands, Feet, Organs of Excretion & Procreation
7. Principal Objectives	*Dharma* (righteous living), *Artha* (earning wealth through proper and legitimate means), *Kaama* (supreme desire), *Mokhsha* (liberation from bondage)

Let the petty wishes for which you now approach God be realised or not, let the plans for promotion or progress which you place before God, be fulfilled or not; they are not so important after all. The primary aim should be to become Masters of yourselves, to hold intimate and constant communion with the Divine that is in you as well as in the Universe of which you are a part. Welcome disappointments, for they toughen you and test your fortitude.

– Sri Sathya Sai Baba

APPENDIX D

KEY TO ALPHABETICAL CODE

The key to the alphabetical code as appearing in the *Vedic* Mathematics is as follows :

"Ka–aadi nav, Ta–aadi nav, Pa–aadi panchak,
Ya–aadi ashtak and *Ksha–shunyam"*,

which means :

"*Ka* etc nine, *Ta* etc nine, *Pa* etc five, *Ya* etc eight and count **Ksha** *as* zero."

For ready reference, the key may be tabulated as follows:

Ka	Ta	Pa	Ya	⇨	1
Kha	Tha	Pha	Ra	⇨	2
Ga	Da	Ba	La	⇨	3
Gha	Dha	Bha	Va	⇨	4
Gna	Na	Ma	Sha	⇨	5
Cha	Ta		Sha	⇨	6
Chha	Tha		Sa	⇨	7
Ja	Da		Ha	⇨	8
Jha	Dha			⇨	9
			Ksha	⇨	0

Notes :

(1) Vowels make no difference and are therefore not included in the above table.

(2) In the case of conjunct consonants, count only the last consonant.

(3) In pronouncing the alphabet, treat the ones with the bar on top as "guttural" sounds, the one with dot on top as half mute, and all others as soft or natural sounds.

APPENDIX E

INTERESTING FACTS AND FIGURES
(As abstracted from Swami's discourses)

- Number of life forms in the world : 8 400 000

- A human being takes, on average, 21 600 breaths per day, ie, 900 breaths per hour or 15 breaths per minute. Of these, 10 800 breaths are taken during the day time. With every breath, man repeats *Soham* (I am He). So, the figure 216 and its half 108, have a deep spiritual significance.

- The location of *atma*, the life-principle, is considered as being 10 'inches' above the navel and at the centre of the chest. In other words, the location is given by the intersection of the horizontal line joining the nipples with the vertical line through the centre of the chest. An 'inch' in this measurement is the width of one's thumb at the first joint. The size of atma is taken as the size of one's thumb.

- Average ages of man in the various ages of the Time-Cycle are:

Sat or *Krit Yug*	:	400 years
Treta Yug	:	300 years
Dwapara Yug	:	200 years
Kali Yug	:	100 years

- Norm for the average height of man in the various ages of the Time-Cycle is:

Sat or *Krit Yug*	:	14 Hands
Treta Yug	:	10.5 Hands
Dwapara Yug	:	7 Hands
Kali Yug	:	3.5 Hands

    A 'Hand' is measured as the distance from the finger tip to the elbow.

- Jesus was born on the 24th (December) near midnight and not on the 25th as commonly believed. He realised that he was Christ in his 25th year. For 8 years following his 16th birthday, he travelled in India, Tibet, Iran and Russia.

- The land we now call Sri Lanka is not the same land that existed in the *Treta Yuga* and which was ruled by Ravana at the time of *Ramarajya*. At that time, Lanka was hundreds of miles away to the south from the tip of India; at that time, it was at the equator. As the time passed from *Treta* to *Kali Yuga*, this particular island drifted hundreds of miles northwards. It was recorded in the Greek history that this land which we now call Sri Lanka was completely submerged under water when the oceanic catastrophe called the Atlantis occurred. The Greeks were no ordinary people. They were very advanced in sciences and were very knowledgeable in many fields. They were describing the fact that Lanka was submerged in the ocean and had drifted away and this phenomenon was being accepted by them. At that time, these people were so advanced that they had travelled to the moon and had designed several types of air transport and were such that they had mastered the science of flying.

- Today the entire world refers to the Greenwich Mean Time as the standard of time. In world history, it is known that astrologers of old took the longitude passing through Lanka at that time (ie, when it was at the equator) and when the sun rose on this longitude, they took it as the standard of time for calculations. It is on the basis of this standard of time that *Bharatiyas* (Indians) decided on the birth of Krishna *Avataar*, the time at which Lord Krishna gave up His mortal body and the dates of the *Mahabharata* battle and so on. When the *Pandavas* lived, towards the end of *Dwapara Yuga*, the time scales were determined on the basis of this longitude which passed through Lanka.

- According to this computation, *Kali Yuga* started in the year named *Pramadi*, in the month named *Shravana*, in the fortnight named *Bahula* and on the day called *Ashtami*. According to the English Calendar, this will be described as February 20, 3102 years before the Advent of Christ. As this was the commencing day of the new *Yuga* (Age), it was called *Ugadi*. This particular day called the *Ugadi* is also the day on which the Lord brought His sojourn on earth in the Krishna *Avataar* to an end at a sacred place of pilgrimage called *Prabata* near *Dwarika*..... Between the years 3138 BC when Krishna crowned Dharmaraja, and 3102 BC, a period of 36 years, Krishna enabled the Gopikas to experience the divinity in Krishna.

- It is said that one thinks of all sorts of extraordinary and unusual ideas when one's end is nigh. The *Yadavas*, the community in which Lord Krishna lived, had some such strange ideas then and they brought their end on themselves. Although Lord Krishna was preaching the acceptance of only *sattwic* food, the *Yaadavas* violated this sacred injunction on a holy day. When they were performing a religious ceremony, they used articles which should not have been used and prepared food containing meat and they also partook of alcoholic drinks and consumed these articles. On account of such food and drink, they became intoxicated and lost their balance. They began to fight each other and, in this manner, extinguished the entire *Yaadava* clan. It is in this context, bearing in mind the ideals which Lord Krishna had promulgated, that Gandhi also wanted to forbid meat eating and the use of alcoholic drinks (in India).

- The battle of *Kurukshetra* took place in 3138 BC and lasted 18 days. 4 Million warriors got killed in it. The soldiery on the two sides comprised: eleven *Akshauhinis* for the *Kaurvas* and seven for the *Pandavas*, ie, 18 altogether. An *Akshauhini* consisted of:

109 350	foot soldiers	(50 %)
65 610	horse soldiers	(30 %)
21 870	elephant soldiers	(10 %)
21 870	chariots and their human equipment	(10 %)

    It adds up to a total of 218 700 soldiers in one *Akshauhini*. It is interesting to note that all the digits in the above figures add up to number 9.

- At the time of the *Kurukshetra* battle Bhishma was 116 years of age. He took part in the battle for 9 days and he fell on the 10th day. Thereafter, he lived on the bed of arrows for 58 days. These two together constitute a total of 67 days. He was thinking of the Lord all those days and was waiting for an auspicious time to die. Bhishma finally gave up his life on *Ashtami* (not *Ekadashi* as popularly believed) when the prevailing star was *Rohini*. Thus Bhishma died on a day similar to the one that the Lord took His Krishna *Avataar* on. At the time of battle, Lord Krishna was 86 years of age, Arjuna 84 and Abhimanyu, his son, only 15 years of age. Parikshit, the son of Abhimanyu, was born when Abhimanyu would have been 16 years of age.

- Man alone is endowed with the capacity to discover his divinity. In this context, food habits play an important role. Out of 8 400 000 species of living beings on earth, 8 399 999 species of creatures like insects, birds, animals, beasts, etc, live on what is provided by God in Nature, and hence they do not generally suffer from any diseases. Man is the sole exception in this regard. By becoming a slave to his palate, he relishes only cooked and spicy foods of various kinds, without realising to what extent such foods are curtailing his own longevity.

Besides this, it is significant to note that those who live on vegetarian food are less prone to diseases whereas non-vegetarians are subject to more diseases. Why? Because animal food is incompatible with the needs of the human body. Doctors talk about proteins being present in non-vegetarian food, but the fact is that there are better quality proteins in food articles like vegetables, pulses, milk, curd, etc. Non-vegetarian food not only affects man's body but also has deleterious effect on his mind.

Food, head, God - these three are inter-related. By consuming animal food, animal tendencies are aroused. As is your food, so are your thoughts. Men today are behaving in a manner worse than that of wild animals in the forest. They have become cruel, pitiless and hard-hearted. There is no sympathy or understanding even between man and man. The main reason for this condition lies in the kind of food that is consumed ... . Man needs food which supplies him energy equivalent to about one calorie per minute. Young people should be satisfied with 2 000 calories of food per day. But now-a-days the food intake has increased up to 5 000 calories. As a result, people suffer from indigestion and sleeplessness. Loss of sleep gives rise to many ailments. Don't worry about sleep. If you go to bed without any worry, you will get sound sleep automatically.

Whatever (vegetarian) food we may eat, provided it does not contain too much salt, chilli or acid and if we eat in right proportions, it may be described as *sattwic*. The ideal proportion is 2 parts of solid food, 1 part of liquid and 1 part of air. This kind of food will help us a great deal in our *sadhana* and we will have good health.

- Ills of the body : The human body is subjected to afflictions from three sources: *Vaatha* (the wind element in the body), *Pitha* (bile) and *Slesha* (phlegm). 102 Types of ailments arise from *Vaathas*. 42 Kinds of diseases are caused by bile disorders. Phlegm disorders account for as many as 242 different kinds of ailments. Altogether the body is a sink for hundreds of ailments. In his attachment to the body and the fleeting pleasures derived from the senses, man is forgetting the lasting bliss that can be got from the *atma* within him.

- Ills of the mind : Mind (*antahkarna*) is liable to ailments from three sources: *Mala* (impurities), *Vikshepa* (delusion) and *Aavarna* (covering). It is because of these ailments that man is unable to develop his spiritual nature and acquire knowledge of the *atma*. On account of ignorance of his spiritual nature, he regards his mundane existence as the only reality.

Mala (impurity) is also known by the term *Avidya*, meaning ignorance. Ignorance can be removed by *karmas* (prescribed actions). *Aavarna* (covering) can be removed by *upaasana* (worship). *Vikshepa* (delusion) can be removed by developing the power of discrimination. So, to deal with the maladies of *mala, aavarna* and *vikshepa,* you need work, worship and wisdom. These three paths have been laid down by the *Vedas.* Through *karma* (action), purity of mind is achieved. Through *upaasana* (devotional worship), one-pointed concentration of mind is promoted. And through wisdom, liberation is attained.

The primary cause of sorrow for man is birth itself. *Karma* (past action) is the cause of birth. Desire is the impelling cause of all actions. Desire is prompted by attachment, which proceeds from lack of understanding. Ego is the cause of this ignorance. When ignorance goes, the ego subsides. Absence of egoism leads to right understanding. The desires abate. With the decline of desires, actions get sanctified. Then life becomes meaningful. Thus ignorance is called *aavarna* (that which covers or envelops an object).

Mala (impurity) is a stage anterior to *aavarna*. It is a state of mind in which the body, made up of five elements and the senses of perception and action, is regarded as the real Self. Because of this mental condition, man has delusions regarding the body which are false and unreal. The passing of excreta and urine is described as '*malavisarjanam*' (getting rid of filthy things from the body). '*Mala*' means that which is impure. As a state of mind, '*mala*' refers to the condition in which one regards the impermanent, the false and the unsacred as permanent, true and holy.

Aavarna means enveloping or covering something. The six vices, lust, anger, greed, pride, delusion and envy, have enveloped man. Attachment and aversion have gripped him. Because of this, man has forgotten his real nature and filled himself with pride of all sorts. Losing his powers of discrimination, he indulges in all kinds of misbehaviour towards his betters. The *Vedas* prescribe *upaasana* (devotional worship) as a means of getting rid of these bad qualities. As a lighted joss stick removes, by its fragrance, the bad odour in a place, devotional repetition of the name of God drives away the impurities of the mind.

The state of mind depends on the type of food that is consumed. After digestion, the grossest part of the food is given out as excreta. A subtle part becomes blood and flesh and provides sustenance for the body. The subtlest part goes to the mind. Hence the tendencies of the mind are based on the type of food that is eaten.

- *Avataars* seldom give advice directly. What they wish to convey they give indirectly. The reason is: there is divinity present in each human being and it is by making man realise it that he should be enabled to correct himself. If the correctives are applied directly, man will never try to realise his (innate) divinity. The indirect method is used to give to man the capacity to understand his (native) divinity.

- The Wright brothers are declared to be the pioneers, the very first to fly a heavier-than-air plane in the sky. Their powered flight took place on December 17, 1903. But a German had actually forestalled them by his flight on September 13, 1896. We must note that even earlier than this German, on August 14, 1895, an Indian hailing from Bombay, Shivaram Bapuji Kadalekar had succeeded in a similar feat. His name failed to draw public admiration and his feat was not acclaimed because of the envy, selfishness and the quarrelsome nature of certain people.

> *I am the Truth of Truths. Why has Truth come on earth in human form? To plant in the heart of man the yearning for Truth, to place man on the road to Truth, to help man reach Truth, by loving instruction and by the final gift of Illumination.*
> — Sri Sathya Sai Baba

APPENDIX F

BIBLIOGRAPHY

Books and Discourses by Bhagawan Sri Sathya Sai Baba:

Bhagvatha Vahini.
Dhyana Vahini.
Discourses on Bhagavad Gita.
Geetha Vahini.
Indian Culture and Spirituality; Summer Course, May-June 1990.
Prasnottar Vahini.
Sandeha Nivarini.
Sathya Sai Speaks, Vols. II, IV, VI.
Seva Sadhana.
Summer Roses on the Blue Mountains.
Summer Showers in Brindavan, 1972; 1974; 1978.
Sutra Vahini.
Upanishad Vahini.

Books by other authors:

Chinmayananda, Swami; Vedanta - The Science of Life, Part III.
Cohen, S. S; Guru Ramana.
Devi Indra; Sai Baba and Sai Yoga.
Fanibunda, Dr. E; Vision of the Divine.
Ferris, Timothy; Frontiers of Physics; SPAN, March 1983.
Gokak, Dr. V. K; In Defence of Jesus Christ and other Avatars.
Hislop, Dr. J. S; Conversations with Bhagavan Sri Sathya Sai Baba.
Hislop, Dr. J. S; My Baba and I.
Huxley, Aldous; Perennial Philosophy.
Krishnananda, Swami; The Mandukya Upanishad.
Lao Tzu; Tr. of Tao Teh King in The Way and Its Power by Arthur Waley (London, 1933).
Lowenberg, R; The Grace of Sai.
Nikhilananda, Swami; Atma Bodh : Self-knowledge of Sri Sankaracarya.
Nikhilananda, Swami; Vedanta of Sadananda.
Page, V. S; Dialogues with the Divine.
Paramananda, Swami; Silence as Yoga.
Prabhavananda, Swami; Patanjali Yoga Sutr.
Ra. Ganapati; Baba: Satya Sai, Part I.
Raghavan, Smt. Kaushalyarani; Guide to Indian Culture and Spirituality.
Rodrigo, Lenny P (Ed); He, Sathya Sai Baba.

Rumi, Jalal-uddin; Masnavi; Translated by E. H. Whinfield (London, 1898).
Sen, Gautam; The Mind of Swami Vivekananda.
Swami Sri Bharati Krishna Tirthaji Maharaja; Vedic Mathematics.
Swami Sri Ramananda Saraswathi: Tr; Tripura Rahasya, or, The Mystery Beyond the Trinity.
Taimni, I. K; Gayatri.
Thakkar, Hirabhai; Theory of Karma.
Venkatavardan, Dr. V. S; Vedic Thought and Modern Cosmology.
Watts, Alan W; The Spirit of Zen (London, 1936).
Vimuktananda, Swami; Aparoksanubhuti or Self-realisation of Sri Sankaracarya.
Yatiswarananda, Swami; Universal Prayers.

Other Books and Journals;

Adi Sankara, The Saviour of Mankind; Project BHISHMA.
Amrit Bindu Upanishad.
Bhagavad Geeta.
Brahadaranyaka Upanishad 3-7-3.
Brahma Sutras; with comments by Swami Vishweshvarananda; Advaita Ashram.
Chandogya Upanishad.
Dakshinamurti Stotram.
Katha Upanishad.
Laghu Vakyavrtti of Sri Sankaracarya with commentary; Advaita Ashrama.
Maharshi's Gospel (Books I & II); Sri Ramanasramam.
Manusmrithi.
Pancikaranam of Sri Sankaracarya; Advaita Ashram.
Praarthana Preeti; Shreemad Bhagawad Geeta Paathshaala.
Sanathana Sarathis.
Self - enquiry.
Speeches of Swami Ram Tirth.
Spirituality and Science; Sri Sathya Sai Trust.
Sri Sathya Sai Seva Organisations - Seva Dal; Central Office, Prashanthi Nilayam (AP).
Stories for children; Education in Human Values series.
The Complete Works of Swami Vivekananda, Vol. 1.
The Divine Master; Sairatan Publication.
The Path Divine; Sri Sathya Sai Bal Vikas Education Trust.
The Ten Principal Upanishads; Tr. by Shree Purohit and W. B. Yeats (London,1937).
"What is Life and Mind and Matter"; Cambridge University Press. 1967.
Works of Meister Eckhart; Translated by C. B. Evans (London, 1936).

APPENDIX (G)

GLOSSARY OF SANSKRIT WORDS

Aachaarya	: Teacher; Preceptor.
Aadhaara	: Support; Basis.
Aadaaya	: Taking away; Subtracting; Coming out.
Aadi	: Etc; First.
Aadityaas	: Luminaries.
Aagaami	: Yet to come; Yet to bear fruit; Would be.
Aagama	: Exhaling of the Lord's breath (ie *Vedas*).
Aakaara	: Form; Shape.
Aakaash	: Sky; Ether; Space.
Aamnaaya	: Constant contemplation of the root syllable *"na"* in the study of the *Vedas*.
Aanand	: Bliss. (Not to be confused with pleasure which comes hand-in-hand with pain.)
Aanandamaya	: Blissful; Full of Bliss.
Aarati	: Waving of flame at the end of *bhajan* session.
Aasana	: Posture.
Aaseet	: Was; Stay; Remain.
Aavarna	: Veil; Layer (of ignorance); Unreality; Covering or enveloping something
Abhan	: Delusion.
Abhaya	: Without fear; Fear not; Fearlessness.
Abhinivesha	: Complete identification of ones's consciousness with the body; The feeling that one is young/old, tall/short, etc; Owning.
Achalam	: Immovable; Unshakable; Mountain.
Acharam	: Immovable.
Achyuta	: One of the many names of Lord Krishna.
Adah	: That (God).
Adhyaropa	: Superimposition.
Adreshta	: Not the object of sight; Destiny.
Adwaita	: Non-dual; Monism.
Agni	: Fire.
Agra	: In the beginning; First; Foremost; In front of; Before.
Aham	: 'I'; In its purest sense, it represent the Self.
Ahamkaar	: Ego; Mistaken notion of body as the real 'I'.
Ahimsa	: Non-violence in thought, word, & deed.
Ahoraatra	: Day and night.
Aikam	: One; Single; Alone; Only.

Aikyam	:	One-ness with God.
Aisha	:	Such; This. *(Fem.)*
Ajapa	:	Without deliberate repetition; Repetition on its own without any external or deliberate effort; *SO-HAM* mantra which is recited automatically with every breath is referred to as the *Ajapa or Hamsa Gayatri*.
Ajna	:	Frontal.
Ajnaana	:	Ignorance; Darkness.
Akarma	:	Action without the assumption of doership; Inaction in action.
Akarmani	:	In inaction.
Akshara	:	Alphabet; Without death; Imperishable; Unchanging.
Alakshyam	:	Negligence.
Amaatra	:	Letterless resonance.
Amrit	:	Not mortal; Ambrosia; Not subject to death; Nectar that confers immortality.
Anaadi	:	Without beginning.
Anaahata	:	Ever new; Incessant; Irrespective of conscious will.
Anaatma	:	Non-self; Materialistic; Non-spiritual.
Ananta	:	Without end.
Anapeksha	:	Unwanted; Without desire (Beyond *Preyas* and *Shreyas*; Actions as offering to God).
Andhakaara	:	Darkness; Ignorance.
Anga	:	Part of the body.
Aneema	:	Ability to assume a very small form.
Anna, Annam	:	Food; Sustenance.
Annamaya	:	Food related; Sustained by food.
Anoraniyaan	:	Smaller than the smallest; Subtler than the subtlest.
Anrtam	:	Untrue; False.
Antahkarana	:	Inner senses; *(Man, Buddhi, Chitta, Ahamkaar)*.
Antaram	:	Another; In between.
Anuswara	:	Practice of repeating a *mantra*.
Apaana	:	One of the five vital airs.
Apeksha	:	Liking.
Api	:	Too; Also; As well.
Apriyam	:	Unpleasant; Lacking pleasantness.
Ardha	:	Half; Semi.
Arishta	:	Transgression.
Artha	:	Wealth; Meaning; Product; Earning; Accumulation.
Asabhyata	:	Lack of social etiquette.
Asat	:	Untruth; False; Of no permanent existence.
Ashrotra	:	Not the object of hearing.
Ashta	:	Eight.

Ashtavakra	: With eight deformities; Name of a sage.
Assi	: Is.
Asmita	: Turning attention outside; Existence; Individuality.
Asti	: Is; Being.
Astittwa	: Is-ness; Existence.
Astu	: Be; Let (it) be; May (it) be
Asuyah	: Thought of harming others at any cost; Jealousy.
Ateetam	: Beyond; Transcending.
Atithi	: Without appointment; Without prior intimation; Guest.
Atma, Atman	: Soul; Life-force; Real 'I'; Self; Spirit.
Atma-bodh	: Knowledge of self.
Atma-vidyaa	: Knowledge about self.
Avasthaa	: State; Condition.
Avataar	: Appearance of God on the earth plane; Descending.
Avinayam	: Disobedience; Disrespect.
Ayam	: This. *(Masc.)*
Baahavah	: Hands.
Baala	: Boy; Young.
Baalaad	: From a boy.
Bahudaa	: Many; In various ways.
Bahu-syaam	: I want to become many; (I may become several).
Bakaasana	: Crane posture.
Bandhaha	: Bondage; Attachment.
Bandhu	: Relative; Kinsman; Brother.
Bhaaga	: Divide; Part; Portion; Partition; Division.
Bhaajyam	: Which could be divided, Shared. (Division; Partition).
Bhaarakaari	: Weighing heavily; Carrying burden.
Bhaati	: Shining; Splendour; Effulgence.
Bhaava, Bhaavam	: Feeling; Emotion.
Bhaavaateeta	: Beyond feeling.
Bhagavad	: Divine; Of God. (Towards God).
Bhagawan	: God.
Bhaja	: Experience.
Bhakhti	: Devotion; Unconditional attachment to God.
Bhavat	: To happen in the present.
Bhavati	: Becomes; Is; Happens to be.
Bhavishya	: Future.
Bheda	: Difference, discrimination.
Bheeti	: Fear.
Bhojanam	: Food; Act of eating.

Bhojyam	:	Food worth eating; Edible.
Bhokhta	:	Eater; Enjoyer; Reaper; Awardee.
Bhoomi	:	Earth.
Bhoot, Bhootam	:	Past.
Bhrama	:	Delusion; Confusion; Mistake.
Bhraatar	:	Brother.
Bhutaakaasha	:	Gross physical universe; Universe of elements.
Bindu	:	Dot.
Bodha	:	Knowledge; Awareness; Enlightenment.
Brahma	:	The Creator in the Hindu Trinity.
Brahmaananda	:	Divine Bliss. *(Brahma + Aananda)*.
Brahmaasmi	:	I am God.
Brahman	:	Lord; God; Supersoul; Universal Consciousness.
Brahmavid	:	Knower of *Brahma* (God).
Brooyaat	:	Speak; May speak.
Buddhi	:	Intellect; Reasoning faculty which discriminates.
Buddhimaan	:	Wise; Sensible; Intelligent.
Cha	:	And; Also.
Chaartho	:	And wealth. *(Cha + artho)*.
Chaitanya	:	Life - force; Consciousness.
Chakra	:	Wheel, circle.
Chakraasana	:	Circle posture.
Chara	:	Movable.
Chatur	:	Four; Clever.
Chaturyugi	:	Four-age cycle.
Chetanam	:	Energy; Consciousness.
Chhandas	:	Vedas; Knowledge which should be guarded in secret and propagated with care.
Chhinna	:	Bereft; Without; Cut; Removal; Sans; Minus.
Chidaananda	:	Awareness and bliss.
Chin-Mudra	:	Symbol of Wisdom.
Chit	:	Awareness.
Chitta	:	Aspect of mind when it deliberates.
Chittram	:	Picture; Sight; Scene; Various; Wonderful.
Chopastha	:	And genitals. *(Cha + Upastha)*.
Chora	:	Thief; Stealer.
Daasa	:	Servant.
Dadaati	:	Gives; Confers.
Daiva	:	Divine; Of God.
Dama	:	Sense-control.
Dambha	:	Hypocrisy; Vanity.

Danda	:	Stick.
Dandavat	:	Like a stick; Stick posture.
Darbha	:	Kind of grass with medicinal properties.
Darpa	:	Pride of riches.
Dayaa	:	Kindness.
Deha	:	Body.
Dehee	:	Dweller in the Deha (Body).
Dehoham	:	I am body.
Devalaya	:	Abode of God; Temple.
Devo, Devah	:	God.
Dhaarana	:	Concentration; Hold firmly; Keep steadily.
Dhaatu	:	Substance; Verb.
Dhan, Dhanam	:	Wealth; Riches; Money.
Dhanuraasana	:	Bow posture.
Dharma	:	Righteous action; Spiritual, moral duty; Code of conduct in thought, word and deed based on truth; Moral law; Moral act.
Dhee	:	Intelligence.
Dhr	:	To hold. (A root).
Dhyaana	:	Meditation.
Dhyaata	:	Meditator.
Dhyeya	:	Object of meditation.
Dreshtaha	:	Seer.
Duhkham	:	Pain; Unhappiness; Grief; Sorrow.
Durjana	:	Wicked; Evil people.
Dwaita	:	Duality.
Dwandva	:	Duality.
Dwandvaateeta	:	Beyond pairs of opposites.
Dwesha	:	Aversion; Hatred.
Dwitiya	:	Second.
Easitvam	:	The power of creating and destroying the five elements.
Eershyaa	:	Jealousy; Wishing one's grief and misery on others.
Ekam	:	One; Singular; Alone.
Ekoham	:	I am one. *(Eka + Aham).*
Etad	:	This. *(Neu.)*
Eva	:	Also; Alone; Even; Only.
Gagana	:	Sky; Space.
Gahana	:	Mysterious; Deep; Secret.
Gama	:	Inhaling of Lord's breath.
Gamaya	:	Lead into; Go to.

Gandha	:	Smell; Fragrance; Scent.
Ganga	:	River Ganges.
Gata	:	Gone; Free of.
Gatih	:	Nature; Movement.
Gayatri	:	Recitation of which liberates.
Geeta	:	Song.
Ghraana	:	Nose.
Gnaana	:	Knowledge; Wisdom.
Gnaana-moortim	:	Personification of wisdom.
Graahyam	:	Accepted.
Granthi	:	Knot.
Guna	:	Attribute; Characteristic.
Gunaateeta	:	Beyond or transcending gunas
Guru	:	Teacher; Preceptor; Remover of ignorance.
Gurur-Yuvaa	:	Youthful-Master.
Haaryam	:	Stolen; Appropriated; To be taken away.
Hamsa	:	Swan; Celestial swan.
Hasta	:	Hand.
Heenam	:	Bereft; Without; Devoid of.
Hyetad	:	Verily this. *(Hi + etad)*
Ida	:	Ethereal canal to the left of the Sushumna canal connected to the left nostril.
Idam	:	This.
Indrajaalam	:	Magician's art; Magic.
Indriya	:	Senses; Sense-organs.
Indriyaanaam	:	Of senses.
Ishaa	:	God.
Ishwara	:	God; Lord.
Iti	:	Thus; In this way; As such.
Jaagrat	:	Wakeful; Waking.
Jaati	:	Caste.
Jada	:	Inert, Nescient.
Jagat	:	Subject to birth and death; Objective world; Changing.
Jalam	:	Water.
Jalapanchaka	:	Five sub-elements of the primordial element water. *(Jala + panchaka)*
Janah	:	People.
Janma	:	Birth.
Japa	:	Silent recitation; Continual repetition of the name.
Jeevana	:	Life.

Jignyaasa	:	Yearning; Thirst.
Jihvaa	:	Tongue.
Jiva, Jeeva	:	Individual; Embodied soul.
Jnaanam, Jnaana	:	Knowledge.
Jnaanendriyas	:	Senses of knowledge or perception (of sight, sound, smell, touch & taste). (*Jnaana + indriyaas*).
Jnaata	:	Cognizer; Known.
Jyoti	:	Light; Effulgence; Flame.
Kaala	:	Time; Death.
Kaama	:	Lust; Desire.
Kaamaavasaayitvam	:	Ability to acquire anything desired.
Kaarana	:	Cause; Causal.
Kaaranam	:	Cause; Reason.
Kaarmic	:	Of *Karma*.
Kaivalyam	:	Liberation from the pulls of senses.
Kalaa	:	Small part; Portion; One-sixteenth of moon's diameter; Reflected image of Omni-Self through intellect (*buddhi*).
Kara	:	Hand.
Karishye	:	Shall do.
Karma	:	Action (or inaction) which causes a reaction or consequence. (**NOT** to be pronounced as *Kaama*)
Karmakrit	:	Performer of action.
Karmano	:	Of *Karma*.
Karmanyakarma	:	Inaction in action. (Being unattached).
Karmendriyas	:	Senses of action (Hands, Feet, Tongue, organs of procreation & excretion). (*Karma + indreyas*).
Karuna	:	Compassion; Kindness towards afflicted.
Kasmin	:	In what; In which.
Kawalayati	:	Eats.
Kevalam	:	Alone; Only; The Absolute.
Khudaartah	:	Hungry; Famished.
Koham	:	Who am I? (Pronounced *KOHUM*)
Kosha	:	Sheath.
Krite	:	When done; Having done.
Kritsna	:	Entire; Complete; Full.
Krodha	:	Anger.
Kundalini	:	Awesome power (energy) latent at the base of the spine.
Kuru	:	Do.
Labhate	:	Finds; Gets; Attains..

Labdhaa	: Gained; Found.
Lagheema	: Power to become light as cotton fluff.
Lakshana	: Characterization; Symbol; Mark.
Lakshyam	: Aim; goal.
Laya	: Dissolution; Mergence; End; Latency; Disappearance.
Lobha	: Greed.
Loka	: World.
Maarga	: Path.
Maataa, Maatr	: Mother.
Maatra	: Syllable.
Maatsarya	: Extreme jealousy; Malice.
Maya, Maayaa	: Illusion; Grand Illusion; Unreal.
Mada	: Extreme arrogance; Pride; Swagger.
Madhyama	: Middling; Incantation with lips but without audible sound.
Mahabhutas	: Primordial Elements (Earth, Water, Fire, Air, Ether).
Maharshi	: Great sage. *(Maha + rishi)*.
Mahat	: Cosmos.
Mahator-mahiyaan	: Bigger than the biggest; Grosser than the grossest.
Mahayuga	: Great age. *(Maha + yuga)*.
Maheema	: Ability to assume a very big size.
Maheshwara	: Great God; The destroyer aspect. (One of the Hindu Trinity). *(Maha + Ishwara)*.
Maitri	: Friendliness (towards equals).
Mana, Manas	: Mind.
Manana	: Ruminate; Contemplate; Ponder over.
Manipura	: City of jewel.
Manomaya	: Mind related; Mental; Full of mind.
Mantra	: Sacred mystical formula recitation of which liberates.
Manushya	: Man.
Manushyaanaam	: Of men.
Manushyaanand	: Human joy.
Manushyeshu	: Among men.
Matsyaasana	: Fish posture.
May	: To me; Mine.
Mayam	: Full of.
Mayuraasana	: Peacock posture.
Mithyaa	: Myth; Illusory; Unreal; Neither true nor untrue; Mixture of truth and falsehood.
Mitram	: Friend.
Moha	: Attachment; Infatuation; Delusion.
Mokhsha	: Liberation from the cycle fo birth and death.

Mokhshayoh	:	Of Liberation.
Mooka	:	Silent; Sound of silence.
Moola	:	Root; Base.
Moortim	:	Idol; Statue; Personification.
Mounam	:	Silence.
Mrityu	:	Death; Mortality.
Mudita	:	Freedom from envy; Enjoying.
Mudraa	:	Gesture; Symbol; Posture.
Muhurtam	:	Auspicious period of time; Propitious moment.
Mukhti	:	Liberation; Freedom from the cycle of birth and death.
Na	:	No.
Naada	:	Sound.
Naadi	:	Cord.
Naama	:	Name.
Naanrtm	:	Not untrue. *(Na + anrtam)*.
Na-cha	:	And not. *(Na + cha)*.
Naiva	:	Not even; Never; Not at all. *(Na + eva)*.
Namaami	:	I bow down to.
Namaskaar	:	Salutation.
Namaste	:	Salutation (to you).
Nartaki	:	Danceuse.
Nashta	:	Destroyed.
Na vaa	:	Nor.
Neeti	:	Ethics; Moral.
Neti	:	Not only this; Nihilistic approach.
Netra	:	Eyes.
Nidhidhyaasana	:	Absorbing what has been listened to and putting it into practice.
Nilayam	:	Abode.
Niraakaar	:	Without form; Formless.
Nirvikalpa	:	Without doubt; With full control over the activity of senses; Without option; Without remaining separate. *(Nir + vikalpa)*.
Nishkaama	:	Self-less; Without attachment; Without an eye on the reward.
Nissamshaya	:	Without doubt; Free from reservations.
Nityaananda	:	Eternal bliss.
Nityam	:	Always; Ever.
Nivaaranah	:	To remove.
Paadau	:	Two feet.

Paani	: Hand; Palm.
Paapam	: Sin.
Paayu	: Excretory organs.
Padma	: Lotus.
Padmaasana	: Lotus posture.
Pancha, Panchaka	: Five.
Pankaja	: Born out of mud; Lotus.
Para	: Beyond; Supra; Ultimate.
Paraat Para	: Beyond all Ultimates.
Parabrahma	: Supreme Lord.
Paramaatma	: Supersoul; God.
Paramam	: Supreme; Greatest.
Parityajya	: Abandoning; Giving up.
Paschimothana	: Posterior stretching.
Pashyanti	: Soundless; Seen not heard.
Pashyed, Pashyet	: Seeth.
Pati	: Lord; Master; Husband.
Pibati	: Drinks.
Pingala	: Ethereal canal to the right of the *Sushumna* canal connected to the right nostril.
Pitaa, Pitru	: Father.
Poornaat	: From infinite.
Poornam	: Complete; Infinite; Full.
Poornasya	: Out of infinite; Of infinite.
Praakaamyam	: Power to enter fire or immerse in acid as harmlessly as bathing in water.
Praana	: Vital Air (of five types); Life breath.
Praanamaya	: Life breath related.
Praapti	: Attainment; Power to acquire any object from any quarter.
Praarabdha	: Consequence of past actions come to fruition; Destiny.
Pradeepte	: Kindled.
Pradhaanam	: Superior.
Pragnaanam	: Self-effulgent consciousness.
Praja	: Masses; Subjects.
Prajapati	: Lord of the masses; King; Creator; *Brahma*.
Prajnaanam	: See *Pragnaanam*
Prakriti	: Creation; Female aspect; Matter.
Pralaya	: Dissolution.
Pranava	: Primordial sound AUM; which pervades all life.
Pranu	: To vibrate.
Prapancha	: Proliferation; Manifestation; Relative existence; World.
Prasaad	: Grace; Gift.

Prashanti	: Supreme peace.
Prateekaaro	: Counteraction.
Preeti	: Love.
Prema	: Love - unconditional & unconditioned (as opposed to infatuation; affection, etc.,)
Preyas	: Pleasant; Pleasurable; Binding.
Priyam	: Joyous; Attractive; Charming; Pleasant; Dear.
Prthvi	: Earth.
Punya, Punyam	: Meritorious deed; Virtuous act.
Purusha	: Creator; Male aspect; Immortal self; Spirit.
Purushaartha	: Principle objectives of human life.
Raaga	: Fondness for sense objects.
Raagaagnau	: In the fire of desire; In Passion.
Rahitam	: Without.
Raja	: King.
Rajas	: Attribute of activity.
Rasa	: Taste; Essence.
Rishi	: Sage.
Roopa	: Form.
Sa	: With.
Saadhana	: Disciplined spiritual practice.
Saadhu	: Good; Noble; Virtuous.
Saakshi	: Witness.
Saalokyam	: Continuous contemplation of Divine.
Saamaanya	: Ordinary; General.
Saameepyam	: Nearness to God.
Saankhya	: A school of thought.
Saayujyam	: Mergence in the Divine.
Sadaa	: Always; Ever.
Sadguru	: True teacher. (*Sat + Guru*).
Sadhana	: See *Saadhana*
Sadrsham	: Like; Comparable to; Equal to.
Sah	: He; That.
Sahasra	: Thousand.
Sahit	: Together with; In the company of.
Salilam	: Water.
Sama	: Mind control.
Samaadhi, Samadhi	: State of equal mindedness; Equanimity; State of oneness with God.
Samaagama	: Meeting with; Association of.
Samaamnaaya	: Acquiring the knowledge of the *Vedas* by constant

		contemplation.
Samaana	:	One type of vital air in the body; Equal.
Samattwam	:	Equipoise; Equanimity.
Sampatha	:	Treasure.
Samsaara	:	World.
Samsargam	:	Company.
Samshaya	:	Doubt; Reservation.
Samshayaatma	:	Doubter; Doubtful soul; Suspicious self.
San	:	Having been.
Sanathana	:	Eternal; Universal; Changeless; Perennial.
Sanchita	:	Fruit or consequence yet to face, of action(s) already committed.
Sandeha	:	Doubt; Reservation.
Sandhya	:	Contact period; Prayer appropriate to that period; Twilight.
Sangha, Sanga	:	Company.
Sangyo	:	With the company of.
Sankhyaa	:	Number.
Sapta	:	Seven.
Saptaaha	:	Week.
Sarva	:	All.
Sarvaangaasana	:	All - parts posture. (*Sarva + Anga + Aasana*).
Sarvadhee	:	All mental activity. (*Sarva + dhee*).
Sarvam	:	Everything; All.
Sarvatra	:	Everywhere; All over.
Sat	:	Truth; Eternal existence.
Sattwa	:	Attribute of harmony; Piousness.
Satyam	:	Truth; Truthful.
Shaaka	:	Vegetables.
Shaaleen	:	Grain (like rice etc).
Shaastra	:	Scripture; Discipline; Faculty; Science.
Shabda	:	Sound.
Shabdaateetam	:	Beyond sound.
Shakti	:	Power; Divine energy; Strength.
Shankaa	:	Doubt.
Shanti	:	Peace.
Sharanagati	:	Surrender.
Sharanam	:	Refuge.
Shareeram	:	That which wastes away; Perishable Body.
Shariri	:	Dweller in the body; Soul; God.
Shatkarma	:	Six actions (exercises) of (body) purification.
Shavam	:	Corpse.
Shira	:	Heads.

Shirshaasana	: Head - stand posture.
Shishya	: Disciple; Taught; Student; Pupil.
Shishyaa	: Disciples *(plural)*.
Shivam	: Purity; Auspiciousness; Goodness.
Shlishyati	: Embraces.
Shloka	: Stanza; Verse.
Shraddhaa	: Faith.
Shraddhaavaan	: One full of faith.
Shravanam	: Listen; Hearing.
Shree	: Truth; Goodness; Beauty.
Shreyas	: Superior; Liberating; The good.
Shrotaha	: Listeners.
Shrotra	: Ears.
Shruti	: Heard; Process of learning the *Vedas* by word of mouth from a preceptor by practising the precise manner of chanting the *mantra*.
Shuchah	: Grieve.
Shuka	: Parrot; Sage Shuka.
Shunya	: Zero; Void; Nothingness.
Shushyati	: Parched; dries up (with thirst).
Siddhanta	: Principle; Doctrine.
Smara	: Remember.
Smriti	: Memory; Recollection.
Soham	: Unity of He and I. (Pronounced *SOHUM*).
Sookshma	: Subtle.
Sookshama	: See *Sookshma*.
Soukhyam	: Pleasure; Happiness; Contentment.
Soyam	: This is that.
Sparsha	: Touch.
Sphota	: Outburst.
Srishti	: Creation.
Stamba	: Pillar.
Sthitah	: Standing.
Sthiti	: Preservation; Maintenance.
Sthula	: Gross; External.
Stotram	: Song of praise.
Sudridhataram	: Tightly; Firmly.
Sukhaasana	: Comfortable (easy) posture.
Sukhadam	: Bestower of happiness.
Sukhamiti	: Happiness as such. (*Sukham + iti*).
Sundaram	: Beauty.
Surabhi	: Scented; Fragrant; Cow.
Sushumna	: Ethereal cord of the subtle body.

Sushupti	: Deep sleep state.
Sutra	: Exposition; Aphorism.
Swaadhishthaana	: Generative.
Swaadhyaayam	: Acquisition of *Vedic* knowledge through geneological succession.
Swadu	: Sweet; Tasty.
Swami	: Lord; Master. (An appellative used by devotees for Sai Baba).
Swapna	: Dream.
Tad, Tatt, Tam	: That.
Tamas	: Attribute of inertia; Sloth; Ignorance; Darkness.
Tamaso	: From *Tamas* (ignorance); From darkness.
Tanmaatraas	: Subtleties.
Tasya	: His.
Tatt-twam-Assi	: That Thou Art.
Tava	: Thine.
Teertham	: Holy place.
Tejo	: Fire; Effulgence; Radiance; Glow.
Titiksha	: Forbearance.
Trayee	: Triad.
Tri	: Three.
Tri-Kaalaateetam	: Beyond the three stages of time.
Tri-guna	: Three attributes.
Trishaa	: Thirst.
Turiya	: Beyond state; Fourth; Final; Ultimate.
Twam	: Thou.
Twat	: Thy.
Tyaaga	: Give up; Caste away; Renounce; Eliminate.
Tyaajyam	: To be rejected; To be discarded; Fit for being left away; To be given up.
Tyaja	: Give up; Relinquish.
Udaana	: One of the five vital airs.
Udachyate	: Come out; Has emerged.
Upaasana	: Be seated close (to God); Worship. (*Upa* + *aasana*).
Upanishad	: Sit close; Literature dealing with the innate Truth; Philosophy.
Upastha	: Genitals.
Upeksha	: Disinterestedness; Non-involvement; Feeling of unconcern at the wicked, neither loving them nor hating them; Negligence.

Vaa	:	Even; Or.
Vaachakah	:	Name.
Vaak	:	Sound; Word; Tongue.
Vaang	:	Spoken word.
Vaasana	:	Past residual impression; Recollection.
Vaasyam	:	Lives in; Permeates; Being lived upon.
Vaayu	:	Air.
Vacho	:	Spoken; Speech.
Vachanam	:	Word; Command; Bidding.
Vadanti	:	Speak; Call.
Vai	:	Verily; Indeed.
Vaidika	:	Of *Vedas*.
Vaikhari	:	Loud incantation, ie, audible.
Vairagya	:	Detachment; Renunciation.
Vardhata	:	Increasing; May increase; Develop.
Varjitah	:	Without.
Varna	:	Sound made by the spoken word (vernacular); Caste.
Vashishyate	:	Remains.
Vasitvam	:	Mastery over five elements & control them at will.
Vata-taruh	:	Banyan tree.
Veda	:	Knowledge, which once known everything else becomes known.
Vedanta	:	End of *Vedas*; Final portions of the *Vedas*; Philosophy.
Vettaa, Vettaha	:	Who has known.
Vetti	:	Knows; Understands.
Vibhur	:	Supreme; Lord.
Vichaar	:	Earnest enquiry; deep thought.
Vichakshana	:	Intelligent.
Vidyaa	:	Knowledge.
Vignaanamaya	:	Intellect related.
Vijnaana	:	Knowledge; Wisdom; Science.
Vijnaate	:	When known.
Vikshepa	:	Projecting.
Vimalam	:	Pure; Pristine; Without blemish.
Vinaasha	:	Destruction; Ruin.
Vinashyati	:	Perishes.
Vinayam	:	Humility; Humbleness.
Viparyasyati	:	Misunderstood; Mistaken.
Viprah	:	Wise; Brahmin.
Vishishta	:	Qualified; Special.
Vishnu	:	The preserver aspect, (one of the Hindu Trinity).
Vishuddha	:	Laryngeal.

Viveka	:	Discrimination; Wisdom; Analytical reasoning.
Vraja	:	Come to; Arrive.
Vriddaad	:	From elderly person.
Vriddha	:	Elderly; Old.
Vritti	:	Function; Activity; Agitation of mind.
Vyaakhyaanam	:	Exposition; Description; Speech; Commentary.
Vyaana	:	One of the five vital airs.
Vyaapi	:	Immanent; Extant.
Vyadhih	:	Disease; Pain.
Vyaye	:	By spending; By giving away.
Vyoma	:	Sky.
Wadhoo	:	Wife; Bride.
Walitaan	:	Mixed with; Cooked.
Yad	:	Which.
Yadchaanyat	:	Whatever.
Yagyaha, Yagnyaha	:	Sacrifice.
Yah	:	Whoever.
Yajna	:	Sacrifice; A spiritual exercise; Offerings for the glory of God, in an atmosphere of thankfulness and awe, of humility and holiness.
Yam	:	That which; Whom.
Yamuna	:	River Jamuna.
Yat	:	Whatever; That.
Yatna	:	Effort.
Yoga	:	Union of the human with the divine consciousness; Union of the individual self with the Universal Self; Exercises helpful towards achieving the union.
Yogi, Yogin	:	God-centred man.
Yuktah	:	Capable; A *Yogin*; United (with Spirit); Absorbed.
Yuktam	:	Full of.
Yukti	:	Reasoning; Means of attainment.
Yuvaa	:	Youth; Young.

I am the Truth of truths, I guide towards the Truth, I manifest Truth and when men realise Truth, they realise Me.
— Sri Sathya Sai Baba

NOTES

NOTES

NOTES

NOTES

NOTES

NOTES

NOTES